FREE FOR ALL

FREE FOR ALL

• • •

How Linux and the Free Software Movement
Undercut the High-Tech Titans

PETER WAYNER

HarperBusiness
An Imprint of HarperCollins*Publishers*

HarperCollins books may be purchased for educational, business, or sales promotional use. For information please write: Special Markets Department, HarperCollins Publishers Inc., 10 East 53rd Street, New York, NY 10022.

FIRST EDITION

Designed by William Ruoto

Printed on acid-free paper.

Library of Congress Cataloging-in-Publication Data

Wayner, Peter, 1964–
    Free for all : how Linux and the free software movement undercut the high-tech titans / Peter Wayner.
        p. cm.
    ISBN 0-06-662050-3
    1. Linux. 2. Operating systems (Computers) 3. Free computer software. I. Title.
QA76.76.063 W394 2000
005.4'469—dc21   00-023919

00 01 02 03 04 ❖/RRD 10 9 8 7 6 5 4 3 2 1

CONTENTS

ACKNOWLEDGMENTS

This is just a book about the free software movement. It wouldn't be possible without the hard work and the dedication of the thousands if not millions of people who like to spend their free time hacking code. I salute you. Thank you.

Many people spoke to me during the process of assembling this book, and it would be impossible to cite them all. The list should begin with the millions of people who write and contribute to the various free software lists. The letters, notes, and postings to these lists are a wonderful history of the evolution of free software and an invaluable resource.

The list should also include the dozens of journalists at places like *Slashdot.org*, *LinuxWorld*, *Linux* magazine, *Linux Weekly News*, *Kernel Traffic*, *Salon*, and the *New York Times*. I should specifically mention the work of Joe Barr, Jeff Bates, Janelle Brown, Zack Brown, Jonathan Corbet, Elizabeth Coolbaugh, Amy Harmon, Andrew Leonard, Rob Malda, John Markoff, Mark Nielsen, Nicholas Petreley, Harald Radke, and Dave Whitinger. They wrote wonderful pieces that will make a great first draft of the history of the open source movement. Only a few of the pieces are cited directly in the footnotes, largely for practical reasons. The entire body of websites like *Slashdot*, *Linux Journal*, *Linux World*, *Kernel Notes*, or *Linux Weekly News* should be required reading for anyone interested in the free software movement.

There are hundreds of folks at Linux trade shows who took the time to show me their products, T-shirts, or, in one case, cooler filled with beer. Almost everyone I met at the conferences was happy to speak about their experiences with open source software. They were all a great source of information, and I don't even know most of their names.

Some people went beyond the call of duty. John Gilmore, Ethan Rasiel, and Caroline McKeldin each read drafts when the book was quite unfinished. Their comments were crucial.

Many friends, acquaintances, and subjects of the book were kind enough to read versions that were a bit more polished, but far from complete: L. David Baron, Jeff Bates, Brian Behlendorf, Alan Cox, Robert Dreyer, Theo de Raadt, Telsa Gwynne, Jordan Hubbard, James Lewis Moss, Kirk McKusick, Sam Ockman, Tim O'Reilly, Sameer Parekh, Bruce Perens, Eric Raymond, and Richard Stallman.

There are some people who deserve a different kind of thanks. Daniel Greenberg and James Levine did a great job shaping the conception of the book. When I began, it was just a few ideas on paper. My editors, David Conti, Laureen Rowland, Devi Pillai, and Adrian Zackheim, were largely responsible for this transition. Kimberly Monroe suffered through my mistakes as she took the book through its production stages. They took a bunch of rambling comments about a social phenomenon and helped turn it into a book.

Finally, I want to thank everyone in my family for everything they've given through all of my life. And, of course, Caroline, who edited large portions with a slavish devotion to grammar and style.

Visit http://www.wayner.org/books/ffa/ for updates, corrections, and additional comments.

1. BATTLE

The world where cash was king, greed was good, and money was power fell off its axis and stopped rotating, if only for a second, in January 1999. Microsoft, the great software giant and unstoppable engine of cash, was defending itself in a courtroom in Washington, D.C. The Department of Justice claimed that Microsoft was a monopoly and was using this power to cut off competitors. Microsoft denied it all and claimed that the world was hurling threat after competitive threat its way. They weren't a monopoly, they were just a very competitive company that managed to withstand the slings and arrows of other equally ruthless competitors out to steal its market share.

The trial quickly turned into everyone's worst nightmare as the lawyers, the economists, and the programmers filled the courtroom with a thick mixture of technobabble and legal speak. On the stands, the computer nerds spewed out three-letter acronyms (TLAs) as they talked about creating operating systems. Afterward, the legal nerds started slicing them up into one-letter acronyms and testing to see just which of the three letters was really the one that committed the crime. Then the economists came forward and offered their theories on just when a monopoly is a monopoly. Were three letters working in collusion enough? What about two? Everyone in the courtroom began to dread spending the day cooped up in a small room as Microsoft tried to deny what was obvious to practically everyone.

In the fall and early winter of 1998 and 1999, the Department of Justice had presented its witnesses, who explained how Microsoft had slanted contracts, tweaked software, and twisted arms to ensure that it and it alone got the lion's share of the computer business. Many watching the trial soon developed the opinion that Microsoft had adopted a mixture of tactics from the schoolyard bully, the local mob boss, and the mother from hell. The Department of Justice trotted out a number of witnesses who produced ample evidence that suggested the computer customers of the world will buy Microsoft products unless Microsoft decides otherwise. Competitors must be punished.

By January, the journalists covering the trial were quietly complaining about this endless waste of time. The Department of Justice's case was so compelling that they saw the whole trial as just a delay in what would eventually come to be a ruling that would somehow split or shackle Microsoft.

But Microsoft wasn't going to be bullied or pushed into splitting up. The trial allowed them to present their side of the story, and they had one ready. Sure, everyone seemed to use Microsoft products, but that was because they were great. It wasn't because there weren't any competitors, but because the competitors just weren't good enough.

In the middle of January, Richard Schmalensee, the dean of the Sloan School of Management at the Massachusetts Institute of Technology, took the stand to defend Microsoft. Schmalensee had worked for the Federal Trade Commission and the Department of Justice as an economist who examined the marketplace and the effects of anti-competitive behavior. He studied how monopolies behave, and to him Microsoft had no monopoly power. Now, he was being paid handsomely by Microsoft as an expert witness to repeat this view in court.

Schmalensee's argument was simple: competitors are popping up all over the place. Microsoft, he said in his direct testimony, "is in a constant struggle for competitive survival. That struggle—the race to win and the victor's perpetual fear of being displaced—is the source of competitive vitality in the microcomputer software industry."

Schmalensee even had a few competitors ready. "The iMac clearly competes directly and fiercely with Intel-compatible computers running Windows," he said without mentioning that Microsoft had bailed out Apple several months before with hundreds of millions of dollars in an investment. When Steve Jobs, the iCEO of Apple, announced the deal to a crowd of Mac lovers, the crowd booed. Jobs quieted them and tried to argue that the days of stiff competition with Microsoft were over. The scene did such a good job of capturing the total domination of Microsoft that the television movie *The Pirates of Silicon Valley* used it to illustrate how Bill Gates had won all of the marbles.

After the announcement of the investment, Apple began shipping Microsoft's Internet Explorer web browser as the preferred browser on its machines. Microsoft's competitor Netscape became just a bit harder to find on the iMac. After that deal, Steve Jobs even began making statements that the old sworn enemies, Apple and Microsoft, were now more partners than competitors. Schmalensee didn't focus on this facet of Apple's new attitude toward competition.

Next, Schmalensee trotted out BeOS, an operating system made by Be, a small company with about 100 employees run by ex-Apple executive Jean-Louis Gassée. This company had attracted millions of dollars in funding, he said, and some people really liked it. That made it a competitor.

Schmalensee didn't mention that Be had trouble giving away the BeOS operating system. Gassée approached a number of PC manufacturers to see if they would include BeOS on their machines and give users the chance to switch between two operating systems. Gassée found, to no one's real surprise, that Microsoft's contracts with manufacturers made it difficult, if not practically impossible, to get BeOS in customers' hands. Microsoft controlled much of what the user got to see and insisted on almost total control over the viewer's experience. Schmalensee didn't mention these details in his testimony. BeOS may have been as locked up as a prisoner in a windowless cell in a stone-walled asylum on an island in the middle of the ocean, but BeOS was still a competitor for the love of the fair maiden.

The last competitor, though, was the most surprising to everyone. Schmalensee saw Linux, a program given away for free, as a big potential competitor. When he said Linux, he really meant an entire collection of programs known as "open source" software. These were written by a loose-knit group of programmers who shared all of the source code to the software over the Internet.

Open source software floated around the Internet controlled by a variety of licenses with names like the GNU General Public License (GPL). To say that the software was "controlled" by the license is a bit of a stretch. If anything, the licenses were deliberately worded to prohibit control. The GNU GPL, for instance, let users modify the program and give away their own versions. The license did more to enforce sharing of all the source code than it did to control or constrain. It was more an anti-license than anything else, and its author, Richard Stallman, often called it a "copyleft."

Schmalensee didn't mention that most people thought of Linux as a strange tool created and used by hackers in dark rooms lit by computer monitors. He didn't mention that many people had trouble getting Linux to work with their computers. He forgot to mention that Linux manuals came with subheads like "Disk Druid-like 'fstab editor' available." He didn't delve into the fact that for many of the developers, Linux was just a hobby they dabbled with when there was nothing interesting on television. And he certainly didn't mention that most people thought the whole Linux project was the work of a mad genius and his weirdo disciples who still hadn't caught on to the fact that the Soviet Union had already failed big-time. The Linux folks actually thought sharing would make the world a better place. Fat-cat programmers who spent their stock-option riches on Porsches and balsamic vinegar laughed at moments like this.

Schmalensee didn't mention these facts. He just offered Linux as an alternative to Windows and said that computer manufacturers might switch to it at any time. Poof. Therefore, Microsoft had competitors. At the trial, the discourse quickly broke down into an argument over what is really a worthy competitor and what isn't. Were there enough applications available for Linux or the Mac? What qualifies as "enough"? Were these really worthy?

Under cross-examination, Schmalensee explained that he wasn't holding up the Mac, BeOS, or Linux as competitors who were going to take over 50 percent of the marketplace. He merely argued that their existence proved that the barriers produced by the so-called Microsoft monopoly weren't that strong. If rational people were investing in creating companies like BeOS, then Microsoft's power wasn't absolute.

Afterward, most people quickly made up their minds. Everyone had heard about the Macintosh and knew that back then conventional wisdom dictated that it would soon fail. But most people didn't know anything about BeOS or Linux. How could a company be a competitor if no one had heard of it? Apple and Microsoft had TV commercials. BeOS, at least, had a charismatic chairman. There was no Linux pitchman, no

Linux jingle, and no Linux 30-second spot in major media. At the time, only the best-funded projects in the Linux community had enough money to buy spots on late-night community-access cable television. How could someone without money compete with a company that hired the Rolling Stones to pump excitement into a product launch?

When people heard that Microsoft was offering a free product as a worthy competitor, they began to laugh even louder at the company's chutzpah. Wasn't money the whole reason the country was having a trial? Weren't computer programmers in such demand that many companies couldn't hire as many as they needed, no matter how high the salary? How could Microsoft believe that anyone would buy the supposition that a bunch of pseudo-communist nerds living in their weird techno-utopia where all the software was free would ever come up with software that could compete with the richest company on earth? At first glance, it looked as if Microsoft's case was sinking so low that it had to resort to laughable strategies. It was as if General Motors were to tell the world "We shouldn't have to worry about fixing cars that pollute because a collective of hippies in Ithaca, New York, is refurbishing old bicycles and giving them away for free." It was as if Exxon waved away the problems of sinking oil tankers by explaining that folksingers had written a really neat ballad for teaching birds and otters to lick themselves clean after an oil spill. If no one charged money for Linux, then it was probably because it wasn't worth buying.

But as everyone began looking a bit deeper, they began to see that Linux was being taken seriously in some parts of the world. Many web servers, it turned out, were already running on Linux or another free cousin known as FreeBSD. A free webserving tool known as Apache had controlled more than 50 percent of the web servers for some time, and it was gradually beating out Microsoft products that cost thousands of dollars. Many of the web servers ran Apache on top of a Linux or a FreeBSD machine and got the job done. The software worked well, and the nonexistent price made it easy to choose.

Linux was also winning over some of the world's most serious physicists, weapons designers, biologists, and hard-core scientists. Some of the nation's top labs had wired together clusters of cheap PCs and turned them into supercomputers that were highly competitive with the best machines on the market. One upstart company started offering "supercomputers" for $3,000. These machines used Linux to keep the data flowing while the racks of computers plugged and chugged their way for hours on complicated simulations.

There were other indications. Linux users bragged that their system rarely crashed. Some claimed to have machines that had been running for a year or more without a problem. Microsoft (and Apple) users, on the other hand, had grown used to frequent crashes. The "Blue Screen of Death" that appears on Windows users' monitors when something goes irretrievably wrong is the butt of many jokes.

Linux users also bragged about the quality of their desktop interface. Most of the uninitiated thought of Linux as a hacker's system built for nerds. Yet recently two very good operating shells called GNOME and KDE had taken hold. Both offered the user an environment that looked just like Windows but was better. Linux hackers started bragging that they were able to equip their girlfriends, mothers, and friends with Linux boxes without grief. Some people with little computer experience were adopting Linux with little trouble.

Building websites and supercomputers is not an easy task, and it is often done in back rooms out of the sight of most people. When people began realizing that the free software hippies had slowly managed to take over a large chunk of the web server and supercomputing world, they realized that perhaps Microsoft's claim was viable. Web servers and supercomputers are machines built and run by serious folks with bosses who want something in return for handing out paychecks. They aren't just toys sitting around the garage.

If these free software guys had conquered such serious arenas, maybe they could handle the office and the desktop. If the free software world had created something usable by the programmers' mothers, then maybe they were viable competitors. Maybe Microsoft was right.

Sleeping In

While Microsoft focused its eyes and ears upon Washington, one of its biggest competitors was sleeping late. When Richard Schmalensee was prepping to take the stand in Washington, D.C., to defend Microsoft's outrageous fortune against the slings and arrows of a government inquisition, Alan Cox was still sleeping in. He didn't get up until 2:00 P.M. at his home in Swansea on the south coast of Wales. This isn't too odd for him. His wife, Telsa, grouses frequently that it's impossible to get him moving each morning without a dose of Jolt Cola, the kind that's overloaded with caffeine.

The night before, Cox and his wife went to see *The Mask of Zorro*, the latest movie that describes how Don Diego de la Vega assumed the secret identity of Zorro to free the Mexican people from the tyranny of Don Rafael Montero. In this version, Don Diego, played by Anthony Hopkins, chooses an orphan, Alejandro Murrieta, played by Antonio Banderas, and teaches him to be the next Zorro so the fight can continue. Its theme resonates with writers of open source software: a small band of talented, passionate warriors warding off the evil oppressor.

Cox keeps an open diary and posts the entries on the web. "It's a nice-looking film, with some great stunts and character play," he wrote, but

You could, however, have fitted the plot, including all the twists, on the back of a matchbox. That made it feel a bit ponderous so it only got a 6 out of 10 even though I'm feeling extremely smug because I spotted one of the errors in the film while watching it not by consulting imdb later.

By the imdb, he meant the Internet Movie Database, which is one of the most complete listings of film credits, summaries, and glitches available on the Net. Users on the Internet write in with their own reviews and plot synopses, which the database dutifully catalogs and makes available to everyone. It's a reference book with thousands of authors.

In this case, the big glitch in the film is the fact that one of the train gauges uses the metric system. Mexico converted to this system in 1860, but the film is set in 1841. Whoops. Busted.

Telsa wrote in her diary, which she also posts to the Net under the title "The More Accurate Diary. Really."

Dragged him to cinema to see Zorro. I should have remembered he'd done some fencing and found something different. He also claimed he'd spotted a really obscure error. I checked afterward on IMDB, and was amazed. How did he see this?

Cox is a big bear of a man who wears a long, brown wizard's beard. He has an agile, analytic mind that constantly picks apart a system and probes it for weaknesses. If he's playing a game, he plays until he finds a trick or a loophole that will give him the winning edge. If he's working around the house, he often ends up meddling with things until he fixes and improves them. Of course, he also often breaks them. His wife loves to complain about the bangs and crashes that come from his home office, where he often works until 6:30 in the morning.

To his wife, this crashing, banging, and late-night hacking is the source of the halfhearted grousing inherent in every marriage. She obviously loves both his idiosyncrasies and the opportunity to discuss just how strange they can be. In January, Telsa was trying to find a way to automate her coffeepot by hooking it up to her computer.

She wrote in her diary,

Alan is reluctant to get involved with any attempt to make a coffee-maker switch on via the computer now because he seems to think I will eventually switch it on with no water in and start a fire. I'm not the one who welded tinned spaghetti to the non-stick saucepan. Or set the wok on fire. More than once. Once with fifteen guests in the house. But there we are.

To the rest of the world, this urge to putter and fiddle with machines is more than a source of marital comedy. Cox is one of the great threats to the continued dominance of Microsoft, despite the fact that he found a way to weld spaghetti to a nonstick pan. He is one of the core developers who help maintain the Linux kernel. In other words, he's one of the group of programmers who helps guide the development of the Linux operating system, the one Richard Schmalensee feels is such a threat to Microsoft. Cox is one of the few people whom Linus Torvalds, the creator of Linux, trusts to make important decisions about future directions. Cox is an expert on the networking guts of the system and is responsible for making sure that most of the new ideas that people suggest for Linux are considered carefully and integrated correctly. Torvalds defers to Cox on many matters about how Linux-based computers talk with other computers over a network. Cox works long and hard to find efficient ways for Linux to juggle multiple connections without slowing down or deadlocking.

The group that works with Cox and Torvalds operates with no official structure. Millions of people use Linux to keep their computers running, and all of them have copies of the source code. In the 1980s, most companies began keeping the source code to their software as private as possible because they worried that a competitor might come along and steal the ideas the source spelled out. The source code, which is written in languages like C, Java, FORTRAN, BASIC, or Pascal, is meant to be read by programmers. Most companies didn't want other programmers understanding too much about the guts of their software. Information is power, and the companies instinctively played their cards close to their chests.

When Linus Torvalds first started writing Linux in 1991, however, he decided to give away the operating system for free. He included all the source code because he *wanted* others to read it, comment upon it, and perhaps improve it. His decision was as much a radical break from standard programming procedure as a practical decision. He was a poor student at the time, and this operating system was merely a hobby. If he had tried to sell it, he wouldn't have gotten anything for it. He certainly had no money to build a company that could polish the software and market it. So he just sent out copies over the Internet.

Sharing software had already been endorsed by Richard Stallman, a legendary programmer from MIT who believed that keeping source code private was a sin and a crime against humanity. A programmer who shares the source code lets others learn, and those others can contribute their ideas back into the mix. Closed source code leaves users frustrated because they can't learn about the software or fix any bugs. Stallman broke away from MIT in 1984 when he founded the Free Software Foundation. This became the organization that sponsored Stallman's grand project to free source code, a project he called GNU. In the 1980s, Stallman created very advanced tools like the GNU Emacs text editor, which people could use to write programs and articles. Others donated their work and the GNU project soon included a wide range of tools, utilities, and games. All of them were distributed for free.

Torvalds looked at Stallman and decided to follow his lead with open source code. Torvalds's free software began to attract people who liked to play around with technology. Some just glanced at it. Others messed around for a few hours. Free is a powerful incentive. It doesn't let money, credit cards, purchase orders, and the boss's approval get in the way of curiosity. A few, like Alan Cox, had such a good time taking apart an operating system that they stayed on and began contributing back to the project.

In time, more and more people like Alan Cox discovered Torvalds's little project on the Net. Some slept late. Others kept normal hours and worked in offices. Some just found bugs. Others fixed the bugs. Still others added new features that they wanted. Slowly, the operating system grew from a toy that satisfied the curiosity of computer scientists into a usable tool that powers supercomputers, web servers, and millions of other machines around the world.

Today, about a thousand people regularly work with people like Alan Cox on the development of the Linux kernel, the official name for the part of the operating system that Torvalds started writing back in 1991. That may not be an accurate estimate because many people check in for a few weeks when a project requires their participation. Some follow everything, but most people are just interested in little corners. Many other programmers have contributed various pieces of software such as word processors or spreadsheets. All of these are bundled together into packages that are often called plain Linux or GNU/Linux and shipped by companies like Red Hat or more ad hoc groups like Debian.[1] While Torvalds only wrote the core kernel, people use his name, Linux, to stand for a whole body of software written by thousands of others. It's not exactly fair, but most let it slide. If there hadn't been the Linux kernel, the users wouldn't have the

---

[1]*Linux Weekly News* keeps a complete list of distributors. These range from the small, one- or two-man operations to the biggest, most corporate ones like Red Hat: Alzza Linux, Apokalypse, Armed Linux, Bad Penguin Linux, Bastille Linux, Best Linux (Finnish/Swedish), Bifrost, Black Cat Linux (Ukrainian/Russian), Caldera OpenLinux, CCLinux, Chinese Linux Extension, Complete Linux, Conectiva Linux (Brazilian), Debian GNU/Linux, Definite Linux, DemoLinux, DLD, DLite, DLX, DragonLinux, easyLinux, Enoch, Eridani Star System, Eonova Linux, e-smith server and gateway, Eurielec Linux (Spanish), eXecutive Linux, floppyfw, Floppix, Green Frog Linux, hal91, Hard Hat Linux, Immunix, Independence, Jurix, KhaOs Linux, KRUD, KSI-

ability to run software on a completely free system. The free software would need to interact with something from Microsoft, Apple, or IBM. Of course, if it weren't for all of the other free software from Berkeley, the GNU project, and thousands of other garages around the world, there would be little for the Linux kernel to do.

Officially, Linus Torvalds is the final arbiter for the kernel and the one who makes the final decisions about new features. In practice, the group runs like a loosely knit "ad-hocracy." Some people might care about a particular feature like the ability to interface with Macintoshes, and they write special code that makes this task easier. Others who run really big databases may want larger file systems that can store more information without limits.

All of these people work at their own pace. Some work in their homes, like Alan Cox. Some work in university labs. Others work for businesses that use Linux and encourage their programmers to plug away so it serves their needs.

The team is united by mailing lists. The Linux Kernel mailing list hooks up Cox in Britain, Torvalds in Silicon Valley, and the others around the globe. They post notes to the list and discuss ideas. Sometimes verbal fights break out, and sometimes everyone agrees. Sometimes people light a candle by actually writing new code to make the kernel better, and other times they just curse the darkness.

Cox is now one of several people responsible for coordinating the addition of new code. He tests it for compatibility and guides Linux authors to make sure they're working together optimally. In essence, he tests every piece of incoming software to make sure all of the gauges work with the right system of measurement so there will be no glitches. He tries to remove the incompatibilities that marred Zorro.

Linux, Laetos, LEM, Linux Cyrillic Edition, LinuxGT, Linux-Kheops (French), Linux MLD (Japanese), LinuxOne OS, LinuxPPC, LinuxPPP (Mexican), Linux Pro Plus, Linux Router Project, LOAF, LSD, Mandrake, Mastodon, MicroLinux, MkLinux, muLinux, nanoLinux II, NoMad Linux, OpenClassroom, Peanut Linux, Plamo Linux, PLD, Project Ballantain, PROSA, QuadLinux, Red Hat, Rock Linux, RunOnCD, ShareTheNet, Skygate, Slackware, Small Linux, Stampede, Stataboware, Storm Linux, SuSE, Tomsrtbt, Trinux, TurboLinux, uClinux, Vine Linux, WinLinux 2000, Xdenu, XTeamLinux, and Yellow Dog Linux.

Often, others will duplicate Cox's work. Some new features are very popular and have many cooks minding the stew. The technology for speeding up computers with multiple CPUs lets each computer harness the extra power, so many list members test it frequently. They want the fastest machines they can get, and smoothing the flow of data between the CPUs is the best way to let the machines cooperate.

Other features are not so popular, and they're tackled by the people who need the features. Some people want to hook their Linux boxes up to Macintoshes. Doing that smoothly can require some work in the kernel. Others may want to add special code to enable a special device like a high-speed camera or a strange type of disk drive. These groups often work on their own but coordinate their solutions with the main crowd. Ideally, they'll be able to come up with some patches that solve their problem without breaking some other part of the system.

It's a very social and political process that unrolls in slow motion through e-mail messages. One person makes a suggestion. Others may agree. Someone may squabble with the idea because it seems inelegant, sloppy, or, worst of all, dangerous. After some time, a rough consensus evolves. Easy problems can be solved in days or even minutes, but complicated decisions can wait as the debate rages for years.

Each day, Cox and his virtual colleagues pore through the lists trying to figure out how to make Linux better, faster, and more usable. Sometimes they skip out to watch a movie. Sometimes they go for hikes. But one thing they don't do is spend months huddled in conference rooms trying to come up with legal arguments. Until recently, the Linux folks didn't have money for lawyers, and that means they didn't get sidetracked by figuring out how to get big and powerful people like Richard Schmalensee to tell a court that there's no monopoly in the computer operating system business.

Suits Against Hackers

Schmalensee and Cox couldn't be more different from each other. One is a career technocrat who moves easily between the government and MIT. The other is what used to be known as an absentminded professor—the kind who works when he's really interested in a problem. It just so happens that Cox is pretty intrigued with building a better operating system than the various editions of Windows that form the basis of Microsoft's domination of the computer industry.

The battle between Linux and Microsoft is lining up to be the classic fight between the people like Schmalensee and the people like Cox. On one side are the armies of lawyers, lobbyists, salesmen, and expensive executives who are armed with patents, lawsuits, and legislation. They are skilled at moving the levers of power until the gears line up just right and billions of dollars pour into their pockets. They know how to schmooze, toady, beg, or even threaten until they wear the mantle of authority and command the piety and devotion of the world. People buy Microsoft because it's "the standard." No one decreed this, but somehow it has come to be.

On the other side are a bunch of guys who just like playing with computers and will do anything to take them apart. They're not like the guy in the song by John Mellencamp who sings "I fight authority and authority always wins." Some might have an attitude, but most just want to look at the insides of their computers and rearrange them to hook up to coffee machines or networks. They want to fidget with the guts of their machines. If they weld some spaghetti to the insides, so be it.

Normally, these battles between the suits and the geeks don't threaten the established order. There are university students around the world building solar-powered cars, but they don't actually pose a threat to the oil or auto industries. "21," a restaurant in New York, makes a great hamburger, but they're not going to put McDonald's out of business. The experimentalists and the perfectionists don't usually knock heads with the corporations who depend upon world domination for their profits. Except when it comes to software.

Software is different from cars or hamburgers. Once someone writes the source code, copying the source costs next to nothing. That makes it much easier for tinkerers like Cox to have a global effect. If Cox, Stallman, Torvalds, and his chums just happen to luck upon something that's better than Microsoft, then the rest of the world can share their invention for next to nothing. That's what makes Cox, Torvalds, and their buddies a credible threat no matter how often they sleep late.

It's easy to get high off of the idea alone. A few guys sleeping late and working in bedrooms aren't supposed to catch up to a cash engine like Microsoft. They aren't supposed to create a webserving engine that controls more than half of the web. They aren't supposed to create a graphical user interface for drawing windows and icons on the screen that's much better than Windows. They aren't supposed to create supercomputers with sticker prices of $3,000. Money isn't supposed to lose.

Of course, the folks who are working on free software projects have advantages that money can't buy. These programmers don't need lawyers to create licenses, negotiate contracts, or argue over terms. Their software is free, and lawyers lose interest pretty quickly when there's no money around. The free software guys don't need to scrutinize advertising copy. Anyone can download the software and just try it. The programmers also don't need to sit in the corner when their computer crashes and complain about the idiot who wrote the software. Anyone can read the source code and fix the glitches.

The folks in the free source software world are, in other words, grooving on freedom. They're high on the original American dream of life, liberty, and the pursuit of happiness. The founders of the United States of America didn't set out to create a wealthy country where citizens spent their days worrying whether they would be able to afford new sport utility vehicles when the stock options were vested. The founders just wanted to secure the blessings of liberty for posterity. Somehow, the wealth followed.

This beautiful story is easy to embrace: a group of people started out swapping cool software on the Net and ended up discovering that their free sharing created better software than what a corporation could produce with a mountain of cash.

The programmers found that unrestricted cooperation made it easy for everyone to contribute. No price tags kept others away. No stereotypes or biases excluded anyone. The software and the source code were on the Net for anyone to read.

Wide-open cooperation also turned out to be wide-open competition because the best software won the greatest attention. The corporate weasels with the ear of the president could not stop a free source software project from shipping. No reorganization or downsizing could stop people from working on free software if they wanted to hack. The freedom to create was more powerful than money.

That's an idyllic picture, and the early success of Linux, FreeBSD, and other free packages makes it tempting to think that the success will build. Today, open source servers power more than 50 percent of the web servers on the Internet, and that is no small accomplishment. Getting thousands, if not millions, of programmers to work together is quite amazing given how quirky programmers can be. The ease of copying makes it possible to think that Alan Cox could get up late and still move the world.

But the 1960s were also an allegedly idyllic time when peace, love, and sharing were going to create a beautiful planet where everyone gave to everyone else in an eternal golden braid of mutual respect and caring. Everyone assumed that the same spirit that so quickly and easily permeated the college campuses and lovefests in the parks was bound to sweep the world. The communes were really happening, man. But somehow, the groovy beat never caught on beyond those small nests of easy caring and giving. Somehow, the folks started dropping back in, getting real jobs, taking on real mortgages, and buying back into the world where money was king.

Over the years, the same sad ending has befallen many communes, utopian visions, and hypnotic vibes. Freedom is great. It allows brilliant inventors to work independently of the wheels of power. But capital is another powerful beast that drives innovation. The great communes often failed because they never converted their hard work into money, making it difficult for them to save and invest. Giving things away may be, like, really groovy, but it doesn't build a nest egg.

Right now, the free software movement stands at a crucial moment in its history. In the past, a culture of giving and wide-open sharing let thousands of programmers build a great operating system that was, in many ways, better than anything coming from the best companies. Many folks began working on Linux, FreeBSD, and thousands of other projects as hobbies, but now they're waking up to find IBM, Hewlett-Packard, Apple, and all the other big boys pounding on their door. If the kids could create something as nice as Linux, everyone began to wonder whether these kids really had enough good stuff to go the distance and last nine innings against the greatest power hitters around.

Perhaps the free software movement will just grow faster and better as more people hop on board. More users mean more eyes looking for bugs. More users mean more programmers writing new source code for new features. More is better.

On the other hand, sharing may be neat, but can it beat the power of capital? Microsoft's employees may be just serfs motivated by the dream that someday their meager stock options will be worth enough to retire upon, but they have a huge pile of cash driving them forward. This capital can be shifted very quickly. If Bill Gates wants 1,000 programmers to create something, he can wave his hand. If he wants to buy 1,000 computers, it takes him a second. That's the power of capital.

Linus Torvalds may be on the cover of magazines, but he can't do anything with the wave of a hand. He must charm and cajole the thousands of folks on the Linux mailing list to make a change. Many of the free software projects may generate great code, but they have to beg for computers. The programmers might even surprise him and come up with an even better solution. They've done it in the past. But no money means that no one has to do what anyone says.

In the past, the free software movement was like the movies in which Mickey Rooney and Judy Garland put on a great show in the barn. That part won't change. Cool kids with a dream will still be spinning up great programs that will be wonderful gifts for the world.

But shows that are charming and fresh in a barn can become thin and weak on a big stage on Broadway. The glitches and raw functionality of Linux and free software don't seem too bad if you know that they're built by kids in their spare time. Building real tools for real companies, moms, police stations, and serious users everywhere is another matter. Everyone may be hoping that sharing, caring, and curiosity are enough, but no one knows for certain. Maybe capital will end up winning. Maybe it won't. It's freedom versus assurance; it's wide-open sharing versus stock options; it's cooperation versus intimidation; it's the geeks versus the suits, all in one knockdown, hack-till-you-drop, winner-take-everything fight.

2. LISTS

While Alan Cox was sleeping late and Microsoft was putting Richard Schmalensee on the stand, the rest of the open source software world was tackling their own problems. Some were just getting up, others were in the middle of their day, and still others were just going to sleep. This is not just because the open source hackers like to work at odd times around the clock. Some do. But they also live around the globe in all of the different time zones. The sun never sets on the open source empire.

On January 14, 1999, for instance, Peter Jeremy, an Australian, announced that he had just discovered a potential Y2K problem in the control software in the central database that helped maintain the FreeBSD source code. He announced this by posting a note to a mailing list that forwarded the message to many other FreeBSD users. The problem was that the software simply appended the two characters "19" to the front of the year. When the new millennium came about a year later, the software would start writing the new date as "19100." Oops. The problem was largely cosmetic because it only occurred in some of the support software used by the system.

FreeBSD is a close cousin to the Linux kernel and one that predates it in some ways. It descends from a long tradition of research and development of operating systems at the University of California at Berkeley. The name BSD stands for "Berkeley Software Distribution," the name given to one of the first releases of operating system source code that Berkeley made for the world. That small package grew, morphed, and absorbed many other contributions over the years.

Referring to Linux and FreeBSD as cousins is an apt term because they share much of the same source code in the same way that cousins share some of the same genes. Both borrow source code and ideas from each other. If you buy a disk with FreeBSD, which you can do from companies like Walnut Creek, you may get many of the same software packages that you get from a disk from Red Hat Linux. Both include, for instance, some of the GNU compilers that turn source code into something that can be understood by computers.

FreeBSD, in fact, has some of its own fans and devotees. The FreeBSD site lists thousands of companies large and small that use the software. Yahoo, the big Internet directory, game center, and news operation, uses FreeBSD in some of its servers. So does Blue Mountain Arts, the electronic greeting card company that is consistently one of the most popular sites on the web. There are undoubtedly thousands more who aren't listed on the FreeBSD site. The software produced by the FreeBSD project is, after all, free, so people can give it away, share it with their friends, or even pretend they are "stealing" it by making a copy of a disk at work. No one really knows how many copies of FreeBSD are out there because there's no reason to count. Microsoft may need to count heads so they can bill everyone for using Windows, but FreeBSD doesn't have that problem.

That morning, Peter Jeremy's message went out to everyone who subscribed to the FreeBSD mailing list. Some users who cared about the Y2K bug could take Jeremy's patch and use it to fix their software directly. They didn't need to wait for some central bureaucracy to pass judgment on the information. They didn't need to wait for the Y2K guy at FreeBSD to get around to vetting the change. Everyone could just insert the fix because they had all of the source code available to them.

Of course, most people never use all their freedoms. In this case, most people didn't have to bother dealing with Jeremy's patch because they waited for the official version. The FreeBSD infrastructure absorbed the changes into its source code vaults, and the changes appeared in the next fully updated version. This new complete version is where most people first started using the fix. Jeremy is a programmer who created a solution that was easy for other programmers to use. Most people, however, aren't programmers, and they want their software to be easy to use. Most programmers aren't even interested in poking around inside their machines. Everyone wants the solution to either fix itself or come as close to that as possible.

Jeremy's message was just one of the hundreds percolating through the FreeBSD community that day. Some fell on deaf ears, some drew snotty comments, and a few gathered some real attention. The mailing lists were fairly complex ecologies where ideas blossomed and grew before they faded away and died.

Of course, it's not fair to categorize the FreeBSD world as a totally decentralized anarchy. There is one central team led by one man, Jordan Hubbard, who organizes the leadership of a core group of devoted programmers. The group runs the website, maintains an up-to-date version of FreeBSD, and sponsors dozens of lists devoted to different corners or features. One list focuses on hooking up the fast high-performance SCSI hard disks that are popular with people who demand high-performance systems. Another concentrates on building in enough security to keep out attackers who might try to sneak in through the Internet.

That January 14, a man in Great Britain, Roger Hardiman, was helping a man in Switzerland, Reto Trachsel, hook up a Hauppauge video card to his system. They were communicating on the Multimedia mailing list devoted to finding ways to add audio and video functions to FreeBSD systems. Trachsel posted a note to the list asking for information on how to find the driver software that would make sure that the data coming out of the Hauppauge television receiver would be generally available to the rest of the computer. Hardiman pointed out a solution, but cautioned, "If your Hauppauge card has the MSP34xx Stereo Decoder audio chip, you may get no sound when watching TV. I should get this fixed in the next week or two."

Solutions like these float around the FreeBSD community. Most people don't really care if they can watch television with their computer, but a few do. The easy access to source code and drivers means that the few can go off and do their own thing without asking some major company for permission. The big companies like Microsoft and Apple, for instance, have internal projects that are producing impressive software for creating and displaying multimedia extravaganzas on computers. But they have a strict view of the world: the company is the producer of high-quality tools that make their way to the consumer who uses them and pays for them in one way or another.

The list ecology is more organic and anti-hierarchical. Everyone has access to the source code. Everyone can make changes. Everyone can do what they want. There is no need for the FreeBSD management to meet and decide "Multimedia is good." There is no need for a project team to prioritize and list action items and best-of-breed deliverables. Someone in Switzerland decides he wants to hook up a television receiver to his computer and, what do you know, someone in Great Britain has already solved the problem. Well, he's solved it if you don't have an MSP34xx stereo decoder chip in your card. But that should be fixed sooner or later, too.

Free Doesn't Mean Freeloading

There are thousands of other mailing lists linking thousands of other projects. It's hard to actually put a number to them because the projects grow, merge, and fade as people's interests wax and wane. The best flourish, and the others just drift away.

Life on the mailing lists is often a bit more brutal and short than life on earth. The work on the project needs to split up. The volunteers need to organize themselves so that great software can be written.

On that January 14, a new member of the WINE list was learning just how volunteering works. The guy posted a note to the list that described his Diamond RIO portable music device that lets you listen to MP3 files whenever you want. "I think the WINE development team should drop everything and work on getting this program to work as it doesn't seem like Diamond wants to release a Linux utility for the Rio," he wrote.

WINE stands for "WINE Is Not an Emulator," which is a joke that only programmers and free software lovers can get. It's first a play on the recursive acronym for the GNU project ("GNU is not UNIX"). It's also a bit of a political statement for programmers. An emulator is a piece of software that makes one computer act like another. A company named Connectix, for instance, sells an emulator that lets a Macintosh behave like a Windows PC so anyone can use their Windows software on the Mac. Emulators, however, are pretty slow because they're constantly translating information on the fly. Anyone who has tried to hold a conversation with someone who speaks a different language knows how frustrating it can be to require a translator.

The WINE project is an ambitious attempt to knock out one of the most important structural elements of the Microsoft monopoly. Software written for Windows only functions when people buy a version of Windows from Microsoft. When you purchase a Connectix emulator for the Mac, you get a version of Windows bundled with it.

The WINE project is a group of people who are trying to clone Windows. Well, not clone all of it. They just want to clone what is known as the Win32 API, a panoply of features that make it easier to write software for a Microsoft machine. A programmer who wants to create a new button for a Windows computer doesn't need to write all of the instructions for drawing a frame with three-dimensional shading. A Microsoft employee has already bundled those instructions into the Win32 API. There are millions of functions in these kits that help programmers. Some play audio files, others draw complex images or movies. These features make it easy for programmers to write software for Windows because some of the most repetitive work is already finished.

The WINE clone of the Win32 is a fascinating example of how open source starts slowly and picks up steam. Bob Amstadt started the project in 1993, but soon turned it over to Alexandre Julliard, who has been the main force behind it. The project, although still far from finished, has produced some dramatic accomplishments, making it possible to run major programs like Microsoft Word or Microsoft Excel on a Linux box without using Windows. In essence, the WINE software is doing a good enough job acting like Windows that it's fooling Excel and Word. If you can trick the cousins, that's not too bad.

The WINE home page (www.winehq.com) estimates that more than 90,000 people use WINE regularly to run programs for Microsoft Windows without buying Windows. About 140 or more people regularly contribute to the project by writing code or fixing bugs. Many are hobbyists who want the thrill of getting their software to run without Windows, but some are corporate programmers. The corporate programmers want to sell their software to the broadest possible marketplace, but they don't want to take the time to rewrite everything. If they can get their software working well with WINE, then people who use Linux or BSD can use the software that was written for Microsoft Windows.

The new user who wanted to get his RIO player working with his Linux computer soon got a rude awakening. Andreas Mohr, a German programmer, wrote back,

Instead of suggesting the WINE team to "drop everything" in order to get a relatively minor thing like PMP300 to work, would you please install *WINE, test it, read documentation/bug reports and post a* useful *bug report here? There are* zillions *of very useful and impressing Windoze apps out there . . . (After all that's only my personal opinion, maybe that was a bit too harsh ;-)*

Most new free software users soon discover that freedom isn't always easy. If you want to get free software, you're going to have to put in some work. Sometimes you get lucky. The man in Switzerland who posted his note on the same day found out that someone in Britain was solving his problems for him. There was no one, however, working on the RIO software and making sure it worked with WINE.

Mohr's suggestion was to file a bug report that ranks the usability of the software so the programmers working on WINE can tweak it. This is just the first step in the free software experience. Someone has to notice the problem and fix it. In this case, someone needs to hook up their Diamond RIO MP3 player to a Linux box and try to move MP3 files with the software written for Windows. Ideally, the software will work perfectly, and now all Linux users will be able to use RIO players. In reality, there might be problems or glitches. Some of the graphics on the screen might be wrong. The software might not download anything at all. The first step is for someone to test the product and write up a detailed report about what works and what doesn't.

At the time of this writing, no one has stepped up to the plate. There are no reports about the Diamond player in the WINE database. Maybe the new user didn't have time. Maybe he wasn't technically sophisticated enough to get WINE running in the first place. It's still not a simple system to use. In any case, his bright idea fell by the wayside.

The mailing lists buzz with idle chatter about neat, way-out ideas that never come to fruition. Some people see this as a limitation of the free software world. A corporation, however, is able to dispatch a team of programmers to create solutions. These companies have money to spend on polishing a product and making sure it works. Connectix, for instance, makes an emulator that lets Mac users play games written for the Sony PlayStation. The company employs a substantial number of people who simply play all the Sony games from beginning to end until all of the bugs are gone. It's a rough job, but someone has to do it.

WINE can't pay anyone, and that means that great ideas sometimes get ignored. The free software community, however, doesn't necessarily see this as a limitation. If the RIO player were truly important, someone else would come along and pick up the project. Someone else would do the work and file a bug report so everyone could use the software. If there's no one else, then maybe the RIO software isn't that important to the Linux community. Work gets done when someone really cares enough to do it.

These mailing lists are the fibers that link the open source community into the network of minds. Before e-mail, they were just a bunch of rebels haunting the moors and rattling around their basements inventing monstrous machines. Now they're smoothly tuned mechanisms coordinated by messages, notes, and missives. They're not madmen who roar at dinner parties about the bad technology from Borg-like corporations. They've got friends now. One person may be a flake, but a group might be on to something.

3. IMAGE

Consider this picture: Microsoft is a megalith built by one man with a towering ego. It may not be fair to lump all of the serfs in the corporate cubicle farms in Redmond into one big army of automatons, but it sure conjures a striking image that isn't altogether inaccurate. Microsoft employees are fiercely loyal and often more dedicated to the cause than the average worker bee. Bill Gates built the company from scratch with the help of several college friends, and this group maintains tight control over all parts of the empire. The flavor of the organization is set by one man with the mind and the ego to micromanage it all.

Now consider the image of the members of the free software revolution. Practically every newspaper article and colorful feature describing the group talks about a ragtag army of scruffy, bearded programmers who are just a bit too pale from spending their days in front of a computer screen. The writers love to conjure up a picture of a group that looks like it came stumbling out of some dystopian fantasy movie like *Mad Max* or *A Boy and His Dog*. They're the outsiders. They're a tightly knit band of rebel outcasts who are planning to free the people from their Microsoft slavery and return to the people the power usurped by Mr. Gates. What do they want? Freedom! When do they want it? Now!

There's only one problem with this tidy, Hollywood-ready image: it's far from true. While Microsoft is one big corporation with reins of control that keep everyone in line, there is no strong or even weak organization that binds the world of open source software. The movement, if it could be called that, is comprised of individuals, each one free to do whatever he wants with the software. That's the point: no more shackles. No more corporate hegemony. Just pure source code that runs fast, clean, and light, straight through the night.

This doesn't mean that the image is all wrong. Some of the luminaries like Richard Stallman and Alan Cox have been known to sport long, Rip van Winkle–grade beards. Some folks are strikingly pale. A few could bathe a bit more frequently. Caffeine is a bit too popular with them. Some people look as if they were targets for derision by the idiots on the high school football team.

But there are many counterexamples. Linus Torvalds drives a Pontiac and lives in a respectable home with a wife and two children. He works during the day at a big company and spends his evenings shopping and doing errands. His life would be perfectly categorized as late 1950s sitcom if his wife, Tove, weren't a former Finnish karate champion and trucks weren't driving up to his house to deliver top-of-the-line computers like a 200-pound monstrosity with four Xeon processors. He told *VAR Business*, "A large truck brought it to our house and the driver was really confused. He said, 'You don't have a loading dock?'" On second thought, those are the kind of shenanigans that drive most sitcoms.

There's no easy way to classify the many free source code contributors. Many have children, but many don't. Some don't mention them, some slip in references to them, and others parade them around with pride. Some are married, some are not. Some are openly gay. Some exist in sort of a presexual utopia of early teenage boyhood. Some of them *are* still in their early teens. Some aren't.

Some contributors are fairly described as "ragtag," but many aren't. Many are corporate droids who work in cubicle farms during the day and create free software projects at night. Some work at banks. Some work on databases for human resource departments. Some build websites. Everyone has a day job, and many keep themselves clean and ready to be promoted to the next level. Bruce Perens, one of the leaders of the Debian group, used to work at the Silicon Valley glitz factory Pixar and helped write some of the software that created the hit *Toy Story*.

Still, he told me, "At the time *Toy Story* was coming out, there was a space shuttle flying with the Debian GNU/Linux distribution on it controlling a biological experiment. People would say 'Are you proud of working at Pixar?' and then I would say my hobby software was running on the space shuttle now. That was a turnaround point when I realized that Linux might become my career."

In fact, it's not exactly fair to categorize many of the free software programmers as a loosely knit band of rebel programmers out to destroy Microsoft. It's a great image that feeds the media's need to highlight conflict, but it's not exactly true. The free software movement began long before Microsoft was a household word. Richard Stallman wrote his manifesto setting out some of the precepts in 1984. He was careful to push the notion that programmers always used to share the source code to software until the 1980s, when corporations began to develop the shrink-wrapped software business. In the olden days of the 1950s, 1960s, and 1970s, programmers always shared. While Stallman has been known to flip his middle finger out at the name Bill Gates for the reporting pleasure of a writer from *Salon* magazine, he's not after Microsoft per se. He just wants to return computing to the good old days when the source was free and sharing was possible.

The same holds for most of the other programmers. Some contribute source code because it helps them with their day job. Some stay up all night writing code because they're obsessed. Some consider it an act of charity, a kind of noblesse oblige. Some want to fix bugs that bother them. Some want fame, glory, and the respect of all other computer programmers. There are thousands of reasons why new open source software gets written, and very few of them have anything to do with Microsoft.

In fact, it's a bad idea to see the free software revolution as having much to do with Microsoft. Even if Linux, FreeBSD, and other free software packages win, Microsoft will probably continue to fly along quite happily in much the same way that IBM continues to thrive even after losing the belt of the Heavyweight Computing Champion of the World to Microsoft. Anyone who spends his or her time focused on the image of a ragtag band of ruffians and orphans battling the Microsoft leviathan is bound to miss the real story.

The fight is really just a by-product of the coming of age of the information business. The computer trade is rapidly maturing and turning into a service industry. In the past, the manufacture of computers and software took place on assembly lines and in cubicle farms. People bought shrink-wrapped items from racks. These were *items* that were *manufactured*. Now both computers and software are turning into dirt-cheap commodities whose only source of profit is customization and handholding. The real money now is in *service*.

Along the way, the free software visionaries stumbled onto a curious fact. They could give away software, and people would give back improvements to it. Software cost practically nothing to duplicate, so it wasn't that hard to just give it away after it was written. At first, this was sort of a pseudo-communist thing to do, but today it seems like a brilliant business decision. If the software is turning into a commodity with a price falling toward zero, why not go all the way and gain whatever you can by freely sharing the code? The profits could come by selling services like programming and education. The revolution isn't about defeating Microsoft; it's just a change in the whole way the world buys and uses computers.

The revolution is also the latest episode in the battle between the programmers and the suits. In a sense, it's a battle for the hearts and minds of the people who are smart enough to create software for the world. The programmers want to write challenging tools that impress their friends. The suits want to rein in programmers and channel their energy toward putting more money in the pockets of the corporation. The suits hope to keep programmers devoted by giving them fat paychecks, but it's not clear that programmers really want the cash. The freedom to do whatever you want with source code is intrinsically rewarding. The suits want to keep software under lock and key so they can sell it and maximize revenues. The free software revolution is really about a bunch of programmers saying, "Screw the cash. I really want the source code."

The revolution is also about defining wealth in cyberspace. Microsoft promises to build neat tools that will help us get wherever we want to go today—if we keep writing larger and larger checks. The open source movement promises software with practically no limitations. Which is a better deal? The Microsoft millionaires probably believe in proprietary software and suggest that the company wouldn't have succeeded as it did if it didn't provide something society wanted. They created good things, and the people rewarded them.

But the open source movement has also created great software that many think is better than anything Microsoft has built. Is society better off with a computer infrastructure controlled by a big corporate machine driven by cash? Or does sharing the source code create better software? Are we at a point where money is not the best vehicle for lubricating the engines of societal advancement? Many in the free software world are pondering these questions.

Anyone who tunes in to the battle between Microsoft and the world expecting to see a good old-fashioned fight for marketplace domination is going to miss the real excitement. Sure, Linux, FreeBSD, OpenBSD, NetBSD, Mach, and the thousands of other free software projects are going to come out swinging. Microsoft is going to counterpunch with thousands of patents defended by armies of lawyers. Some of the programmers might even be a bit weird, and a few will be entitled to wear the adjective "ragtag." But the real revolution has nothing to do with whether Bill Gates keeps his title as King of the Hill. It has nothing to do with whether the programmers stay up late and work in the nude. It has nothing to do with poor grooming, extravagant beards, Coke-bottle glasses, black trench coats, or any of the other stereotypes that fuel the media's image.

It's about the gradual commodification of software and hardware. It's about the need for freedom and the quest to create cool software. It's about a world just discovering how much can be accomplished when information can be duplicated for next to nothing.

The real struggle is finding out how long society can keep hanging ten toes off the edge of the board as we get carried by the wave of freedom. Is there enough energy in the wave and enough grace in society to ride it all the way to the shore? Or will something wicked, something evil, or something sloppy come along and mess it up?

• • •

4. COLLEGE

Speaking in Tongues

I was part of the free software movement for many years, but I didn't know it. When I was a graduate student, I released the source code to a project. In 1991, that was the sort of thing to do in universities. Publishing the source code to a project was part of publishing a paper about it. And the academy put publishing pretty high on its list.

My first big release came in May 1991 when I circulated a program that let people hide secret messages as innocuous text. My program turned any message into some cute play-by-play from a baseball game, like "No contact in Mudsville! It's a fastball with wings. No wood on that one. He's uncorking what looks like a spitball. Whooooosh! Strike! He's out of there." The secret message was encoded in the choices of phrases. "He's out of there" meant something different from "He pops it up to Orville Baskethands." The program enabled information to mutate into other forms, just like the shapeshifting monsters from *The X-Files*. I sent out an announcement to the influential newsgroup comp.risks and soon hundreds of people were asking for free copies of the software.

I created this program because Senator Joe Biden introduced a bill into the Senate that would require the manufacturers of all computer networks to provide a way for the police to get copies of any message. The Federal Bureau of Investigation, among others, was afraid that they would have trouble obtaining evidence if people were able to encode data. My software illustrated how hard it would be to stop the flow of information.

The best, and perhaps most surprising, part of the whole bloom of e-mail came when a fellow I had never met, D. Jason Penney, converted the program from the fading Pascal into the more popular C. He did this on his own and sent the new, converted software back to me. When I asked him whether I could distribute his version, he said that it was my program. He was just helping out.

I never thought much more about that project until I started to write this book. While two or three people a month would write asking for copies of the software, it never turned into more than a bit of research into the foundations of secret codes and a bit of a mathematical parlor trick. It was more an academic exercise than a prototype of something that could rival Microsoft and make me rich.

In the past, I thought the project never developed into more than a cute toy because there was no market for it. The product wasn't readily useful for businesses, and no one starts a company without the hope that millions of folks desperately need a product. Projects needed programmers and programmers cost money. I just assumed that other free software projects would fall into the same chasm of lack of funding.

Now, after investigating the free software world, I am convinced that my project was a small success. Penney's contribution was not just a strange aberration but a relatively common event on the Internet. People are quite willing to take a piece of software that interests them, modify it to suit their needs, and then contribute it back to the world. Sure, most people only have a few hours a week to work on such projects, but they add up. Penney's work made my software easier to use for many C programmers, thus spreading it further.

In fact, I may have been subconsciously belittling the project. It took only three or four days of my time and a bit more of Penney's, but it was a complete version of a powerful encryption system that worked well. Yes, there was no money flowing, but that may have made it more of a success. Penney probably wouldn't have given me his C version if he knew I was going to sell it. He probably would have demanded a share. Lawyers would have gotten involved. The whole project would have been gummed up with contracts, release dates, distribution licenses, and other hassles that just weren't worth it for a neat way to hide messages. Sure, money is good, but money also brings hassles.

Cash Versus Sharing

In the 1980s and 1990s, programmers in universities still shared heavily with the world. The notion of sharing source code with the world owes a great deal to the academic tradition of publishing results so others can read them, think about them, critique them, and ultimately extend them. Many of the government granting agencies like the National Science Foundation and the Defense Advanced Research Projects Agency fostered this sharing by explicitly requiring that people with grants release the source code to the world with no restrictions. Much of the Internet was created by people who gave out these kinds of contracts and insisted upon shared standards that weren't proprietary. This tradition has fallen on harder times as universities became more obsessed with the profits associated with patents and contract research, but the idea is so powerful that it's hard to displace.

The free software movement in particular owes a great deal to the Massachusetts Institute of Technology. Richard Stallman, the man who is credited with starting the movement, began working in MIT's computer labs in the 1970s. He gets credit for sparking the revolution because he wrote the GNU *Manifesto* in 1984. The document spelled out why it's essential to share the source code to a program with others. Stallman took the matter to heart because he also practiced what he wrote about and contributed several great programs, including a text editor with thousands of features.

Of course, Stallman doesn't take credit for coming up with the idea of sharing source code. He remembers his early years at MIT quite fondly and speaks of how people would share their source code and software without restrictions. The computers were new, complicated, and temperamental. Cooperation was the only way that anyone could accomplish anything. That's why IBM shared the source code to the operating systems on their mainframes though the early part of the 1960s.

This tradition started to fade by the early 1980s as the microcomputer revolution began. Companies realized that most people just wanted software that worked. They didn't need the source code and all the instructions that only programmers could read. So companies quickly learned that they could keep the source code to themselves and keep their customers relatively happy while locking out competitors. They were kings who built a wall to keep out the intruders.

The *GNU Manifesto* emerged as the most radical reaction to the trend toward locking up the source code. While many people looked at the *GNU Manifesto* with confusion, others became partial converts. They began donating code that they had written. Some tossed random utility programs into the soup, some offered games, and some sent in sophisticated packages that ran printers, networks, or even networks of printers. A few even became complete disciples and started writing code full-time for the GNU project. This growth was largely ignored by the world, which became entranced with the growth of Microsoft. More and more programmers, however, were spending more time mingling with the GNU project, and it was taking hold.

In the early 1980s, an operating system known as UNIX had grown to be very popular in universities and laboratories. AT&T designed and built it at Bell Labs throughout the 1970s. In the beginning, the company shared the source code with researchers and computer scientists in universities, in part because the company was a monopoly that was only allowed to sell telephone service. UNIX was just an experiment that the company started to help run the next generation of telephone switches, which were already turning into specialized computers.

In the beginning, the project was just an academic exercise, but all of the research and sharing helped create a nice operating system with a wide audience. UNIX turned out to be pretty good. When the phone company started splitting up in 1984, the folks at AT&T wondered how they could turn a profit from what was a substantial investment in time and money. They started by asking people who used UNIX at the universities to sign nondisclosure agreements.

Stallman looked at this as mind control and the death of a great tradition. Many others at the universities were more pragmatic. AT&T had given plenty of money and resources to the university. Wasn't it fair for the university to give something back?

Stallman looked at this a bit differently. Yes, AT&T was being nice when they gave grants to the university, but weren't masters always kind when they gave bowls of gruel to their slaves? The binary version AT&T started distributing to the world was just gruel for Stallman. The high priests and lucky few got to read the source code. They got to eat the steak and lobster spread. Stallman saw this central, controlling, corporate force as the enemy, and he began naming his work GNU, which was a recursive acronym that stood for "GNU's Not UNIX." The GNU project aimed to produce a complete working operating system that was going to do everything that UNIX did for none of the moral, emotional, or ethical cost. Users would be able to read the source code to Stallman's OS and modify it without signing a tough nondisclosure agreement drafted by teams of lawyers. They would be able to play with their software in complete freedom. Stallman notes that he never aimed to produce an operating system that didn't cost anything. The world may be entranced with the notion of a price tag of zero, but for Stallman, that was just a side effect of the unrestricted sharing.

Creating a stand-alone system that would do everything with free software was his dream, but it was a long way from fruition, and Stallman was smart enough to start off with a manageable project. He began by producing a text editor known as GNU Emacs. The program was a big hit because it was highly customizable. Some people just used the program to edit papers, but others programmed it to accomplish fancier tasks such as reading their e-mail and generating automatic responses. One programmer was told by management that he had to include plenty of comments in his source code, so he programmed GNU Emacs to insert them automatically. One professor created a version of GNU Emacs that would automatically insert random praise into requests to his secretary.[1] Practically everything in Emacs could be changed or customized. If you didn't like hitting the delete key to fix a mistyped character, then you could arrange for the 6 key to do the same thing. This might make it hard to type numbers, but the user was free to mess up his life as much as he wanted.

It took Microsoft years to catch up with Stallman's solution, and even then they implemented it in a dangerous way. They let people create little custom programs for modifying documents, but they forgot to pre-

---

[1] "Where are those reports I asked you to copy? You're doing a great job. Thanks for all the help," on one day. "Are you ever going to copy those reports? You're doing a great job. Thanks for all the help," on the next.

vent malicious code from crying havoc. Today, Microsoft Word allows little programs named macro viruses to roam around the planet. Open up a Word document, and a virus might be lurking.

In the 1980s, the free software world devoted itself to projects like this. GNU Emacs became a big hit in the academic world where system administrators could install it for free and not worry about counting students or negotiating licenses. Also, smart minds were better able to appreciate the cool flexibility Stallman had engineered into the system. Clever folks wasted time by adding filters to the text editor that would scan their text and translate it into, like, Valley Girl talk or more urban jive.

The GNU project grew by accepting contributions from many folks across the country. Some were fairly sophisticated, eye-catching programs like GNU Chess, a program that was quite competitive and as good as all but the best packages. Most were simple tools for handling many of the day-to-day chores for running a computer system. System administrators, students, and programmers from around the country would often take on small jobs because they felt compelled to fix something. When they were done, a few would kick the source code over to the GNU project.

Stallman's biggest programming project for GNU during the 1980s was writing the GNU C compiler (GCC). This program was an important tool that converted the C source code written by humans into the machine code understood by computers. The GCC package was an important cornerstone for the GNU project in several ways. First, it was one of the best compilers around. Second, it could easily move from machine to machine. Stallman personally ported it to several different big platforms like Intel's x86 line of processors. Third, the package was free, which in the case of GNU software meant that anyone was free to use and modify the software.

The GCC provided an important harmonizing effect to the GNU project. Someone could write his program on a machine built by Digital, compile it with GCC, and be fairly certain that it would run on all other machines with GCC. That allowed the GNU software to migrate freely throughout the world, from machine to machine, from Sun to Apollo to DEC to Intel.

The GCC's license also attracted many developers and curious engineers. Anyone could use the source code for their projects, and many did. Over time, the compiler moved from machine to machine as users converted it. Sometimes a chip company engineer would rework the compiler to make it work on a new chip. Sometimes a user would do it for a project. Sometimes a student would do it when insomnia struck. Somehow, it moved from machine to machine, and it carried all of the other GNU software with it.

The next great leap forward came in the early 1990s as people began to realize that a completely free operating system was a serious possibility. Stallman had always dreamed of replacing UNIX with something that was just as good and accompanied by the source code, but it was a large task. It was the reason he started the GNU project. Slowly but surely, the GNU project was assembling the parts to make it work. There were hundreds of small utilities and bigger tools donated to the GNU project, and those little bits were starting to add up.

The free software movement also owes a great deal to Berkeley, or more precisely to a small group in the Department of Computer Science at the University of California at Berkeley. The group of hardcore hackers, which included professors, research associates, graduate students, and a few undergraduates, had developed a version of UNIX known as BSD (Berkeley Software Distribution). AT&T shared their version of UNIX with Berkeley, and the programmers at Berkeley fixed, extended, and enhanced the software. These extensions formed the core of BSD. Their work was part experimental and part practical, but the results were widely embraced. Sun Microsystems, one of Silicon Valley's UNIX workstation companies, used a version on its machines through the early 1990s when they created a new version known as Solaris by folding in some of AT&T's System V. Many feel that BSD and its approach remain the foundation of the OS.

The big problem was that the team built their version on top of source code from AT&T. The folks at Berkeley and their hundreds, if not thousands, of friends, colleagues, and students who contributed to the project gave their source code away, but AT&T did not. This gave AT&T control over anyone who wanted to use BSD, and the company was far from ready to join the free software movement. Millions of dollars were spent on the research developing UNIX. The company wanted to make some money back.

The team at Berkeley fought back, and Keith Bostic, one of the core team, began organizing people together to write the source code that could replace these bits. By the beginning of the 1990s, he had cajoled enough of his friends to accomplish it. In June 1991, the group produced "Networking Release 2," a version that included almost all of a complete working version of UNIX. All you needed to do was add six files to have a complete operating system.

AT&T was not happy. It had created a separate division known as the UNIX Systems Laboratory and wanted to make a profit. Free source code from Berkeley was tough competition. So the UNIX Systems Laboratory sued.

This lawsuit marked the end of universities' preeminent role in the development of free software. Suddenly, the lawsuit focused everyone's attention and made them realize that taking money from corporations came into conflict with sharing software source code. Richard Stallman left MIT in 1984 when he understood that a university's need for money would eventually trump his belief in total sharing of source code. Stallman was just a staff member who kept the computers running. He wasn't a tenured professor who could officially do anything. So he started the Free Software Foundation and never looked back. MIT helped him at the beginning by loaning him space, but it was clear that the relationship was near the end. Universities needed money to function. Professors at many institutions had quotas specifying how much grant money they needed to raise. Stallman wasn't bringing in cash by giving away his software.

Meanwhile, on the other coast, the lawsuit tied up Berkeley and the BSD project for several years, and the project lost valuable energy and time by devoting them to the legal fight. In the meantime, several other completely free software projects started springing up around the globe. These began in basements and depended on machines that the programmer owned. One of these projects was started by Linus Torvalds and would eventually grow to become Linux, the unstoppable engine of hype and glory. He didn't have the money of the

Berkeley computer science department, and he didn't have the latest machines that corporations gave them. But he had freedom and the pile of source code that came from unaffiliated, free projects like GNU that refused to compromise and cut intellectual corners. Although Torvalds might not have realized it at the time, freedom turned out to be most valuable of all.

• • •

5. QUICKSAND

The story of the end of the university's preeminence in the free software world is a tale of greed and corporate power. While many saw an unhappy ending coming for many years, few could do much to stop the inevitable collision between the University of California at Berkeley and its former patron, AT&T.

The lawsuit between AT&T and the University of California at Berkeley had its roots in what marriage counselors love to call a "poorly conceived relationship." By the end of the 1980s, the computer science department at Berkeley had a problem. They had been collaborating with AT&T on the UNIX system from the beginning. They had written some nice code, including some of the crucial software that formed the foundation of the Internet. Students, professors, scientists, and even Wall Street traders loved the power and flexibility of UNIX. Everyone wanted UNIX.

The problem was that not everyone could get UNIX. AT&T, which had sponsored much of the research at Berkeley, kept an iron hand on its invention. If you wanted to run UNIX, then you needed to license some essential software from AT&T that sat at the core of the system. They were the supreme ruler of the UNIX domain, and they expected a healthy tithe for the pleasure of living within it.

One of the people who wanted UNIX was the Finnish student Linus Torvalds, who couldn't afford this tithe. He was far from the first one, and the conflict began long before he started to write Linux in 1991.

Toward the end of the 1980s, most people in the computer world were well aware of Stallman's crusade against the corporate dominance of AT&T and UNIX. Most programmers knew that GNU stood for

"GNU's Not UNIX." Stallman was not the only person annoyed by AT&T's attitude toward secrecy and nondisclosure agreements. In fact, his attitude was contagious. Some of the folks at Berkeley looked at the growth of tools emerging from the GNU project and felt a bit used. They had written many pieces of code that found their way into AT&T's version of UNIX. They had contributed many great ideas. Yet AT&T was behaving as if AT&T alone owned it. They gave and gave, while AT&T took.

Stallman got to distribute his source code. Stallman got to share with others. Stallman got to build his reputation. Programmers raved about Stallman's Emacs. People played GNU Chess at their offices. Others were donating their tools to the GNU project. Everyone was getting some attention by sharing except the folks at Berkeley who collaborated with AT&T. This started to rub people the wrong way.

Something had to be done, and the folks at Berkeley started feeling the pressure. Some at Berkeley wondered why the professors had entered into such a Faustian bargain with a big corporation. Was the payoff great enough to surrender their academic souls? Just where did AT&T get off telling us what we could publish?

Others outside of Berkeley looked in and saw a treasure trove of software that was written by academics. Many of them were friends. Some of them had studied at Berkeley. Some had even written some of the UNIX code before they graduated. Some were companies competing with AT&T. All of them figured that they could solve their UNIX problems if they could just get their hands on the source code. There had to be some way to get it released.

Slowly, the two groups began making contact and actively speculating on how to free Berkeley's version of UNIX from AT&T's grip.

Breaking the Bond

The first move to separate Berkeley's version of UNIX from AT&T's control wasn't really a revolution. No one was starting a civil war by firing shots at Fort Sumter or starting a revolution by dropping tea in the harbor. In fact, it started long before the lawsuit and Linux. In 1989, some people wanted to start hooking their PCs and other devices up to the Internet, and they didn't want to use UNIX.

Berkeley had written some of the software known as TCP/IP that defined how computers on the Internet would communicate and share packets. They wrote the software for UNIX because that was one of the favorite OSs around the labs. Other companies got a copy of the code by buying a source license for UNIX from AT&T. The TCP/IP code was just part of the mix. Some say that the cost of the license reached $250,000 or more and required that the customer pay a per-unit fee for every product that was shipped. Those prices didn't deter the big companies like IBM or DEC. They thought of UNIX as an OS for the hefty workstations and minicomputers sold to businesses and scientists. Those guys had the budget to pay for big hardware, so it was possible to slip the cost of the UNIX OS in with the package.

But the PC world was different. It was filled with guys in garages who wanted to build simple boards that would let a PC communicate on the Internet. These guys were efficient and knew how to scrounge up cheap parts from all over the world. Some of them had gone to Berkeley and learned to program on the VAXes and Sun workstations running Berkeley's version of UNIX. A few of them had even helped write or debug the code. They didn't see why they had to buy such a big license for something that non-AT&T folks had written with the generous help of large government grants. Some even worked for corporations that gave money to support Berkeley's projects. Why couldn't they get at the code they helped pay to develop?

Kirk McKusick, one of the members of the Computer Systems Research Group at the time, remembers, "People came to us and said, 'Look, you wrote TCP/IP. Surely you shouldn't require an AT&T license for that?' These seemed like reasonable requests. We decided to start with something that was clearly not part of the UNIX we got from AT&T. It seemed very clear that we could pull out the TCP/IP stack and distribute that without running afoul of AT&T's license."

So the Berkeley Computer Systems Research Group (CSRG) created what they called Network Release 1 and put it on the market for $1,000 in June 1989. That wasn't really the price because the release came with one of the first versions of what would come to be known as the BSD-style license. Once you paid the $1,000, you could do whatever you wanted with the code, including just putting it up on the Net and giving it away.

"We thought that two or three groups would pay the money and then put the code on the Internet, but in fact, hundreds of sites actually paid the one thousand dollars for it," says McKusick and adds, "mostly so they could get a piece of paper from the university saying, 'You can do what you want with this.'"

This move worked out well for Berkeley and also for UNIX. The Berkeley TCP/IP stack became the best-known version of the code, and it acted like a reference version for the rest of the Net. If it had a glitch, everyone else had to work around the glitch because it was so prevalent. Even today, companies like Sun like to brag that their TCP/IP forms the backbone of the Net, and this is one of the reasons to buy a Sun instead of an NT workstation. Of course, the code in Sun's OS has a rich, Berkeley-based heritage, and it may still contain some of the original BSD code for controlling the net.

In for a Penny, in for a Pound

In time, more and more companies started forming in the Bay Area and more and more realized that Berkeley's version of UNIX was the reference for the Internet. They started asking for this bit or that bit.

Keith Bostic heard these requests and decided that the Berkeley CSRG needed to free up as much of the source code as possible. Everyone agreed it was a utopian idea, but only Bostic thought it was possible to accomplish. McKusick writes, in his history of BSD, "Mike Karels [a fellow software developer] and I pointed out that releasing large parts of the system was a huge task, but we agreed that if he could sort out how to deal with re-implementing the hundreds of utilities and the massive C library, then we would tackle the kernel. Privately, Karels and I thought that would be the end of the discussion."

Dave Hitz, a good friend of Bostic's, remembers the time. "Bostic was more of a commanding type. He just rounded up all of his friends to finish up the code. You would go over to his house for dinner and he would say, 'I've got a list. What do you want to do?' I think I did the cp command and maybe the look command." Hitz, of course, is happy that he took part in the project. He recently founded Network Appliance, a company that packages a stripped-down version of BSD into a file server that is supposed to be a fairly bulletproof appliance for customers. Network Appliance didn't need to do much software engineering when they began. They just grabbed the free version of BSD and hooked it up.

Bostic pursued people far and wide to accomplish the task. He gave them the published description of the utility or the part of the library from the documentation and then asked them to reimplement it without looking at the source code. This cloning operation is known as a cleanroom operation because it is entirely legal if it takes place inside a metaphorical room where the engineers inside don't have any information about how the AT&T engineers built UNIX.

This was not an easy job, but Bostic was quite devoted and pursued people everywhere. He roped everyone who could code into the project and often spent time fixing things afterward. The task took 18 months and included more than 400 people who received just notoriety and some thanks afterward. The 400-plus names are printed in the book he wrote with McKusick and Karels in 1996.

When Bostic came close to finishing, he stopped by McKusick's office and asked how the kernel was coming along. This called McKusick and Karels's bluff and forced them to do some hard engineering work. In some respects, Bostic had the easier job. Writing small utility programs that his team used was hard work, but it was essentially preorganized and segmented. Many folks over the years created manual files that documented exactly what the programs were supposed to do. Each program could be assigned separately and people didn't need to coordinate their work too much. These were just dishes for a potluck supper.

Cleaning up the kernel, however, was a different matter. It was much larger than many of the smaller utilities and was filled with more complicated code that formed a tightly coordinated mechanism. Sloppy work in one of the utility files would probably affect only that one utility, but a glitch in the kernel would routinely bring down the entire system. If Bostic was coordinating a potluck supper, McKusick and Karels had to find a way to create an entire restaurant that served thousands of meals a day to thousands of customers. Every detail needed to work together smoothly.

To make matters more complicated, Berkeley's contributions to the kernel were mixed in with AT&T's contributions. Both had added on parts, glued in new features, and created new powers over the years. They were de facto partners on the project. Back in the good old days, they had both shared their source code without any long-term considerations or cares. But now that AT&T claimed ownership of it all, they had to find a way to unwind all of the changes and figure out who wrote what.

McKusick says, "We built a converted database up line by line. We took every line of code and inserted it into the database. You end up finding pretty quickly where the code migrated to and then you decide whether it is sufficiently large enough to see if it needed recoding."

This database made life much easier for them and they were able to plow through the code, quickly recoding islets of AT&T code here and there. They could easily pull up a file filled with source code and let the database mark up the parts that might be owned by AT&T. Some parts went quickly, but other parts dragged on. By late spring of 1991, they had finished all but six files that were just too much work.

It would be nice to report that they bravely struggled onward, forgoing all distractions like movies, coffeehouses, and friends, but that's not true. They punted and tossed everything out the door and called it "Network Release 2." The name implied that this new version was just a new revision of their earlier product, Network Release 1, and this made life easier with the lawyers. They just grabbed the old, simple license and reused it. It also disguised the fact that this new pile of code was only about six files short of a full-grown OS.

The good news about open source is that projects often succeed even when they initially fail. A commercial product couldn't ship without the complete functionality of the six files. Few would buy it. Plus, no one could come along, get a bug under his bonnet, and patch up the holes. Proprietary source code isn't available and no one wants to help someone else in business without compensation.

The new, almost complete UNIX, however, was something different. It was a university project and so university rules of camaraderie and sharing seemed to apply. Another programmer, Bill Jolitz, picked up Network Release 2 and soon added the code necessary to fill the gap. He became fascinated with getting UNIX up and running on a 386 processor, a task that was sort of like trying to fit the latest traction control hardware and anti-lock brakes on a go-cart. At the time, serious computer scientists worked on serious machines from serious workstation and minicomputer companies. The PC industry was building toys. Of course, there was something macho to the entire project. Back then I remember joking to a friend that we should try to get UNIX running on the new air-conditioning system, just to prove it could be done.

Jolitz's project, of course, found many people on the Net who didn't think it was just a toy. Once he put the source code on the Net, a bloom of enthusiasm spread through the universities and waystations of the world. People wanted to experiment with a high-grade OS and most could only afford relatively cheap hardware like the 386. Sure, places like Berkeley could get the government grant money and the big corporate donations, but 2,000-plus other schools were stuck waiting. Jolitz's version of 386BSD struck a chord.

While news traveled quickly to some corners, it didn't reach Finland. Network Release 2 came in June 1991, right around the same time that Linus Torvalds was poking around looking for a high-grade OS to use in experiments. Jolitz's 386BSD came out about six months later as Torvalds began to dig into creating the OS he would later call Linux. Soon afterward, Jolitz lost interest in the project and let it lie, but others came along. In fact, two groups called NetBSD and FreeBSD sprang up to carry the torch.

Although it may seem strange that three groups building a free operating system could emerge without knowing about each other, it is important to realize that the Internet was a very different world in 1991 and 1992. The World Wide Web was only a gleam in some people's eyes. Only the best universities had general access to the web for its students, and most people didn't understand what an e-mail address was. Only a few computer-related businesses like IBM and Xerox put their researchers on the Net. The community was small and insular.

The main conduits for information were the USENET newsgroups, which were read only by people who could get access through their universities. This technology was an efficient way of sharing information, although quite flawed. Here's how it worked: every so often, each computer would call up its negotiators and swap the latest articles. Information traveled like gossip, which is to say that it traveled quickly but with very uneven distribution. Computers were always breaking down or being upgraded. No one could count on every message getting to every corner of the globe.

The NetBSD and the FreeBSD forks of the BSD kernel continue to exist separately today. The folks who work on NetBSD concentrate on making their code run on all possible machines, and they currently list 21 different platforms that range from the omnipresent Intel 486 to the gone but not forgotten Commodore Amiga.

The FreeBSD team, on the other hand, concentrates on making their product work well on the Intel 386. They added many layers of installation tools to make it easier for the average Joe to use, and now it's the most popular version of BSD code around.

Those two versions used the latest code from Berkeley. Torvalds, on the other hand, didn't know about the 386BSD, FreeBSD, or NetBSD. If he had found out, he says, he probably would have just downloaded the versions and joined one of those teams. Why run off and reinvent the wheel?

AT&T Notices the Damage

Soon after Network Release 2 hit the world, the real problems began for BSD. While AT&T didn't really notice 386BSD, NetBSD, or FreeBSD, they did notice a company called Berkeley Software Design Incorporated. This corporation created their own OS by taking Network Release 2 and adding their own versions of the missing six files, but they didn't release this for free on the Net. They started putting advertisements in the trade press offering the source code for $995, a price they claimed was a huge discount over AT&T's charge.

The modern, post-Internet reader should find this hilarious. Two to three groups and countless splinter factions were distributing the BSD software over the Internet for free and this didn't seem to catch AT&T's

attention, but the emergence of BSDI selling the same product for almost $1,000 rang alarm bells. That was the time, though, before the Internet infrastructure became ubiquitous. In the early 1990s, people only half-joked that FedEx was the most efficient Internet Service Provider around. It was much faster to copy hundreds of megabytes of data onto a magnetic tape and drop it in FedEx than to actually try to copy it over the Internet. Back then only real nerds were on the Internet. Managers and lawyers wore suits and got their news from the trade press and advertisements.

BSDI's cost-cutting was a major headache for AT&T. This small company was selling a product that AT&T felt it had shepherded, organized, and coordinated over time.

AT&T started off by claiming UNIX as a trademark and threatening BSDI with infringing upon it. BSDI countered by changing the ads to emphasize that BSDI was a separate company that wasn't related to AT&T or the subsidiary AT&T created to market UNIX known as UNIX System Laboratories, or USL.

That didn't work. USL saw its cash cow melting away and assumed folks would jump at the chance to buy a complete OS with all the source code for $995. The price seems outrageously high today, but that's only after the stiff price competition of the 1990s. It was still a good deal at the time. So USL sued BSDI for actually stealing proprietary source code from AT&T.

This argument didn't work, either. BSDI turned around and waved the Network Release 2 license they got from Berkeley. They bought all but six of the files from Berkeley, and Berkeley claimed that all of the source code was theirs to sell. BSDI wrote the missing six files themselves and they were quite sure that they got no help from AT&T or USL. Therefore, BSDI didn't steal anything. If AT&T thought it was stolen, they should take it up with Berkeley. The judge bought BSDI's argument and narrowed the case to focus on the six files.

This was a crucial moment in the development of the free software movement and its various kernels. AT&T found itself cornered. Backing down meant giving up its claim to UNIX and the wonderful stream of license fees that kept pouring in. Pressing ahead meant suing the University of California, its old friend, partner, and author of lots of UNIX code. Eventually, the forces of greed and omnipotent corporate power won out and AT&T's USL filed a lawsuit naming both BSDI and the University of California.

Taking sides in this case was pretty easy for most folks in the academic and free software world. The CSRG at Berkeley did research. They published things. University research was supposed to be open and freely distributed. AT&T was trying to steal the work of hundreds if not thousands of students, researchers, professors, and others. That wasn't fair.

In reality, AT&T did pay something for what they got. They sent their employees to Berkeley to get master's degrees, they shared the original Versions 5, 6, and 7 and 32/V source code, and they even sent some hardware to the computer science department. The original creators of UNIX lived and worked at Bell Labs drawing AT&T paychecks. Berkeley students got summer jobs at AT&T. There wasn't an official quid-pro-quo. It wasn't very well spelled out, but AT&T was paying something.

Some folks on AT&T's side might even want to paint the CSRG at Berkeley as filled with academic freeloaders who worked hard to weasel money out of the big corporations without considering the implications. The folks at Berkeley should have known that AT&T was going to want something for its contributions. There's no such thing as a free lunch.

There's something to this argument because running a high-rent research project at a top-notch school requires a fair amount of guile and marketing sophistication. By the 1990s, the top universities had become very good at making vague, unofficial promises with their pleas for corporate gifts. This sort of coquetry and teasing was bound to land someone in a fight. McKusick, for instance, says that the CSRG designed the BSD license to be very liberal to please the corporate donors. "Hewlett-Packard put in hundreds of thousands of dollars and they were doing so under the understanding that they were going to use the code," he said. If the BSD hadn't kept releasing code like Network Release 2 in a clear, easy-to-reuse legal form, he says, some of the funding for the group would have dried up.

But there's also a bit of irony here. McKusick points out that AT&T was far from the most generous company to support the CSRG. "In fact, we even had to pay for our license to UNIX," he says before adding, "although it was only ninety-nine dollars at the time."

AT&T's support of the department was hardly bountiful. The big checks weren't grants outright. They paid for the out-of-state tuition for AT&T employees who came to Berkeley to receive their master's degrees. While AT&T could have sent their employees elsewhere, there's no doubt that there are more generous ways to send money to researchers.

McKusick also notes that AT&T didn't even send along much hardware. The only hardware he remembers receiving from them were some 5620 terminals and a Datakit circuit-based switch that he says "was a huge headache that really did us very little good." Berkeley was on the forefront of developing the packet-based standards that would dominate the Internet. If anything, the older circuit-based switch convinced the Berkeley team that basing the Internet on the old phone system would be a major mistake.

To make matters worse, AT&T often wanted the BSD team to include features that would force all the BSD users to buy a newer, more expensive license from AT&T. In addition, license verification was never a quick or easy task. McKusick says, "We had a person whose full-time job was to keep the AT&T licensing person happy."

In the end, he concludes, "They paid us next to nothing and got a huge windfall."

Choosing sides in this battle probably isn't worth the trouble at this point because Berkeley eventually won. The hard work of Bostic's hundreds of volunteers and the careful combing of the kernel by the CSRG paid off. AT&T's case slowly withered away as the University of California was able to show how much of the distribution came from innocent, non-AT&T sources.

Berkeley even landed a few good blows of its own. They found that AT&T had stripped copyrights from Berkeley code that they had imported to System V and had failed to provide due credit to Berkeley. The BSD license is probably one of the least restrictive ones in the world. Companies like Apple use BSD source code all the time. The license has few requirements beyond keeping the copyright notice intact and including some credit for the University of California. AT&T didn't pay attention to this and failed to cite Berkeley's contributions in their releases. Oops. The CSRG countersued claiming that AT&T had violated a license that may be one of the least restrictive in the world.

The battle raged in the courts for more than a year. It moved from federal to California state court. Judges held hearings, lawyers took depositions, clerks read briefs, judges heard arguments presented by briefs written by lawyers who had just held depositions. The burn rate of legal fees was probably larger than most Internet start-ups.

Any grown-up should take one look at this battle and understand just how the free software movement got so far. While the Berkeley folks were meeting with lawyers and worrying about whether the judges were going to choose the right side, Linus Torvalds was creating his own kernel. He started Linux on his own, and that made him a free man.

In the end, the University of California settled the lawsuit after the USL was sold to Novell, a company run by Ray Noorda. McKusick believes that Noorda's embrace of free competition made a big difference, and by January 1994 the legal fight was over. Berkeley celebrated by releasing a completely free and unencumbered 4.4BSD-Lite in June 1994.

The terms of the settlement were pretty minor. Net Release 2 came with about 18,000 files. 4.4BSD-Lite contained all but three of them. Seventy of them included a new, expanded copyright that gave some credit to AT&T and USL, but didn't constrain anyone's right to freely distribute them. McKusick, Bostic, and the hundreds of volunteers did a great job making sure that Net Release 2 was clean. In fact, two people familiar with the settlement talks say that Berkeley just deleted a few files to allow USL's lawyers to save face. We'll never know for sure because the details of the settlement are sealed. McKusick and the others can't talk about the details. That's another great example of how the legal system fails the American people and inadvertently gives the free software world another leg up. There's no information in the record to help historians or give future generations some hints on how to solve similar disputes.

6. OUTSIDER

The battle between the University of California at Berkeley's computer science department and AT&T did not reach the court system until 1992, but the friction between the department's devotion to sharing and the corporation's insistence on control started long before.

While the BSD team struggled with lawyers, a free man in Finland began to write his own operating system without any of the legal or institutional encumbrance. At the beginning he said it was a project that probably wouldn't amount to much, but only a few years later people began to joke about "Total World Domination." A few years after that, they started using the phrase seriously.

In April 1991, Linus Torvalds had a problem. He was a relatively poor university student in Finland who wanted to hack in the guts of a computer operating system. Microsoft's machines at the time were the cheapest around, but they weren't very interesting. The basic Disk Operating System (DOS) essentially let one program control the computer. Windows 3.1 was not much more than a graphical front end to DOS featuring pretty pictures—icons—to represent the files. Torvalds wanted to experiment with a real OS, and that meant UNIX or something that was UNIX-like. These real OSs juggled hundreds of programs at one time and often kept dozens of users happy. Playing with DOS was like practicing basketball shots by yourself. Playing with UNIX was like playing with a team that had 5, 10, maybe as many as 100 people moving around the court in complicated, clockwork patterns.

But UNIX machines cost a relative fortune. The high-end customers requested the OS, so generally only high-end machines came with it. A poor university student in Finland didn't have the money for a top-notch Sun Sparc station. He could only afford a basic PC, which came with the 386 processor. This was a top-of-the-line PC at the time, but it still wasn't particularly exciting. A few companies made a version of UNIX for this low-end machine, but they charged for it.

In June 1991, soon after Torvalds[1] started his little science project, the Computer Systems Research Group at Berkeley released what they thought was their completely unencumbered version of BSD UNIX known as Network Release 2. Several projects emerged to port this to the 386, and the project evolved to become the FreeBSD and NetBSD versions of today. Torvalds has often said that he might never have started Linux if he had known that he could just download a more complete OS from Berkeley.

But Torvalds didn't know about BSD at the time, and he's lucky he didn't. Berkeley was soon snowed under by the lawsuit with AT&T claiming that the university was somehow shipping AT&T's intellectual property. Development of the BSD system came to a screeching halt as programmers realized that AT&T could shut them down at any time if Berkeley was found guilty of giving away source code that AT&T owned.

If he couldn't afford to buy a UNIX machine, he would write his own version. He would make it POSIX-compatible, a standard for UNIX designers, so others would be able to use it. Minix was another UNIX-like OS that a professor, Andrew Tanenbaum, wrote for students to experiment with the guts of an OS. Torvalds initially considered using Minix as a platform. Tanenbaum included the source code to his project, but he charged for the package. It was like a textbook for students around the world.

Torvalds looked at the price of Minix ($150) and thought it was too much. Richard Stallman's GNU General Public License had taken root in Torvalds's brain, and he saw the limitations in charging for software. GNU had also produced a wide variety of tools and utility programs that he could use on his machine. Minix was controlled by Tanenbaum, albeit with a much looser hand than many of the other companies at the time.

---

[1]Everyone in the community, including many who don't know him, refers to him by his first name. The rules of style prevent me from using that in something as proper as a book.

People could add their own features to Minix and some did. They did get a copy of the source code for $150. But few changes made their way back into Minix. Tanenbaum wanted to keep it simple and grew frustrated with the many people who, as he wrote back then, "want to turn Minix into BSD UNIX."

So Torvalds started writing his own tiny operating system for this 386. It wasn't going to be anything special. It wasn't going to topple AT&T or the burgeoning Microsoft. It was just going to be a fun experiment in writing a computer operating system that was all his. He wrote in January 1992, "Many things should have been done more portably if it would have been a real project. I'm not making overly many excuses about it though: it was a design decision, and last April when I started the thing, I didn't think anybody would actually want to use it."

Still, Torvalds had high ambitions. He was writing a toy, but he wanted it to have many, if not all, of the features found in full-strength UNIX versions on the market. On July 3, he started wondering how to accomplish this and placed a posting on the USENET newsgroup comp.os.minix, writing:

Hello netlanders,
Due to a project I'm working on (in minix), I'm interested in the posix standard definition. Could somebody please point me to a (preferably) machine-readable format of the latest posix rules? Ftp-sites would be nice.

Torvalds's question was pretty simple. When he wrote the message in 1991, UNIX was one of the major operating systems in the world. The project that started at AT&T and Berkeley was shipping on computers from IBM, Sun, Apple, and most manufacturers of higher-powered machines known as workstations. Wall Street banks and scientists loved the more powerful machines, and they loved the simplicity and hackability of UNIX machines. In an attempt to unify the marketplace, computer manufacturers created a way to standardize UNIX and called it POSIX. POSIX ensured that each UNIX machine would behave in a standardized way.

Torvalds worked quickly. By September he was posting notes to the group with the subject line "What would you like to see most in Minix?" He was adding features to his clone, and he wanted to take a poll about where he should add next.

Torvalds already had some good news to report. "I've currently ported bash(1.08) and GCC(1.40), and things seem to work. This implies that I'll get something practical within a few months," he said.

At first glance, he was making astounding progress. He created a working system with a compiler in less than half a year. But he also had the advantage of borrowing from the GNU project. Stallman's GNU project group had already written a compiler (GCC) and a nice text user interface (bash). Torvalds just grabbed these because he could. He was standing on the shoulders of the giants who had come before him.

The core of an OS is often called the "kernel," which is one of the strange words floating around the world of computers. When people are being proper, they note that Linus Torvalds was creating the Linux *kernel* in 1991. Most of the other software, like the desktop, the utilities, the editors, the web browsers, the games, the compilers, and practically everything else, was written by other folks. If you measure this in disk space, more than 95 percent of the code in an average distribution lies outside the kernel. If you measure it by user interaction, most people using Linux or BSD don't even know that there's a kernel in there. The buttons they click, the websites they visit, and the printing they do are all controlled by other programs that do the work.

Of course, measuring the importance of the kernel this way is stupid. The kernel is sort of the combination of the mail room, boiler room, kitchen, and laundry room for a computer. It's responsible for keeping the data flowing between the hard drives, the memory, the printers, the video screen, and any other part that happens to be attached to the computer.

In many respects, a well-written kernel is like a fine hotel. The guests check in, they're given a room, and then they can order whatever they need from room service and a smoothly oiled concierge staff. Is this new job going to take an extra 10 megabytes of disk space? No problem, sir. Right away, sir. We'll be right up with it. Ideally, the software won't even know that other software is running in a separate room. If that other program is a loud rock-and-roll MP3 playing tool, the other software won't realize that when it crashes and burns up its own room. The hotel just cruises right along, taking care of business.

In 1991, Torvalds had a short list of features he wanted to add to the kernel. The Internet was still a small network linking universities and some advanced labs, and so networking was a small concern. He was only aiming at the 386, so he could rely on some of the special features that weren't available on other chips. High-end graphics hardware cards were still pretty expensive, so he concentrated on a text-only interface. He would later fix all of these problems with the help of the people on the Linux kernel mailing list, but for now he could avoid them.

Still, hacking the kernel means anticipating what other programmers might do to ruin things. You don't know if someone's going to try to snag all 128 megabytes of RAM available. You don't know if someone's going to hook up a strange old daisy-wheel printer and try to dump a PostScript file down its throat. You don't know if someone's going to create an endless loop that's going to write random numbers all over the memory. Stupid programmers and dumb users do these things every day, and you've got to be ready for it. The kernel of the OS has to keep things flowing smoothly between all the different parts of the system. If one goes bad because of a sloppy bit of code, the kernel needs to cut it off like a limb that's getting gangrene. If one job starts heating up, the kernel needs to try to give it all the resources it can so the user will be happy. The kernel hacker needs to keep all of these things straight.

Creating an operating system like this is no easy job. Many of the commercial systems crash frequently for no perceptible reason, and most of the public just takes it.[2] Many people somehow assume that it must be their fault that the program failed. In reality, it's probably the

---

[2]Microsoft now acknowledges the existence of a bug in the tens of millions of copies of Windows 95 and Windows 98 that will cause your computer to 'stop responding (hang)'—you know, what you call crash—after exactly 49 days, 17 hours, 2 minutes, and 47.296 seconds of continuous operation . . . . Why 49.7? days? Because computers aren't counting the days. They're counting the milliseconds. One counter begins when Windows starts up; when it gets to 232 milliseconds—which happens to be 49.7 days—well, that's the biggest number this counter can handle. And instead of gracefully rolling over and starting again at zero, it manages to bring the entire operating system to a halt."—James Gleick in the *New York Times*.

kernel's. Or more precisely, it's the kernel designer's fault for not anticipating what could go wrong.

By the mid-1970s, companies and computer scientists were already experimenting with many different ways to create workable operating systems. While the computers of the day weren't very powerful by modern standards, the programmers created operating systems that let tens if not hundreds of people use a machine simultaneously. The OS would keep the different tasks straight and make sure that no user could interfere with another.

As people designed more and more operating systems, they quickly realized that there was one tough question: how big should it be? Some people argued that the OS should be as big as possible and come complete with all the features that someone might want to use. Others countered with stripped-down designs that came with a small core of the OS surrounded by thousands of little programs that did the same thing.

To some extent, the debate is more about semantics than reality. A user wants the computer to be able to list the different files stored in one directory. It doesn't matter if the question is answered by a big operating system that handles everything or a little operating system that uses a program to find the answer. The job still needs to be done, and many of the instructions are the same. It's just a question of whether the instructions are labeled the "operating system" or an ancillary program.

But the debate is also one about design. Programmers, teachers, and the Lego company all love to believe that any problem can be solved by breaking it down into small parts that can be assembled to create the whole. Every programmer wants to turn the design of an operating system into thousands of little problems that can be solved individually. This dream usually lasts until someone begins to assemble the parts and discovers that they don't work together as perfectly as they should.

When Torvalds started crafting the Linux kernel, he decided he was going to create a bigger, more integrated version that he called a "monolithic kernel." This was something of a bold move because the academic community was entranced with what they called "microkernels." The difference is partly semantic and partly real, but it can be summarized by analogy with businesses. Some companies try to build large, smoothly integrated operations where one company controls all the steps of production. Others try to create smaller operations that subcontract much of the production work to other companies. One is big, monolithic, and all-encompassing, while the other is smaller, fragmented, and heterogeneous. It's not uncommon to find two companies in the same industry taking different approaches and thinking they're doing the right thing.

The design of an operating system often boils down to the same decision. Do we want to build a monolithic core that handles all the juggling internally, or do we want a smaller, more fragmented model that should be more flexible as long as the parts interact correctly?

In time, the OS world started referring to this core as the *kernel* of the operating system. People who wanted to create big OSs with many features wrote monolithic kernels. Their ideological enemies who wanted to break the OS into hundreds of small programs running on a small core wrote microkernels. Some of the most extreme folks labeled their work a nanokernel because they thought it did even less and thus was even more pure than those bloated microkernels.

The word "kernel" is a bit confusing for most people because they often use it to mean a fragment of an object or a small fraction. An extreme argument may have a kernel of truth to it. A disaster movie always gives the characters and the audience a kernel of hope to which to cling.

Mathematicians use the word a bit differently and emphasize the word's ability to let a small part define a larger concept. Technically, a kernel of a function f is the set of values, $x_1, x_2, \ldots x_n$ such that $f(x_i)=1$, or whatever the identity element happens to be. The action of the kernel of a function does a good job of defining how the function behaves with all the other elements. The algebraists study a kernel of a function because it reveals the overall behavior.[3]

The OS designers use the word in the same way. If they define the kernel correctly, then the behavior of the rest of the OS will follow. The small part of the code defines the behavior of the entire computer. If the kernel does one thing well, the entire computer will do it well. If it does one thing badly, then everything will suffer.

Many computer users often notice this effect without realizing why it

---

[3] The kernel of $f(x)=x_2$ is (-1, 1) and it illustrates how the function has two branches.

exists. Most Macintosh computers, for instance, can be sluggish at times because the OS does not do a good job juggling the workload between processes. The kernel of the OS has not been completely overhauled since the early days when the machines ran one program at a time. This sluggishness will persist for a bit longer until Macintosh releases a new version known as MacOS X. This will be based on the Mach kernel, a version developed at Carnegie-Mellon University and released as open source software. Steve Jobs adopted it when he went to NeXT, a company that was eventually folded back into Apple. This kernel does a much better job of juggling different tasks because it uses preemptive multitasking instead of cooperative multitasking. The original version of the MacOS let each program decide when and if it was going to give up control of the computer to let other programs run. This low-rent version of juggling was called cooperative multitasking, but it failed when some program in the hotel failed to cooperate. Most software developers obeyed the rules, but mistakes would still occur. Bad programs would lock up the machine. Preemptive multitasking takes this power away from the individual programs. It swaps control from program to program without asking permission. One pig of a program can't slow down the entire machine. When the new MacOS X kernel starts offering preemptive multitasking, the users should notice less sluggish behavior and more consistent performance.

Torvalds plunged in and created a monolithic kernel. This made it easier to tweak all the strange interactions between the programs. Sure, a microkernel built around a clean, message-passing architecture was an elegant way to construct the guts of an OS, but it had its problems. There was no easy way to deal with special exceptions. Let's say you want a web server to run very quickly on your machine. That means you need to treat messages coming into the computer from the Internet with exceptional speed. You need to ship them with the equivalent of special delivery or FedEx. You need to create a special exception for them. Tacking these exceptions onto a clean microkernel starts to make it look bad. The design starts to get cluttered and less elegant. After a few special exceptions are added, the microkernel can start to get confused.

Torvalds's monolithic kernel did not have the elegance or the simplicity of a microkernel OS like Minix or Mach, but it was easier to hack. New tweaks to speed up certain features were relatively easy to add. There was no need to come up with an entirely new architecture for the message-passing system. The downside was that the guts could grow remarkably byzantine, like the bureaucracy of a big company.

In the past, this complexity hurt the success of proprietary operating systems. The complexity produced bugs because no one could understand it. Torvalds's system, however, came with all the source code, making it much easier for application programmers to find out what was causing their glitch. To carry the corporate bureaucracy metaphor a bit further, the source code acted like the omniscient secretary who is able to explain everything to a harried executive. This perfect knowledge reduced the cost of complexity.

By the beginning of 1992, Linux was no longer a Finnish student's part-time hobby. Several influential programmers became interested in the code. It was free and relatively usable. It ran much of the GNU code, and that made it a neat, inexpensive way to experiment with some excellent tools. More and more people downloaded the system, and a significant fraction started reporting bugs and suggestions to Torvalds. He rolled them back in and the project snowballed.

A Hobby Begets a Project that Begets a Movement

On the face of it, Torvalds's decision to create an OS wasn't extraordinary. Millions of college-age students decide that they can do anything if they just put in a bit more elbow grease. The college theater departments, newspapers, and humor magazines all started with this impulse, and the notion isn't limited to college students. Millions of adults run Little League teams, build model railroads, lobby the local government to create parks, and take on thousands of projects big and small in their spare time.

Every great idea has a leader who can produce a system to sustain it. Every small-town lot had kids playing baseball, but a few guys organized a Little League program that standardized the rules and the competition. Every small town had people campaigning for parks, but one small group created the Sierra Club, which fights for parks throughout the world.

This talent for organizing the work of others is a rare commodity, and Torvalds had a knack for it. He was gracious about sharing his system with the world and he never lorded it over anyone. His messages were filled with jokes and self-deprecating humor, most of which were carefully marked with smiley faces (:-)) to make sure that the message was clear. If he wrote something pointed, he would apologize for being a "hothead." He was always gracious in giving credit to others and noted that much of Linux was just a clone of UNIX. All of this made him easy to read and thus influential.

His greatest trick, though, was his decision to avoid the mantle of power. He wrote in 1992, "Here's my standing on 'keeping control,' in 2 words (three?): I won't. The only control I've effectively been keeping on Linux is that I know it better than anybody else."

He pointed out that his control was only an illusion that was caused by the fact that he did a good job maintaining the system. "I've made my changes available to ftp-sites etc. Those have become effectively official releases, and I don't expect this to change for some time: not because I feel I have some moral right to it, but because I haven't heard too many complaints."

As he added new features to his OS, he shipped new copies frequently. The Internet made this easy to do. He would just pop a new version up on a server and post a notice for all to read: come download the latest version.

He made it clear that people could vote to depose him at any time. "If people feel I do a bad job, they can do it themselves." They could just take all of his Linux code and start their own version using Torvalds's work as a foundation.

Anyone could break off from Torvalds's project because Torvalds decided to ship the source code to his project under Richard Stallman's GNU General Public License, or GPL. In the beginning, he issued it with a more restrictive license that prohibited any "commercial" use, but eventually moved to the GNU license. This was a crucial decision because it cemented a promise with anyone who spent a few minutes playing with his toy operating system for the 386. It stated that all of the source code that Torvalds or anyone else wrote would be freely accessible and shared with everyone. This decision was a double-edged sword for the community. Everyone could take the software for free, but if they started circulating some new software built with the code, they would have to donate their changes back to the project. It was like flypaper. Anyone who started working with the project grew attached to it. They couldn't run off into their own corner. Some programmers joke that this flypaper license is like sex. If you make one mistake by hooking up with a project protected by GPL, you pay for it forever. If you ever ship a version of the project, you must include all of the source code. It can be distributed freely forever.

While some people complained about the sticky nature of the GPL, enough saw it as a virtue. They liked Torvalds's source code, and they liked the fact that the GPL made them full partners in the project. Anyone could donate their time and be sure it wasn't going to disappear. The source code became a body of work held in common trust for everyone. No one could rope it off, fence it in, or take control.

In time, Torvalds's pet science project and hacking hobby grew as more people got interested in playing with the guts of machines. The price was right, and idle curiosity could be powerful. Some wondered what a guy in Finland could do with a 386 machine. Others wondered if it was really as usable as the big machines from commercial companies. Others wondered if it was powerful enough to solve some problems in the lab. Still others just wanted to tinker. All of these folks gave it a try, and some even began to contribute to the project.

Torvalds's burgeoning kernel dovetailed nicely with the tools that the GNU project created. All of the work by Stallman and his disciples could be easily ported to work with the operating system core that Torvalds was now calling Linux. This was the power of freely distributable source code. Anyone could make a connection, and someone invariably did. Soon, much of the GNU code began running on Linux. These tools made it easier to create more new programs, and the snowball began to roll.

Many people feel that Linus Torvalds's true act of genius was in coming up with a flexible and responsive system for letting his toy OS grow and change. He released new versions often, and he encouraged everyone to test them with him. In the past, many open source developers using the GNU GPL had only shipped new versions at major landmarks in development, acting a bit like the commercial developers. After they released version 1.0, they would hole up in their basements until they had added enough new features to justify version 2.0.

Torvalds avoided this perfectionism and shared frequently. If he fixed a bug on Monday, then he would roll out a new version that afternoon. It's not strange to have two or three new versions hit the Internet each week. This was a bit more work for Torvalds, but it also made it much easier for others to become involved. They could watch what he was doing and make their own suggestions.

This freedom also attracted others to the party. They knew that Linux would always be theirs, too. They could write neat features and plug them into the Linux kernel without worrying that Torvalds would yank the rug out from under them. The GPL was a contract that lasted long into the future. It was a promise that bound them together.

The Linux kernel also succeeded because it was written from the ground up for the PC platform. When the Berkeley UNIX hackers were porting BSD to the PC platform, they weren't able to make it fit perfectly. They were taking a piece of software crafted for older computers like the VAX, and shaving off corners and rewriting sections until it ran on the PC.

Alan Cox pointed out to me, "The early BSD stuff was by UNIX people for UNIX people. You needed a calculator and familiarity with BSD UNIX on big machines (or a lot of reading) to install it. You also couldn't share a disk between DOS/Windows and 386BSD or the early branches off it.

"Nowadays FreeBSD understands DOS partitions and can share a disk, but at the time BSD was scary to install," he continued.

The BSD also took certain pieces of hardware for granted. Early versions of BSD required a 387, a numerical coprocessor that would speed up the execution of floating point numbers. Cox remembers that the price (about $100) was just too much for his budget. At that time, the free software world was a very lean organization.

Torvalds's operating system plugged a crucial hole in the world of free source software and made it possible for someone to run a computer without paying anyone for a license. Richard Stallman had dreamed of this day, and Torvalds came up with the last major piece of the puzzle.

A Different Kind of Trial

During the early months of Torvalds's work, the BSD group was stuck in a legal swamp. While the BSD team was involved with secret settlement talks and secret depositions, Linus Torvalds was happily writing code and sharing it with the world on the Net. His life wasn't all peaches and cream, but all of his hassles were open. Professor Andy Tanenbaum, a fairly well-respected and famous computer scientist, got in a long, extended debate with Torvalds over the structure of Linux. He looked down at Linux and claimed that Linux would have been worth two F's in his class because of its design. This led to a big flame war that was every bit as nasty as the fight between Berkeley and AT&T's USL. In fact, to the average observer it was even nastier. Torvalds returned Tanenbaum's fire with strong words like "fiasco," "brain-damages," and "suck." He brushed off the bad grades by pointing out that Albert Einstein supposedly got bad grades in math and physics. The high-priced lawyers working for AT&T and Berkeley probably used very expensive and polite words to try and hide the shivs they were trying to stick in each other's back. Torvalds and Tanenbaum pulled out each other's virtual hair like a squawkfest on the Jerry Springer show.

But Torvalds's flame war with Tanenbaum occurred in the open in an Internet newsgroup. Other folks could read it, think about it, add their two cents' worth, and even take sides. It was a wide-open debate that uncovered many flaws in the original versions of Linux and Tanenbaum's Minix. They forced Torvalds to think deeply about what he wanted to do with Linux and consider its flaws. He had to listen to the arguments of a critic and a number of his peers on the Net and then come up with arguments as to why his Linux kernel didn't suck too badly.

This open fight had a very different effect from the one going on in the legal system. Developers and UNIX hackers avoided the various free versions of BSD because of the legal cloud. If a judge decided that AT&T and USL were right, everyone would have to abandon their work on the platform. While the CSRG worked hard to get free, judges don't always make the choices we want.

The fight between Torvalds and Tanenbaum, however, drew people into the project. Other programmers like David Miller, Ted T'so, and

Peter da Silva chimed in with their opinions. At the time, they were just interested bystanders. In time, they became part of the Linux brain trust. Soon they were contributing source code that ran on Linux. The argument's excitement forced them to look at Torvalds's toy OS and try to decide whether his defense made any sense. Today, David Miller is one of the biggest contributors to the Linux kernel. Many of the original debaters became major contributors to the foundations of Linux.

This fight drew folks in and kept them involved. It showed that Torvalds was serious about the project and willing to think about its limitations. More important, it exposed these limitations and inspired other folks on the Net to step forward and try to fix them. Everyone could read the arguments and jump in. Even now, you can dig up the archives of this battle and read in excruciating detail what people were thinking and doing. The AT&T/USL-versus-Berkeley fight is still sealed.

To this day, all of the devotees of the various BSDs grit their teeth when they hear about Linux. They think that FreeBSD, NetBSD, and OpenBSD are better, and they have good reasons for these beliefs. They know they were out the door first with a complete running system. But Linux is on the cover of the magazines. All of the great technically unwashed are now starting to use "Linux" as a synonym for free software. If AT&T never sued, the BSD teams would be the ones reaping the glory. They would be the ones to whom Microsoft turned when it needed a plausible competitor. They would be more famous.

But that's crying over spilled milk. The Berkeley CSRG lived a life of relative luxury in their world made fat with big corporate and government donations. They took the cash, and it was only a matter of time before someone called them on it. Yes, they won in the end, but it came too late. Torvalds was already out of the gate and attracting more disciples.

McKusick says, "If you plot the installation base of Linux and BSD over the last five years, you'll see that they're both in exponential growth. But BSD's about eighteen to twenty months behind. That's about how long it took between Net Release 2 and the unencumbered 4.4BSD-Lite. That's about how long it took for the court system to do its job."

7. GROWTH

Through the 1990s, the little toy operating system grew slowly and quietly as more and more programmers were drawn into the vortex. At the beginning, the OS wasn't rich with features. You could run several different programs at once, but you couldn't do much with the programs. The system's interface was just text. Still, this was often good enough for a few folks in labs around the world. Some just enjoyed playing with computers. Getting Linux running on their PC was a challenge, not unlike bolting an after-market supercharger onto a Honda Civic. But others took the project more seriously because they had serious jobs that couldn't be solved with a proprietary operating system that came from Microsoft or others.

In time, more people started using the system and started contributing their additions to the pot. Someone figured out how to make MIT's free X Window System run on Linux so everyone could have a graphical interface. Someone else discovered how to roll in technology for interfacing with the Internet. That made a big difference because everyone could hack, tweak, and fiddle with the code and then just upload the new versions to the Net.

It goes without saying that all the cool software coming out of Stallman's Free Software Foundation found its way to Linux. Some were simple toys like GNU Chess, but others were serious tools that were essential to the growth of the project. By 1991, the FSF was offering what might be argued were the best text editor and compiler in the world. Others might have been close, but Stallman's were free. These were crucial tools that made it possible for Linux to grow quickly from a tiny experimental kernel into a full-featured OS for doing everything a programmer might want to do.

James LewisMoss, one of the many programmers who devote some time to Linux, says that GCC made it possible for programmers to create, revise, and extend the kernel. "GCC is integral to the success of Linux," he says, and points out that this may be one of the most important reasons why "it's polite to refer to it as GNU/Linux."

LewisMoss points out one of the smoldering controversies in the world of free software: all of the tools and games that came from the GNU project started becoming part of what people simply thought of as plain "Linux." The name for the small kernel of the operating system soon grew to apply to almost all the free software that ran with it. This angered Stallman, who first argued that a better name would be "Lignux." When that failed to take hold, he moved to "GNU/Linux." Some ignored his pleas and simply used "Linux," which is still a bit unfair. Some feel that "GNU/Linux" is too much of a mouthful and, for better or worse, just plain Linux is an appropriate shortcut. Some, like LewisMoss, hold firm to GNU/Linux.

Soon some people were bundling together CD-ROMs with all this software in one batch. The group would try to work out as many glitches as possible so that the purchaser's life would be easier. All boasted strange names like Yggdrasil, Slackware, SuSE, Debian, or Red Hat. Many were just garage projects that never made much money, but that was okay. Making money wasn't really the point. People just wanted to play with the source. Plus, few thought that much money could be made. The GPL, for instance, made it difficult to differentiate the product because it required everyone to share their source code with the world. If Slackware came up with a neat fix that made their version of Linux better, then Debian and SuSE could grab it. The GPL prevented anyone from constraining the growth of Linux.

But only greedy businessmen see sharing and competition as negatives. In practice, the free flow of information enhanced the market for Linux by ensuring that it was stable and freely available. If one key CD-ROM developer gets a new girlfriend and stops spending enough time programming, another distribution will pick up the slack. If a hurricane flattened Raleigh, North Carolina, the home of Red Hat, then another supplier would still be around. A proprietary OS like Windows is like a set of manacles. An earthquake in Redmond, Washington, could cause a serious disruption for everyone.

The competition and the GPL meant that the users would never feel bound to one OS. If problems arose, anyone could always just start a splinter group and take Linux in that direction. And they did. All the major systems began as splinter groups, and some picked up enough steam and energy to dominate. In time, the best splinter groups spun off their own splinter groups and the process grew terribly complicated.

The Establishment Begins to Notice

By the mid-1990s, the operating system had already developed quite a following. In 1994, Jon Hall was a programmer for Digital, a company that was later bought by Compaq. Hall also wears a full beard and uses the name "maddog" as a nickname. At that time, Digital made workstations that ran a version of UNIX. In the early 1990s, Digital made a big leap forward by creating a 64-bit processor version of its workstation CPU chip, the Alpha, and the company wanted to make sure that the chip found widespread acceptance.

Hall remembers well the moment he discovered Linux. He told *Linux Today,*

> I didn't even know I was involved with Linux at first. I got a copy of Dr. Dobb's Journal, *and in there was an advertisement for "get a UNIX operating system, all the source code, and run it on your PC." And I think it was $99. And I go, "Oh, wow, that's pretty cool. For $99, I can do that." So I sent away for it, got the CD. The only trouble was that I didn't have a PC to run it on. So I put it on my Ultrix system, took a look at the main pages, directory structure and stuff, and said, "Hey, that looks pretty cool." Then I put it away in the filing cabinet. That was probably around January of 1994.*

In May 1994, Hall met Torvalds at a DECUS (Digital Equipment Corporation User Society) meeting and became a big fan. Hall is a programmer's programmer who has written code for many different machines over the years, like the IBM 1130 and the DEC PDP–8. He started out as an electrical engineer in college, but took up writing software "after seeing a friend of mine fried by 13,600 volts and 400 amps, which was not a pretty sight." Hall started playing with UNIX when he worked at Bell Labs and fell in love with the OS.

At the meeting, Torvalds helped Hall and his boss set up a PC with Linux. This was the first time that Hall actually saw Linux run, and he was pleasantly surprised. He said, "By that time I had been using UNIX for probably about fifteen years. I had used System V, I had used Berkeley, and all sorts of stuff, and this really felt like UNIX. You know . . . I mean, it's kind of like playing the piano. You can play the piano, even if it's a crappy piano. But when it's a really good piano, your fingers just fly over the keys. That's the way this felt. It felt good, and I was really impressed."

This experience turned Hall into a true convert and he went back to Digital convinced that the Linux project was more than just some kids playing with a toy OS. These so-called amateurs with no centralized system or corporate backing had produced a very, very impressive system that was almost as good as the big commercial systems. Hall was an instant devotee. Many involved in the project recall their day of conversion with the same strength. A bolt of lightning peeled the haze away from their eyes, and they saw.

Hall set out trying to get Torvalds to rewrite Linux so it would work well on the Alpha. This was not a simple task, but it was one that helped the operating system grow a bit more. The original version included some software that assumed the computer was designed like the Intel 386. This was fine when Linux only ran on Intel machines, but removing these assumptions made it possible for the software to run well on all types of machines.

Hall went sailing with Torvalds to talk about the guts of the Linux OS. Hall told me, "I took him out on the Mississippi River, went up and down the Mississippi in the river boat, drinking Hurricanes, and I said to him, 'Linus, did you ever think about porting Linux to a 64-bit processor, like the Alpha?' He said, 'Well, I thought about doing that, but the Helsinki office has been having problems getting me a system, so I guess I'll have to do the PowerPC instead.'

"I knew that was the wrong answer, so I came back to Digital (at the time), and got a friend of mine, named Bill Jackson, to send out a system to Linus, and he received it about a couple weeks after that. Then I found some people inside Digital who were also thinking about porting Linux to an Alpha. I got the two groups together, and after that, we started on the Alpha Linux project."

This was one of the first times that a major corporation started taking note of what was happening in the garages and basements of hard-core computer programmers. It was also one of the first times that a corporation looked at an open source operating system and did not react with fear or shock. Sun was always a big contributor of open source software, but they kept their OS proprietary. Hall worked tirelessly at Digital to ensure that the corporation understood the implications of the GPL and saw that it was a good way to get more interested in the Alpha chip. He says he taught upper management at Digital how to "say the L-word."

Hall also helped start a group called Linux International, which works to make the corporate world safe for Linux. "We help vendors understand the Linux marketplace," Hall told me. "There's a lot of confusion about what the GPL means. Less now, but still there's a lot of confusion. We helped them find the markets."

Today, Linux International helps control the trademark on the name Linux and ensures that it is used in an open way. "When someone wanted to call themselves something like 'Linux University,' we said that's bad because there's going to be more than one. 'Linux University of North Carolina' is okay. It opens up the space."

In the beginning, Torvalds depended heavily on the kindness of strangers like Hall. He didn't have much money, and the Linux project wasn't generating a huge salary for him. Of course, poverty also made it easier for people like Hall to justify giving him a machine. Torvalds wasn't rich monetarily, but he became rich in machines.

By 1994, when Hall met Torvalds, Linux was already far from just a one-man science project. The floppy disks and CD-ROMs holding a version of the OS were already on the market, and this distribution mechanism was one of the crucial unifying forces. Someone could just plunk down a few dollars and get a version that was more or less ready to run. Many simply downloaded their versions for free from the Internet.

Making it Easy to Use

In 1994, getting Linux to run was never really as simple as putting the CD-ROM in the drive and pressing a button. Many of the programs didn't work with certain video cards. Some modems didn't talk to Linux. Not all of the printers communicated correctly. Yet most of the software worked together on many standard machines. It often took a bit of tweaking, but most people could get the OS up and running on their computers.

This was a major advance for the Linux OS because most people could quickly install a new version without spending too much time downloading the new code or debugging it. Even programmers who understood exactly what was happening felt that installing a new version was a long, often painful slog through technical details. These CD-ROMs not only helped programmers, they also encouraged casual users to experiment with the system.

The CD-ROM marketplace also created a new kind of volunteer for the project. Someone had to download the latest code from the author. Someone had to watch the kernel mailing list to see when Torvalds, Cox, and the rest had minted a new version that was stable enough to release. Someone needed to check all the other packages like GNU Emacs or GNU CC to make sure they still worked correctly. This didn't require the obsessive programming talent that created the kernel, but it did take some dedication and devotion.

Today, there are many different kinds of volunteers putting together these packages. The Debian group, for instance, is one of the best known and most devoted to true open source principles. It was started by Ian Murdock, who named it after himself and his girlfriend, Debra. The Debian group, which now includes hundreds of official members, checks to make sure that the software is both technically sound and politically correct. That is, they check the licenses to make sure that the software can be freely distributed by all users. Their guidelines later morphed into the official definition of open source software.

Other CD-ROM groups became more commercial. Debian sold its disks to pay for Internet connection fees and other expenses, but they were largely a garage operation. So were groups with names like Slackware, FreeBSD, and OpenBSD. Other groups like Red Hat actually set out to create a burgeoning business, and to a large extent, they succeeded. They took the money and used it to pay programmers who wrote more software to make Linux easier to use.

In the beginning, there wasn't much difference between the commercially minded groups like Red Hat and the more idealistic collectives like Debian. The marketplace was small, fragmented, and tribal. But by 1998, Red Hat had attracted major funding from companies like Intel, and it plowed more and more money into making the package as presentable and easy to use as possible. This investment paid off because more users turned instinctively to Red Hat, whose CD-ROM sales then exploded.

Most of this development lived in its own Shangri-La. Red Hat, for instance, charged money for its disks, but released all of its software under the GPL. Others could copy their disks for free, and many did. Red Hat may be a company, but the management realized that they depended on thousands if not millions of unpaid volunteers to create their product.

Slowly but surely, more and more people became aware of Linux, the GNU project, and its cousins like FreeBSD. No one was making much money off the stuff, but the word of mouth was spreading very quickly. The disks were priced reasonably, and people were curious. The GPL encouraged people to share. People began borrowing disks from their friends. Some companies even manufactured cheap rip-off copies of the CD-ROMs, an act that the GPL encouraged.

At the top of the pyramid was Linus Torvalds. Many Linux developers treated him like the king of all he surveyed, but he was like the monarchs who were denuded by a popular constitutional democracy. He had always focused on building a fast, stable kernel, and that was what he continued to do. The rest of the excitement, the packaging, the features, and the toys, were the dominion of the volunteers and contributors.

Torvalds never said much about the world outside his kernel, and it developed without him.

Torvalds moved to Silicon Valley and took a job with the very secret company Transmeta in order to help design the next generation of computer chips. He worked out a special deal with the company that allowed him to work on Linux in his spare time. He felt that working for one of the companies like Red Hat would give that one version of Linux a special imprimatur, and he wanted to avoid that. Plus, Transmeta was doing cool things.

In January 1999, the world caught up with the pioneers. Schmalensee mentioned Linux on the witness stand during the trial and served official notice to the world that Microsoft was worried about the growth of Linux. The system had been on the company's radar screen for some time. In October 1998, an internal memo from Microsoft describing the threat made its way to the press. Some thought it was just Microsoft's way of currying favor during the antitrust investigation. Others thought it was a serious treatment of a topic that was difficult for the company to understand.

The media followed Schmalensee's lead. Everyone wanted to know about Linux, GNU, open source software, and the magical effects of widespread, unconditional sharing. The questions came in tidal waves, and Torvalds tried to answer them again and again. Was he sorry he gave it all away? No. If he charged anything, no one would have bought his toy and no one would have contributed anything. Was he a communist? No, he was rather apolitical. Don't programmers have to eat? Yes, but they will make their money selling a service instead of getting rich off bad proprietary code. Was Linux going to overtake Microsoft? Yes, if he had his way. World Domination Soon became the motto.

But there were also difficult questions. How would the Linux world resist the embrace of big companies like IBM, Apple, Hewlett-Packard, and maybe even Microsoft? These were massive companies with paid programmers and schedules to meet. All the open source software was just as free to them as anyone else. Would these companies use their strength to monopolize Linux?

Some were worried that the money would tear apart the open source community. It's easy to get everyone to donate their time to a project when no one is getting paid. Money changes the equation. Would a gulf develop between the rich companies like Red Hat and the poor programmers who just gave away their hard work?

Many wanted to know when Linux would become easier to use for nonprogrammers. Programmers built the OS to be easy to take apart and put back together again. That's a great feature if you like hacking the inside of a kernel, but that doesn't excite the average computer user. How was the open source community going to get the programmers to donate their time to fix the mundane, everyday glitches that confused and infuriated the nonprogrammers? Was the Linux community going to be able to produce something that a nonprogrammer could even understand?

Others wondered if the Linux world could ever agree enough to create a software package with some coherence. Today, Microsoft users and programmers pull their hair out trying to keep Windows 95, Windows 98, and Windows NT straight. Little idiosyncrasies cause games to crash and programs to fail. Microsoft has hundreds of quality assurance engineers and thousands of support personnel. Still, the little details drive everyone crazy.

New versions of Linux appear as often as daily. People often create their own versions to solve particular problems. Many of these changes won't affect anyone, but they can add up. Is there enough consistency to make the tools easy enough to use?

Many wondered if Linux was right for world domination. Programmers might love playing with source code, but the rest of the world just wants something that delivers the e-mail on time. More important, the latter are willing to pay for this efficiency.

Such questions have been bothering the open source community for years and still have no easy answers today. Programmers need food, and food requires money. Making easy-to-use software requires discipline, and discipline doesn't always agree with total freedom.

When the first wave of hype about free software swept across the zeitgeist, no one wanted to concentrate on these difficult questions. The high quality of free operating systems and their use at high-profile sites like Yahoo! was good news for the world. The success of unconditional cooperation was intoxicating. If free software could do so much with so little, it could overcome the difficult questions. Besides, it didn't have to be perfect. It just needed to be better than Microsoft.

8. FREEDOM

The notion embodied by the word "free" is one of the great marketing devices of all time. Cereal manufacturers know that kids will slog through bowls of sugar to get a free prize. Stores know that people will gladly give them their names and addresses if they stand a chance of winning something for free. Car ads love to emphasize the freedom a new car will give to someone.

Of course, Microsoft knows this fact as well. One of their big advertising campaigns stresses the freedom to create new documents, write long novels, fiddle with photographs, and just do whatever you want with a computer. "Where do you want to go today?" the Microsoft ads ask.

Microsoft also recognizes the pure power of giving away something for free. When Bill Gates saw Netscape's browser emerging as a great competitive threat, he first bought a competing version and then wrote his own version of a web browser. Microsoft gave their versions away for free. This bold move shut down the revenue stream of Netscape, which had to cut its price to zero in order to compete. Of course, Netscape didn't have revenues from an operating system to pay the rent. Netscape cried foul and eventually the Department of Justice brought a lawsuit to decide whether the free software from Microsoft was just a plot to keep more people paying big bucks for their not-so-free Windows OS. The fact that Microsoft is now threatened by a group of people who are giving away a free OS has plenty of irony.

The word "free" has a much more complicated and nuanced meaning within the free software movement. In fact, many people who give away their software don't even like the word "free" and prefer to use "open" to describe the process of sharing. In the case of free software, it's not just an ad campaign to make people feel good about buying a product. It's also not a slick marketing sleight of hand to focus people's attention on a free gift while the magician charges full price for a product. The word "free" is more about a way of life. The folks who write the code throw around the word in much the same way the Founding Fathers of the United States used it. To many of them, the free software revolution was also conceived in liberty and dedicated to certain principles like the fact that all men and women have certain inalienable rights to change, modify, and do whatever they please with their software in the pursuit of happiness.

Tossing about the word "free" is easy to do. Defining what it means takes much longer. The Declaration of Independence was written in 1776, but the colonial governments fought and struggled with creating a free government through the ratification of the current United States Constitution in 1787. The Bill of Rights came soon afterward, and the Supreme Court is still continually struggling with defining the boundaries of freedom described by the document. Much of the political history of the United States might be said to be an extended argument about the meaning of the words "free country."

The free software movement is no different. It's easy for one person to simply give their software away for free. It's much harder to attract and organize an army to take on Microsoft and dominate the world. That requires a proper definition of the word "free" so that everyone understands the rights and limitations behind the word. Everyone needs to be on the same page if the battle is to be won. Everyone needs to understand what is meant by "free software."

The history of the free software world is also filled with long, extended arguments defining the freedom that comes bundled with the source code. Many wonder if it is more about giving the user something for nothing, or if is it about empowering him. Does this freedom come with any responsibilities? What should they be? How is the freedom enforced? Is freeloading a proper part of the freedom?

In the early years of computers, there were no real arguments. Software was free because people just shared it with each other. Magazines like *Creative Computing* and *BYTE* published the source code to programs because that was an easy way to share information.

People would even type in the data themselves. Computers cost money, and getting them to run was part of the challenge. Sharing software was just part of being neighborly. If someone needed to borrow your plow, you lent it to them when you weren't using it.

This changed as corporations recognized that they could copyright software and start charging money for it. Most people loved this arrangement because the competition brought new packages and tools to market and people were more than willing to pay for them. How else are the programmers and the manual writers going to eat?

A few people thought this was a disaster. Richard Stallman watched the world change from his office in the artificial intelligence labs of MIT. Stallman is the ultimate hacker, if you use the word in the classical sense. In the beginning, the word only described someone who knows how to program well and loves to poke around in the insides of computers. It only took on its more malicious tone later as the media managed to group all of those with the ability to wrangle computers into the same dangerous camp. Hackers often use the term "cracker" to refer to these people.

Stallman is a model of the hacker. He is strident, superintelligent, highly logical, and completely honest. Most corporations keep their hackers shut off in a back room because these traits seem to scare away customers and investors who just want sweet little lies in their ears. Stallman was never that kind of guy. He looked at the burgeoning corporate control of software and didn't like it one bit. His freedom was slowly being whittled away, and he wasn't the type to simply sit by and not say anything.

When Stallman left the AI lab in 1984, he didn't want to be controlled by its policies. Universities started adopting many of the same practices as the corporations in the 1980s, and Stallman couldn't be a special exception. If MIT was going to be paying him a salary, MIT would own his code and any patents that came from it. Even MIT, which is a much cooler place than most, couldn't accommodate him on staff. He didn't move far, however, because after he set up the Free Software Foundation, he kept an office at MIT, first unofficially and then officially. Once he wasn't "on the staff," the rules became different.

Stallman turned to consulting for money, but it was consulting with a twist. He would only work for companies that wouldn't put any restric-

tions on the software he created. This wasn't an easy sell. He was insisting that any work he did for Corporation X could also be shared with
Corporations Y and Z, even if they were direct competitors.

This wasn't how things were done in the 1980s. That was the decade
when companies figured out how to lock up the source code to a program by only distributing a machine-readable version. They hoped this
would control their product and let them restrain people who might try
to steal their ideas and their intellectual property. Stallman thought it
was shutting down his ability to poke around inside the computer and
fix it. This secrecy blocked him from sharing his thoughts and ideas
with other programmers.

Most programmers looked at the scheme of charging for locked-up
binary versions of a program as a necessary evil. Sure, they couldn't play
around with the guts of Microsoft Windows, but it also meant that no
one could play around with the guts of the programs they wrote. The
scheme locked doors and compartmentalized the world, but it also gave
the creator of programs more power. Most programmers thought having power over their own creation was pretty neat, even if others had
more power. Being disarmed is okay if everyone else is disarmed and
locked in a cage.

Stallman thought this was a disaster for the world and set out to
convince the world that he was right. In 1984, he wrote the *GNU
Manifesto,* which started his GNU project and laid out the conditions
for his revolution. This document stood out a bit in the middle of the
era of Ronald Reagan because it laid out Stallman's plan for creating a
virtual commune where people would be free to use the software. It is
one of the first cases when someone tried to set down a definition of the
word "free" for software users. Sure, software and ideas were quite free
long ago, but no one noticed until the freedom was gone.

He wrote,

> *I consider that the golden rule requires that if I like a program I must
> share it with other people who like it. Software sellers want to divide
> the users and conquer them, making each user agree not to share with
> others. I refuse to break solidarity with other users in this way. . . . So
> that I can continue to use computers without dishonor, I have decided*

to put together a sufficient body of free software so that I will be able to get along without any software that is not free.

The document is a wonderful glimpse at the nascent free software world because it is as much a recruiting document as a tirade directed at corporate business practices. When the American colonies split off from England, Thomas Paine spelled out the problems with the English in the first paragraph of his pamphlet "Common Sense." In his manifesto, Stallman didn't get started using words like "dishonor" until the sixth paragraph. The first several paragraphs spelled out the cool tools he had developed already: "an Emacs text editor with Lisp for writing editor commands, a source level debugger, a yacc-compatible parser generator, a linker, and around 35 utilities." Then he pointed to the work he wanted to complete soon: "A new portable optimizing C compiler has compiled itself and may be released this year. An initial kernel exists but many more features are needed to emulate Unix." He was saying, in effect, that he already had a few juicy peaches growing on the trees of his commune.

If this wasn't enough, he intended to do things a bit better than UNIX. His operating system was going to offer the latest, greatest ideas of computer science, circa 1984. "In particular, we plan to have longer file names, file version numbers, a crashproof file system, file name completion perhaps, terminal-independent display support, and per- haps eventually a Lisp-based window system through which several Lisp programs and ordinary Unix programs can share a screen." The only thing that was missing from every computer nerd's wish list was a secret submarine docking site in the basement grotto.

The fifth paragraph even explained to everyone that the name of the project would be the acronym GNU, which stood for "GNU's Not UNIX," and it should be pronounced with a hard G to make sure that no one would get it confused with the word "new." Stallman has always cared about words, the way they're used and the way they're pro- nounced.

In 1984, UNIX became the focus of Stallman's animus because its original developer, AT&T, was pushing to try to make some money back after paying so many people at Bell Labs to create it. Most people were somewhat conflicted by the fight. They understood that AT&T had paid good money and supported many researchers with the company's beneficence. The company gave money, time, and spare computers. Sure, it was a pain to pay AT&T for something and get only a long license drafted by teams of lawyers. Yes, it would be nice if we could poke around under the hood of UNIX without signing a nondisclosure agreement. It would be nice if we could be free to do whatever we want, but certainly someone who pays for something deserves the right to decide how it is used. We've all got to eat.

Stallman wasn't confused at all. Licenses like AT&T's would constrict his freedom to share with others. To make matters worse, the software companies wanted him to pay for the privilege of getting software without the source code.

Stallman explains that his feelings weren't focused on AT&T per se. Software companies were springing up all over the place, and most of them were locking up their source code with proprietary licenses. It was the 1980s thing to do, like listening to music by Duran Duran and Boy George.

"When I decided to write a free operating system, I did not have AT&T in mind at all, because I had never had any dealings with them. I had never used a UNIX system. They were just one of many companies doing the same discreditable thing," he told me recently. "I chose a Unix-like design just because I thought it was a good design for the job, not because I had any particular feelings about AT&T."

When he wrote the *GNU Manifesto,* he made it clear to the world that his project was more about choosing the right moral path than saving money. He wrote then that the GNU project means "much more than just saving everyone the price of a UNIX license. It means that much wasteful duplication of system programming effort will be avoided. This effort can go instead into advancing the state of the art."

This was a crucial point that kept Stallman from being dismissed as a quasi-communist crank who just wanted everyone to live happily on some nerd commune. The source code is a valuable tool for everyone because it is readable by humans, or at least humans who happen to be good at programming. Companies learned to keep source code proprietary, and it became almost a reflex. If people wanted to use it, they should pay to help defray the cost of creating it. This made sense to programmers who wanted to make a living or even get rich writing their own code. But it was awfully frustrating at times. Many programmers have pulled their hair out in grief when their work was stopped by some bug or undocumented feature buried deep in the proprietary, super-secret software made by Microsoft, IBM, Apple, or whomever. If they had the source code, they would be able to poke around and figure out what was really happening. Instead, they had to treat the software like a black box and keep probing it with test programs that might reveal the secrets hidden inside. Every programmer has had an experience like this, and every programmer knew that they could solve the problem much faster if they could only read the source code. They didn't want to steal anything, they just wanted to know what was going on so they could make their own code work.

Stallman's GNU project would be different, and he explained, "Complete system sources will be available to everyone. As a result, a user who needs changes in the system will always be free to make them himself, or hire any available programmer or company to make them for him. Users will no longer be at the mercy of one programmer or company which owns the sources and is in sole position to make changes."

He was quick to mention that people would be "free to hire any available programmer" to ensure that people understood he wasn't against taking money for writing software. That was okay and something he did frequently himself. He was against people controlling the source with arbitrarily complex legal barriers that made it impossible for him or anyone else to get something done.

When people first heard of his ideas, they became fixated on the word "free." These were the Reagan years. Saying that people should just give away their hard work was sounding mighty communist to everyone, and this was long before the Berlin Wall fell. Stallman reexamined the word "free" and all of its different meanings. He carefully considered all of the different connotations, examined the alternatives, and decided that "free" was still the best word. He began to try to explain the shades of meaning he was after. His revolution was about "free speech," not "free beer." This wasn't going to be a revolution in the sense that frequent flyer miles revolutionized air travel nor in the way that aluminum cans revolutionized beer drinking. No, this was going to be a revolution as Rousseau, Locke, and Paine used the word.

He later codified this into four main principles:

The freedom to run the program, for any purpose (freedom 0).[1]

The freedom to study how the program works, and adapt it to your needs (freedom 1).

The freedom to redistribute copies so you can help your neighbor (freedom 2).

The freedom to improve the program, and release your improvements to the public, so that the whole community benefits (freedom 3).

Free Beer

While Stallman pushed people away from the notion of "free beer," there's little question that this element turned out to be a very important part of the strategy and a foundation of its success. Stallman insisted that anyone could do what they wanted with the software, so he insisted that the source code must be freely distributed. That is, no one could put any restrictions on how you used the software. While this didn't make it free beer, it did mean that you could turn around and give a copy to your friends or your clients. It was pretty close.

The "free beer" nature of Stallman's software also attracted users. If some programmers wanted to check out a new tool, they could download it and try it out without paying for it. They didn't need to ask their boss for a budget, and they didn't need to figure out a way to deal with an invoice. Just one click and the software was there. Commercial software companies continue to imitate this feature by distributing trial versions that come with either a few crippled features or a time lock that shuts them down after a few days.

Of course, the "free beer" nature of the GNU project soon led to money problems. The GNU project took up his time and generated no

---

[1]He numbered them starting at zero because that was what computer scientists did. Someone figured out that it was simpler to start numbering databases at zero because you didn't have to subtract 1 as often.

real revenues at first. Stallman had always lived frugally. He says that he never made more than $20,000 a year at MIT, and still managed to save on that salary. But he was finding it harder and harder to get his assigned jobs done at MIT and write the cool GNU code. While Stallman always supported a programmer's right to make money for writing code, the GNU project wasn't generating any money.

Most folks saw this conflict coming from the beginning. Sure, Stallman would be able to rant and rave about corporate software development for a bit, but eventually he and his disciples would need to eat.

When the MIT support ended, Stallman soon stumbled upon a surprising fact: he could charge for the software he was giving away and make some money. People loved his software, but it was often hard to keep track of it. Getting the package delivered on computer tape or a CD-ROM gave people a hard copy that they could store for future reference or backup. Online manuals were also nice, but the printed book is still a very popular and easy-to-use way of storing information. Stallman's Free Software Foundation began selling printed manuals, tapes, and then CD-ROMs filled with software to make money. Surprisingly, people started paying money for these versions despite the fact that they could download the same versions for free.

Some folks enjoyed pointing out the hypocrisy in Stallman's move. Stallman had run his mouth for so long that many programming "sellouts" who worked for corporations savored the irony. At last that weenie had gotten the picture. He was forced to make money to support himself, and he was selling out, too. These cynics didn't get what Stallman was trying to do.

Most of us would have given up at this time. The free software thing seemed like a good idea, but now that the money was running out it was time to get a real job. In writing this book and interviewing some of the famous and not-so-famous free software developers, I found that some were involved in for-profit, not-so-free software development now. Stallman, though, wasn't going to give up his ideals, and his mind started shifting to accommodate this new measure of reality. He decided that it wouldn't be wrong to sell copies of software or even software services as long as you didn't withhold the source code and stomp on anyone's freedom to use the source code as they wished.

Stallman has always been great at splitting hairs and creating Jesuitical distinctions, and this insight was one of his best. At first glance, it looked slightly nutty. If people were free to do anything they wanted with software, they could just give a copy to their friend and their friend would never send money back to Stallman's Free Software Foundation. In fact, someone could buy a copy from Stallman and then start reselling copies to others to undercut Stallman. The Free Software Foundation and the GNU GPL gave them the freedom to do so. It was as if a movie theater sold tickets to a movie, but also posted a big sign near the exit door that said "Hey, it's absolutely okay for you to prop this open so your friends can sneak in without paying."

While this total freedom befuddled most people, it didn't fail. Many paid for tapes or CD-ROM versions because they wanted the convenience. Stallman's versions came with the latest bug fixes and new features. They were the quasi-official versions. Others felt that paying helped support the work so they didn't feel bad about doing it. They liked the FSF and wanted it to produce more code. Others just liked printed books better than electronic documentation. Buying them from Stallman was cheaper than printing them out. Still others paid for the CD-ROMs because they just wanted to support the Free Software Foundation.

Stallman also found other support. The MacArthur Foundation gave him one of their genius grants that paid him a nice salary for five years to do whatever he wanted. Companies like Intel hired him as a consultant and asked him to make sure that some of his software ran on Intel chips. People were quite willing to pay for convenience because even free software didn't do everything that it should.

Stallman also recognized that this freedom introduced a measure of competition. If he could charge for copies, then so could others. The source code would be a vast commonweal, but the means of delivering it would be filled with people struggling to do the best job of distributing the software. It was a pretty hard-core Reaganaut notion for a reputed communist. At the beginning, few bothered to compete with him, but in time all of the GNU code began to be included with computer operating systems. By the time Linus Torvalds wrote his OS, the GNU code was ready to be included.

Copyleft

If Stallman's first great insight was that the world did not need to put up with proprietary source code, then his second was that he could strictly control the use of GNU software with an innovative legal document entitled GNU General Public License, or GPL. To illustrate the difference, he called the agreement a "copyleft" and set about creating a legal document defining what it meant for software to be "free." Well, defining what he thought it should mean.

The GPL was a carefully crafted legal document that didn't put the software into the "public domain," a designation that would have allowed people to truly do anything they wanted with the software. The license, in fact, copyrighted the software and then extended users very liberal rights for making innumerable copies as long as the users didn't hurt other people's rights to use the software.

The definition of stepping on other people's rights is one that keeps political science departments at universities in business. There are many constituencies that all frame their arguments in terms of protecting someone's rights. Stallman saw protecting the rights of other users in very strong terms and strengthened his grip a bit by inserting a controversial clause. He insisted that a person who distributes an improved version of the program must also share the source code. That meant that some greedy company couldn't download his GNU Emacs editor, slap on a few new features, and then sell the whole package without including all of the source code they created. If people were going to benefit from the GNU sharing, they were going to have to share back. It was freedom with a price.

This strong compact was ready-built for some ironic moments. When Apple began trying to expand the scope of intellectual property laws by suing companies like Microsoft for stealing their "look and feel," Stallman became incensed and decided that he wouldn't develop software for Apple machines as a form of protest and spite. If Apple was going to pollute the legal landscape with terrible impediments to sharing ideas, then Stallman wasn't going to help them sell machines by writing software for the machines. But the GNU copyleft license specifically allowed anyone to freely distribute the source code and use it as they wanted. That meant that others could use the GNU code and convert it to run on the Apple if they wanted to do so. Many did port much of the GNU software to the Mac and distributed the source code with it in order to comply with the license. Stallman couldn't do anything about it. Sure, he was the great leader of the FSF and the author of some of its code, but he had given away his power with the license. The only thing he could do was refuse to help the folks moving the software to the Mac. When it came to principles, he placed freedom to use the source code at the top of the hierarchy.

The GNU Virus

Some programmers soon started referring to the sticky nature of the license as the "GNU virus" because it infected software projects with its freedom bug. If a developer wanted to save time and grab some of the neat GNU software, he was stuck making the rest of his work just as free. These golden handcuffs often scared away programmers who wanted to make money by charging for their work.

Stallman hates that characterization. "To call anything 'like a virus' is a very vicious thing. People who say things like that are trying to find ways to make the GPL look bad," he says.

Stallman did try to work around this problem by creating what he at first called the "Library General Public License" and now refers to as the "Lesser General Public License," a document that allowed software developers to share small chunks of code with each other under less restrictive circumstances. A programmer can use the LGPL to bind chunks of code known as libraries. Others can share the libraries and use them with their source code as long as they don't fully integrate them. Any changes they make to the library itself must be made public, but there is no requirement to release the source code for the main program that uses the library.

This license is essentially a concession to some rough edges at the corners where the world of programming joins the world of law. While Stallman was dead set on creating a perfect collection of free programs that would solve everyone's needs, he was far from finished. If people were going to use his software, they were going to have to use it on machines made by Sun, AT&T, IBM, or someone else who sold a proprietary operating system along with it. He understood that he needed to compromise, at least for system libraries.

The problem is drawing boundaries around what is one pile of software owned by one person and what is another pile owned by someone else. The GPL guaranteed that GNU software would "infect" other packages and force people who used his code to join the party and release theirs as well. So he had to come up with a definition that spelled out what it meant for people to use his code and "incorporate" it with others.

This is often easier said than done. The marketplace has developed ways to sell software as big chunks to people, but these are fictions that camouflage software integration. In modern practice, programmers don't just create one easily distinguished chunk of software known as Microsoft Word or Adobe Photoshop. They build up a variety of smaller chunks known as libraries and link these together. Microsoft Windows, in fact, includes a large collection of libraries for creating the menus, forms, click boxes, and what-not that make the graphical user interfaces. Programmers don't need to write their own instructions for drawing these on the screen and interacting with them. This saves plenty of time and practice for the programmers, and it is a large part of what Microsoft is selling when it sells someone a box with Windows on it.

Stallman recognized that programmers sometimes wrote libraries that they wanted others to use. After all, that was the point of GNU: creating tools that others would be free to use. So Stallman relented and created the Lesser Public License, which would allow people to create libraries that might be incorporated into other programs that weren't fully GNU. The library itself still came with source code, and the user would need to distribute all changes made to the library, but there was no limitation on the larger package.

This new license was also something of a concession to reality. In the most abstract sense, programs are just black boxes that take some input and produce some output. There's no limit to the hierarchies that can be created by plugging these boxes together so that the output for one is the input for another. Eventually, the forest of connections grows so thick that it is difficult to draw a line and label one collection of boxes "ProprietarySoft's SUX–2000" and another collection "GNUSoft's Wombat 3.14.15." The connections are so numerous in well-written, effective software that line-drawing is difficult.

The problem is similar to the one encountered by biologists as they try to define ecosystems and species. Some say there are two different groups of tuna that swim in the Atlantic. Others say there is only one. The distinction would be left to academics if it didn't affect the international laws on fishing. Some groups pushing the vision of one school are worried that others on the other side of the ocean are catching their fish. Others push the two-school theory to minimize the meddling of the other side's bureaucracy. No one knows, though, how to draw a good line.

Stallman's LGPL was a concession to the fact that sometimes programs can be used like libraries and sometimes libraries can be used like programs. In the end, the programmer can draw a strong line around one set of boxes and say that the GPL covers these functions without leaking out to infect the software that links up with the black boxes.

Is the Free Software Foundation Anti-Freedom?

Still, these concessions aren't enough for some people. Many continue to rail against Stallman's definition of freedom and characterize the GPL as a fascist document that steals the rights of any programmer who comes along afterward. Being free means having the right to do anything you want with the code, including keeping all your modifications private.

To be fair, the GPL never forces you to give away your changes to the source code. It just forces you to release your modifications *if* you redistribute it. If you just run your own version in your home, then you don't need to share anything. When you start sharing binary versions of the software, however, you need to ship the source code, too.

Some argue that corporations have the potential to work around this loophole because they act like one person. A company could revise software and "ship it" by simply hiring anyone who wanted to buy it. The new employees or members of the corporation would get access to the software without shipping the source. The source code would never be distributed because it was not publicly shipped. No one seriously believes that anyone would try to exploit this provision with such an extreme interpretation, but it does open the question of whether an airtight license can ever be created.

These fine distinctions didn't satisfy many programmers who weren't so taken with Stallman's doctrinaire version of freedom. They wanted to create free software *and* have the freedom to make some money off of it. This tradition dates back many years before Stallman and is a firm part of academic life. Many professors and students developed software and published a free version before starting up a company that would commercialize the work. They used their professor's salary or student stipend to support the work, and the free software they contributed to the world was meant as an exchange. In many cases, the U.S. government paid for the creation of the software through a grant, and the free release was a gift to the taxpayers who ultimately funded it. In other cases, corporations paid for parts of the research and the free release was seen as a way to give something back to the sponsoring corporation without turning the university into a home for the corporation's low-paid slave programmers who were students in name only.

In many cases, the free distribution was an honest gift made by researchers who wanted to give their work the greatest possible distribution. They would be repaid in fame and academic prestige, which can be more lucrative than everything but a good start-up's IPO. Sharing knowledge and creating more of it was what universities were all about. Stallman tapped into that tradition.

But many others were fairly cynical. They would work long enough to generate a version that worked well enough to convince people of its value. Then, when the funding showed up, they would release this buggy version into the "public domain," move across the street into their own new start-up, and resume development. The public domain version satisfied the university's rules and placated any granting agencies, but it was often close to unusable. The bugs were too numerous and too hidden in the cruft to make it worth someone's time. Of course, the original authors knew where the problems lurked, and they would fix them before releasing the commercial version.

The leader of this academic branch of the free software world became the Computer Systems Research Group at the University of California at Berkeley. The published Berkeley Software Distribution (BSD) versions of UNIX started emerging from Berkeley in the late 1970s. Their work emerged with a free license that gave everyone the right to do what they wanted with the software, including start up a company, add some neat features, and start reselling the whole package. The only catch was that the user must keep the copyright message intact and give the university some credit in the manual and in advertisements. This requirement was loosened in 1999 when the list of people who needed credit on software projects grew too long. Many groups were taking the BSD license and simply replacing the words "University of California" with their name. The list of people who needed to be publicly acknowledged grew with each new project. As the distributions grew larger to include all of these new projects, the process of listing all the names and projects became onerous. The University of California struck the clause requiring advertising credit in the hopes of setting an example that others would follow.

Today, many free software projects begin with a debate of "GNU versus BSD" as the initial founders argue whether it is a good idea to restrict what users can do with the code. The GNU side always believes that programmers should be forced to donate the code they develop back to the world, while the BSD side pushes for practically unlimited freedom.

Rick Rashid is one of the major forces behind the development of Microsoft's Windows NT and also a major contributor to our knowledge of how to build a computer operating system. Before he went to Microsoft, he was a professor at Carnegie-Mellon. While he was there, he spearheaded the team responsible for developing Mach, an operating system that offered relatively easy-to-use multitasking built upon a very tiny kernel. Mach let programmers break their software into multiple "threads" that could run independently of each other while sharing the same access to data.

When asked recently about Mach and the Mach license, he explained that he deliberately wrote the license to be as free as possible.

The GNU GPL, he felt, wasn't appropriate for technology that was developed largely with government grants. The work should be as free as possible and shouldn't force "other people to do things (e.g., give away their personal work) in order to get access to what you had done."

He said, in an e-mail interview, "It was my intent to encourage use of the system both for academic and commercial use and it was used heavily in both environments. Accent, the predecessor to Mach, had already been commercialized and used by a variety of companies. Mach continues to be heavily used today—both as the basis for Apple's new MacOS and as the basis for variants of Unix in the marketplace (e.g., Compaq's 64-bit Unix for the Alpha)."

The Evolution of BSD

The BSD license evolved along a strange legal path that was more like the meandering of a drunken cow than the laser-like devotion of Stallman.

Many professors and students cut their teeth experimenting with UNIX on DEC Vaxes that communicated with old teletypes and dumb terminals. AT&T gave Berkeley the source code to UNIX, and this allowed the students and professors to add their instructions and features to the software. Much of their insight into operating system design and many of their bug fixes made their way back to AT&T, where they were incorporated in the next versions of UNIX. No one really thought twice about the source code being available because the shrink-wrapped software market was still in its infancy. The personal computer market wasn't even born until the latter half of the 1970s, and it took some time for people to believe that source code was something for a company to withhold and protect. In fact, many of the programs still weren't being written in higher-level languages. The programmers would write instructions directly for the computer, and while these often would include some instructions for humans, there was little difference between what the humans wrote and the machine read.

After Bill Joy and others at Berkeley started coming up with several good pieces of software, other universities started asking for copies. At the time, Joy remembers, it was considered a bit shabby for computer science researchers to actually write software and share it with others. The academic departments were filled with many professors who received their formal training in mathematics, and they held the attitude that rigorous formal proofs and analysis were the ideal form of research. Joy and several other students began rebelling by arguing that creating working operating systems was essential experimental research. The physics departments supported experimentalists and theorists.

So Joy began to "publish" his code by sending out copies to other researchers who wanted it. Although many professors and students at Berkeley added bits and pieces to the software running on the DEC Vaxes, Joy was the one who bundled it all together and gave it the name. Kirk McKusick says in his history of Berkeley UNIX, ". . . interest in the error recovery work in the Pascal compiler brought in requests for copies of the system. Early in 1977, Joy put together the 'Berkeley Software Distribution.' This first distribution included the Pascal system, and, in an obscure subdirectory of the Pascal source, the editor *vi*. Over the next year, Joy, acting in the capacity of the distribution secretary, sent out about 30 free copies of the system."

Today, Joy tells the story with a bit of bemused distraction. He explains that he just copied over a license from the University of Toronto and "whited out" "University of Toronto" and replaced it with "University of California." He simply wanted to get the source code out the door. In the beginning, the Berkeley Software Distribution included a few utilities, but by 1979 the code became tightly integrated with AT&T's basic UNIX code. Berkeley gave away the collection of software in BSD, but only AT&T license holders could use it. Many universities were attracted to the package, in part because the Pascal system was easy for its students to use. The personal computer world, however, was focusing on a simpler language known as Basic. Bill Gates would make Microsoft Basic one of his first products.

Joy says that he wrote a letter to AT&T inquiring about the legal status of the source code from AT&T that was rolled together with the BSD code. After a year, he says, "They wrote back saying, 'We take no position' on the matter." Kirk McKusick, who later ran the BSD project through the years of the AT&T lawsuit, explained dryly, "Later they wrote a different letter."

Joy was just one of a large number of people who worked heavily on the BSD project from 1977 through the early 1980s. The work was low-level and grungy by today's standards. The students and professors scrambled just to move UNIX to the new machines they bought. Often, large parts of the guts of the operating system needed to be modified or upgraded to deal with a new type of disk drive or file system. As they did this more and more often, they began to develop more and more higher-level abstractions to ease the task. One of the earliest examples was Joy's screen editor known as vi, a simple package that could be used to edit text files and reprogram the system. The "battle" between Joy's vi and Stallman's Emacs is another example of the schism between MIT and Berkeley. This was just one of the new tools included in version 2 of BSD, a collection that was shipped to 75 different people and institutions.

By the end of the 1970s, Bell Labs and Berkeley began to split as AT&T started to commercialize UNIX and Berkeley stuck to its job of education. Berkeley professor Bob Fabry was able to interest the Pentagon's Defense Advanced Research Projects Agency (DARPA) into signing up to support more development at Berkeley. Fabry sold the agency on a software package that would be usable on many of the new machines being installed in research labs throughout the country. It would be more easily portable so that research would not need to stop every time a new computer arrived. The work on this project became versions 3 and 4 of BSD.

During this time, the relationship between AT&T and the universities was cordial. AT&T owned the commercial market for UNIX and Berkeley supplied many of the versions used in universities. While the universities got BSD for free, they still needed to negotiate a license with AT&T, and companies paid a fortune. This wasn't too much of a problem because universities are often terribly myopic. If they share their work with other universities and professors, they usually consider their sharing done. There may be folks out there without university appointments, but those folks are usually viewed as cranks who can be safely ignored. Occasionally, those cranks write their own OS that grows up to be Linux. The BSD version of freedom was still a far cry from Stallman's, but then Stallman hadn't articulated it yet. His manifesto was still a few years off.

The intellectual tension between Stallman and Berkeley grew during the 1980s. While Stallman began what many thought was a quixotic journey to build a completely free OS, Berkeley students and professors continued to layer their improvements to UNIX on top of AT&T's code. The AT&T code was good, it was available, and many of the folks at Berkeley had either directly or indirectly helped influence it. They were generally happy keeping AT&T code at the core despite the fact that all of the BSD users needed to negotiate with AT&T. This process grew more and more expensive as AT&T tried to make more and more money off of UNIX.

Of course, Stallman didn't like the freedom of the BSD-style license. To him, it meant that companies could run off with the hard work and shared source code of another, make a pile of money, and give nothing back. The companies and individuals who were getting the BSD network release were getting the cumulative hard work of many students and professors at Berkeley (and other places) who donated their time and effort to building a decent OS. The least these companies owed the students were the bug fixes, the extensions, and the enhancements they created when they were playing with the source code and gluing it into their products.

Stallman had a point. Many of these companies "shared" by selling the software back to these students and the taxpayers who had paid for their work. While it is impossible to go back and audit the motives of everyone who used the code, there have been many who've used BSD-style code for their personal gain.

Bill Joy, for instance, went to work at Sun Microsystems in 1982 and brought with him all the knowledge he had gained in developing BSD. Sun was always a very BSD-centered shop, and many of the people who bought Sun workstations ran BSD. At that time, AT&T still controlled much of the kernel and many of the small extra programs that made UNIX a usable system.

But there are counterarguments as well. Joy certainly contributed a lot to the different versions of BSD. If anyone deserves to go off and get rich at a company like Sun, it's he.

Also, the BSD source code was freely available to all comers, and all companies started with the same advantages. The software business is often considered to be one of the most free marketplaces around because of the low barriers to entry. This means that companies should only be able to charge for the value they add to the BSD code. Sure, all of the Internet was influenced by the TCP/IP code, but now Microsoft, Apple, IBM, Be, and everyone else compete on the quality of their interface.

The Price of Total Freedom

The debate between BSD-style freedom and GNU-style freedom is one of the greatest in the free programming world and is bound to continue for a long time as programmers join sides and experiment.

John Gilmore is one programmer who has worked with software developed under both types of licenses. He was employee number five at Sun Microsystems, a cofounder of the software development tool company Cygnus Solutions, and one of the board members of the Electronic Frontier Foundation. His early work at Sun gave him the wealth to pursue many independent projects, and he has spent the last 10 years devoting himself to making it easy for people around the world to use encryption software. He feels that privacy is a fundamental right and an important crime deterrent, and he has funded a number of different projects to advance this right.

Gilmore also runs the cypherpunks mailing list on a computer in his house named Toad Hall near Haight Street in San Francisco. The mailing list is devoted to exploring how to create strong encryption tools that will protect people's privacy and is well known for the strong libertarian tone of the deliberations. Practically the whole list believes (and frequently reiterates) that people need the right to protect their privacy against both the government and private eavesdropping. *Wired* magazine featured Gilmore on the cover, along with fellow travelers Eric Hughes and Tim May.

One of his recent tasks was creating a package of free encryption utilities that worked at the lowest level of the network operating system. These tools, known as Free/SWAN, would allow two computers that meet on the Internet to automatically begin encoding the data they swap with some of the best and most secure codes available. He imagines that banks, scientific laboratories, and home workers everywhere will want to use the toolkit. In fact, AT&T is currently examining how to incorporate the toolkit into products it is building to sell more high-speed services to workers staying at home to avoid the commute.

Gilmore decided to use the GNU license to protect the Free/SWAN software, in part because he has had bad experiences in the past with totally free software. He once wrote a little program called PDTar that was an improvement over the standard version of Tar used on the Internet to bundle together a group of files into one big, easy-to-manage bag of bits often known affectionately as "tarballs." He decided he wasn't going to mess around with Stallman's GNU license or impose any restrictions on the source code at all. He was just going to release it into the public domain and give everyone total freedom.

This good deed did not go unpunished, although the punishment was relatively minor. He recalls, "I never made PDTar work for DOS, but six or eight people did. For years after the release, I would get mail saying, 'I've got this binary for the DOS release and it doesn't work.' They often didn't even have the sources that went with the version so I couldn't help them if I tried." Total freedom, it turned out, brought a certain amount of anarchy that made it difficult for him to manage the project. While the total freedom may have encouraged others to build their own versions of PDTar, it didn't force them to release the source code that went with their versions so others could learn from or fix their mistakes

Hugh Daniel, one of the testers for the Free/SWAN project, says that he thinks the GNU General Public License will help keep some coherency to the project. "There's also a magic thing with GPL code that open source doesn't have," Daniel said. "For some reason, projects don't bifurcate in GPL space. People don't grab a copy of the code and call it their own. For some reason there's a sense of community in GPL code. There seems to be one version. There's one GPL kernel and there's umpty-ump BSD branches."

Daniel is basically correct. The BSD code has evolved, or forked, into many different versions with names like FreeBSD, OpenBSD, and NetBSD while the Linux UNIX kernel released under Stallman's GPL is limited to one fairly coherent package. Still, there is plenty of cross-pollination between the different versions of BSD UNIX. Both NetBSD 1.0 and FreeBSD 2.0, for instance, borrowed code from 4.4 BSD-Lite. Also, many versions of Linux come with tools and utilities that came from the BSD project.

But Daniel's point is also clouded with semantics. There are dozens if not hundreds of different Linux distributions available from different vendors. Many differ in subtle points, but some are markedly different. While these differences are often as great as the ones between the various flavors of BSD, the groups do not consider them psychologically separate. They haven't forked politically even though they've split off their code.

While different versions may be good for some projects, it may be a problem for packages like Free/SWAN that depend upon interoperability. If competing versions of Free/SWAN emerge, then all begin to suffer because the product was designed to let people communicate with each other. If the software can't negotiate secure codes because of differences, then it begins to fail.

But it's not clear that the extra freedom is responsible for the fragmentation. In reality, the different BSD groups emerged because they had different needs. The NetBSD group, for instance, wanted to emphasize multiplatform support and interoperability. Their website brags that the NetBSD release works well on 21 different hardware platforms and also points out that some of these hardware platforms themselves are quite diverse. There are 93 different versions of the Macintosh running on Motorola's 68k chips, including the very first Mac. Eighty-nine of them run some part of NetBSD and 37 of them run all of it. That's why they say their motto is "Of course it runs NetBSD."

The OpenBSD group, on the other hand, is emphasizing security without compromising portability and interoperability. They want to fix all security bugs immediately and be the most secure OS on the marketplace.

There are also deep personal differences in the way Theo de Raadt, the founder of OpenBSD, started the project after the NetBSD group kicked him out of their core group.

For all of these reasons, it may be hard to argue that the freedoms provided by the BSD-style license were largely responsible for the splintering. The GNU software users are just as free to make new versions as long as they kick back the source code into free circulation. In fact, it may be possible to argue that the Macintosh versions of some of the GNU code comprise a splinter group because it occurred despite the ill will Stallman felt for the Mac.

The Synthesis of "Open Source"

The tension between the BSD licenses and the GNU has always festered like the abortion debate. Everyone picked sides and rarely moved from them.

In 1998, a group of people in the free software community tried to unify the two camps by creating a new term, "open source." To make sure everyone knew they were serious, they started an unincorporated organization, registered a trademark, and set up a website (www.open-source.org). Anyone who wanted to label their project "open source" would have to answer to them because they would control the trademark on the name.

Sam Ockman, a Linux enthusiast and the founder of Penguin Computing, remembers the day of the meeting just before Netscape announced it was freeing its source code. "Eric Raymond came into town because of the Netscape thing. Netscape was going to free their software, so we drove down to Transmeta and had a meeting so we could advise Netscape," he said.

He explained that the group considered a number of different options about the structure. Some wanted to choose a leader now. Others wanted to emulate an open source project and let a leader emerge through the display of talent and, well, leadership. Others wanted elections.

The definition of what was open source grew out of the Debian project, one of the different groups that banded together to press CD-ROMs of stable Linux releases. Groups like these often get into debates about what software to include on the disks. Some wanted to be very pure and only include GPL'ed software. In a small way, that would force others to contribute back to the project because they wouldn't get their software distributed by the group unless it was GPL'ed. Others wanted less stringent requirements that might include quasi-commercial projects that still came with their source code. There were some cool projects out there that weren't protected by GPL, and it could be awfully hard to pass up the chance to integrate them into a package.

Over time, one of the leaders of the Debian group, Bruce Perens, came to create a definition of what was acceptable and what wasn't. This definition would be large enough to include the GNU General Public License, the BSD-style licenses, and a few others like MIT's X Consortium license and the Artistic license. The X-windows license covers a graphical windowing interface that began at MIT and was also freely distributed with BSD-like freedom. The Artistic license applies to the Perl programming language, a tool that is frequently used to transform files. The Debian meta-definition would embrace all of these.

The official definition of what was acceptable to Debian leaned toward more freedom and fewer restrictions on the use of software. Of course, that's the only way that anyone could come up with a definition that included both GNU and the much less restrictive BSD. But this was also the intent of the open source group. Perens and Eric Raymond felt that Stallman still sounded too quasi-communist for "conservative businessmen," and they wanted the open source definition to avoid insisting upon the sort of forced sharing that Stallman's GNU virus provided.

Still, the definition borrowed heavily from Stallman's concept of GNU, and Perens credits him by saying that many of the Debian guidelines are derived from the GPL. An official open source license for a product must provide the programmer with source code that is human-readable. It can't restrict what modifications are made to the software or how it is sold or given away.

The definition glossed over the difference between BSD and GPU by stating, "The license must allow modifications and derived works, and must allow them to be distributed under the same terms as the license of the original software."

The definition proved to be the model for more commercial offerings like the Netscape Public License. In 1998, Netscape started distributing the source code to its popular browser in hopes of collecting help from the Internet and stopping Microsoft's gradual erosion of its turf. The license gave users wide opportunities to make changes and tinker with the software, but it also allowed Netscape to use the changes internally and refuse to share what they did with them. This special privilege offended some users who didn't like the imbalance, but it didn't bother many others who thought it was a reasonable compromise for a chance to tinker with commercial code. Netscape, of course, returned some of the favor by allowing people to keep their modifications private in much the same way that the BSD-style license provided.

In June 1999, the Open Source Initiative revealed a startling fact. They were close to failing in their attempts to register the term "open source" as a trademark. The phrase was too common to be registered. Instead, they backed away and offered to check out licenses and classify them officially as "OSI Certified" if they met the terms of the OSI's definition of freedom.

Some reacted negatively. Richard Stallman decided that he didn't like the word "open" as much as "free." Open doesn't capture the essence of freedom. Ockman says, "I don't think it's very fair. For ages, he's always said that the term 'free software' is problematic because people think of 'free beer' when they should be thinking of 'free speech.' We were attempting to solve that term. If the masses are confused, then corporate America is confused even more."

The debate has even produced more terms. Some people now use the phrase "free source" to apply to the general conglomeration of the GPL and the open source world. Using "free software" implies that someone is aligned with Stallman's Free Software Foundation. Using "open source" implies you're aligned with the more business-friendly Open Source Initiative. So "free source" and "open source" both work as a compromise. Others tweak the meaning of free and refer to GPL protected software as "GNUFree."

Naturally, all of this debate about freedom can reach comic proportions. Programmers are almost better than lawyers at finding loopholes, if only because they have to live with a program that crashes.[2] Stallman,

---

[2]Lawyers just watch their clients go to jail.

for instance, applies the GPL to everything coming out of the GNU project except the license itself. That can't be changed, although it can be freely reproduced. Some argue that if it were changeable, people would be able to insert and delete terms at will. Then they could apply the changed GPL to the new version of the software and do what they want. Stallman's original intent would not be changed. The GPL would still apply to all of the GNU software and its descendants, but it wouldn't be the same GPL.

9. SOURCE

Computer programmers love *Star Wars*. So it should be no surprise that practically every single member of the free source community has, at one time or another, rolled out the phrase, "Use the Source, Luke." It does a perfect job of capturing the mythical faith that the free source world places in the ability to access the source code to a program. As everyone points out, in the original version of *Star Wars*, the rebel troops used the plans, *the Source*, to the Death Star carried in R2D2 to look for weaknesses.

The free source realm has been pushing the parallels for some time now. When AT&T unveiled their round logo with an offset dimple, most free source people began to snicker. The company that began the free software revolution by pushing its intellectual property rights and annoying Richard Stallman had chosen a logo that looked just like the Death Star. Everyone said, "Imperialist minds think alike." Some even wondered and hoped that George Lucas would sue AT&T for some sort of look-and-feel, trademark infringement. Those who use the legal intimidation light saber should die by the legal intimidation light saber.

Of course, the free source folks knew that only their loose coalition of rebels spread out around the galaxy would be a strong match for the Empire. The Source was information, and information was power. The Source was also about freedom, one of the best and most consistent reservoirs of revolutionary inspiration around. The rebels might not have teams of lawyers in imperial star cruisers, but they hoped to use the Source to knit together a strong, effective, and more powerful resistance.

The myth of open access to free source code is a powerful one that has made true believers out of many in the community. The source code is a list of instructions for the computer written out in a programming language that is understandable by humans. Once the compilers converted the source code into the string of bits known as the binary or object code, only computers (and some very talented humans) could understand the instructions. I've known several people who could read 8080 binary code by eye, but they're a bit different from the general population.

When companies tried to keep their hard work and research secret by locking up the source code, they built a barrier between the users and their developers. The programmers would work behind secret walls to write the source code. After compilers turned the Source into something that computers could read, the Source would be locked up again. The purchasers would only get the binary code because that's all the companies thought the consumers needed. The source code needed to be kept secret because someone might steal the ideas inside and create their own version.

Stallman saw this secrecy as a great crime. Computer users should be able to share the source code so they can share ways to make it better. This trade should lead to more information-trading in a great feedback loop. Some folks even used the word "bloom" to describe the explosion of interest and cross-feedback. They're using the word the way biologists use it to describe the way algae can just burst into existence, overwhelming a region of the ocean. Clever insights, brilliant bug fixes, and wonderful new features just appear out of nowhere as human curiosity is amplified by human generosity in a grand explosion of intellectual synergy. The only thing missing from the picture is a bunch of furry Ewoks dancing around a campfire.[1]

The Bishop of the Free Marketplace

Eric Raymond, a man who is sort of the armchair philosopher of the open source world, did a great job of summarizing the phenomenon

---

[1]Linux does have many marketing opportunities. Torvalds chose a penguin named Tux as the mascot, and several companies actually manufacture and sell stuffed penguins to the Linux realm. The BSD world has embraced a cute demon, a visual pun on the fact that BSD UNIX uses the word "daemon" to refer to some of the faceless background programs in the OS.

and creating this myth in his essay "The Cathedral and the Bazaar." Raymond is an earnest programmer who spent some time working on projects like Stallman's GNU Emacs. He saw the advantages of open source development early, perhaps because he's a hard-core libertarian. Government solutions are cumbersome. Empowering individuals by not restraining them is great. Raymond comes off as a bit more extreme than other libertarians, in part because he doesn't hesitate to defend the second amendment of the U.S. Constitution as much as the first. Raymond is not ashamed to support widespread gun ownership as a way to further empower the individual. He dislikes the National Rifle Association because they're too willing to compromise away rights that he feels are absolute.

Some people like to call him the Margaret Mead of the free source world because he spent some time studying and characterizing the culture in much the same way that Mead did when she wrote *Coming of Age in Samoa*. This can be a subtle jab because Margaret Mead is not really the same intellectual angel she was long ago. Derek Freeman and other anthropologists raise serious questions about Mead's ability to see without bias. Mead was a big fan of free love, and many contend it was no accident that she found wonderful tales of unchecked sexuality in Samoa. Freeman revisited Samoa and found it was not the guilt-free land of libertine pleasures that Mead described in her book. He documented many examples of sexual restraint and shame that Mead apparently missed in her search for a paradise.

Raymond looked at open source development and found what he wanted to find: the wonderful efficiency of unregulated markets. Sure, some folks loved to label Richard Stallman a communist, a description that has always annoyed Stallman. Raymond looked a bit deeper and saw that the basis of the free software movement's success was the freedom that gave each user the complete power to change and improve their software. Just as Sigmund Freud found sex at the root of everything and Carl Jung uncovered a battle of animus and anima, the libertarian found freedom.

Raymond's essay was one of the first to try to explain why free source efforts can succeed and even prosper without the financial incentives of a standard money-based software company. One of the biggest reasons he cited was that a programmer could "scratch an itch" that bothered him. That is, a programmer might grow annoyed by a piece of software that limited his choices or had an annoying glitch. Instead of cursing the darkness in the brain cavity of the corporate programmer who created the problem, the free source hacker was able to use the Source to try to find the bug.

Itch-scratching can be instrumental in solving many problems. Some bugs in software are quite hard to identify and duplicate. They only occur in strange situations, like when the printer is out of paper and the modem is overloaded by a long file that is coming over the Internet. Then, and only then, the two buffers may fill to the brim, bump into each other, and crash the computer. The rest of the time, the program floats along happily, encountering no problems.

These types of bugs are notoriously hard for corporate testing environments to discover and characterize. The companies try to be diligent by hiring several young programmers and placing them in a room with a computer. The team beats on the software all day long and develops a healthy animosity toward the programming team that has to fix the problems they discover. They can nab many simple bugs, but what happens if they don't have a printer hooked up to their machine? What happens if they aren't constantly printing out things the way some office users are? The weird bug goes unnoticed and probably unfixed.

The corporate development model tries to solve this limitation by shipping hundreds, thousands, and often hundreds of thousands of copies to ambitious users they called "beta testers." Others called them "suckers" or "free volunteers" because once they finish helping develop the software, they get to pay for it. Microsoft even charges some users for the pleasure of being beta testers. Many of the users are pragmatic. They often have no choice but to participate in the scheme because they often base their businesses on some of the software shipped by these companies. If it didn't work, they would be out of a job.

While this broad distribution of beta copies is much more likely to find someone who is printing and overloading a modem at the same time, it doesn't give the user the tools to help find the problem. Their only choice is to write an e-mail message to the company saying "I was printing yesterday and your software crashed." That isn't very helpful for the engineer, and it's no surprise that many of these reports are either ignored or unsolved.

Raymond pointed out that the free source world can do a great job with these nasty bugs. He characterized this with the phrase, "Given enough eyeballs, all bugs are shallow," which he characterized as "Linus's Law." That is, eventually some programmer would start printing and using the Internet at the same time. After the system crashed a few times, some programmer would care enough about the problem to dig into the free source, poke around, and spot the problem. Eventually somebody would come along with the time and the energy and the commitment to diagnose the problem. Raymond named this "Linus's Law" after Linus Torvalds. Raymond is a great admirer of Torvalds and thinks that Torvalds's true genius was organizing an army to work on Linux. The coding itself was a distant second.

Of course, waiting for a user to find the bugs depended on there being someone with enough time and commitment. Most users aren't talented programmers, and most have day jobs. Raymond and the rest of the free source community acknowledge this limitation, but point out that the right person often comes along if the bug occurs often enough to be a real problem. If the bug is serious enough, a nonprogrammer may even hire a programmer to poke into the source code.

Waiting for the bug and the programmer to find each other is like waiting for Arthur to find the sword in the stone. But Raymond and the rest of the free source community have even turned this limitation on its head and touted it as an advantage. Relying on users to scratch itches means that problems only get addressed if they have real constituencies with a big enough population to generate the one true believer with enough time on his hands. It's sort of a free market in people's time for fixing bugs. If the demand is there, the solution will be created. It's Say's Law recast for software development: "the supply of bugs creates the talent for fixes."

Corporate development, on the other hand, has long been obsessed with adding more and more features to programs to give people enough reason to buy the upgrade. Managers have long known that it's better to put more time into adding more doohickeys and widgets to a program than into fixing its bugs. That's why Microsoft Word can do so many different things with the headers and footers of documents but can't stop a Word Macro virus from reproducing. The folks at Microsoft know that when the corporate managers sit down to decide whether to spend the thousands of dollars to upgrade their machines, they'll need a set of new compelling features. People don't like to pay for bug fixes.

Of course, corporations also have some advantages. Money makes sure that someone is actively trying to solve the bugs in the program. The same free market vision guarantees that the companies that consistently disappoint their customers will go out of business. This developer has the advantage of studying the same source code day in and day out. Eventually he'll learn enough about the guts of the Source to be much more effective than the guy with the jammed printer and modem. He should be able to nab the bug 10 times more quickly then the free source hobbyist just because he's an expert in the system.

Raymond acknowledges this problem but proposes that the free source model can still be more effective despite the inexperience of the people who are forced to scratch an itch. Again he taps the world of libertarian philosophy and suggests that the free software world is like a bazaar filled with many different merchants offering their wares. Corporate development, on the other hand, is structured like the religious syndicates that built the medieval cathedrals. The bazaars offered plenty of competition but no order. The cathedrals were run by central teams of priests who tapped the wealth of the town to build the vision of one architect.

The differences between the two were pretty simple. The cathedral team could produce a great work of art if the architect was talented, the funding team was successful, and the management was able to keep everyone focused on doing their jobs. If not, it never got that far. The bazaar, on the other hand, consisted of many small merchants trying to outstrip each other. The best cooks ended up with the most customers. The others soon went out of business.

The comparison to software was simple. Corporations gathered the tithes, employed a central architect with a grand vision, managed the team of programmers, and shipped a product every once and a bit. The Linux world, however, let everyone touch the Source. People would try to fix things or add new features. The best solutions would be adopted by others and the mediocre would fall by the wayside. Many different Linux versions would proliferate, but over time the marketplace of software would coalesce around the best standard version.

"In the cathedral-builder view of programming, bugs and development problems are tricky, insidious, deep phenomena. It takes months of scrutiny by a dedicated few to develop confidence that you've winkled them all out. Thus the long release intervals, and the inevitable disappointment when long-awaited releases are not perfect," Raymond said.

"In the bazaar view, on the other hand, you assume that bugs are generally shallow phenomena—or, at least, that they turn shallow pretty quick when exposed to a thousand eager codevelopers pounding on every single new release. Accordingly you release often in order to get more corrections, and as a beneficial side effect you have less to lose if an occasional botch gets out the door."

They Put a Giant Arrow on the Problem

This bazaar can be a powerful influence on solving problems. Sure, it isn't guided by a talented architect and teams of priests, but it is a great free-for-all. It is quite unlikely, for instance, that the guy with the overloaded printer and modem line will also be a talented programmer with a grand vision to solve the problem. Someone named Arthur only stumbles across the right stone with the right sword every once and a bit. But if the frustrated user can do a good job characterizing it and reporting it, then someone else can solve it.

Dave Hitz was one of the programmers who helped Keith Bostic rewrite UNIX so it could be free of AT&T's copyright. Today, he runs Network Appliance, a company that builds stripped-down file servers that run BSD at their core. He's been writing file systems ever since college, and the free software came in quite handy when he was starting his company. When they started building the big machines, the engineers just reached into the pool of free source code for operating systems and pulled out much of the code that would power his servers. They modified the code heavily, but the body of free software that he helped create was a great starting point.

In his experience, many people would find a bug and patch it with a solution that was good enough for them. Some were just kids in college. Others were programmers who didn't have the time or the energy to read the Source and understand the best way to fix the problem. Some fixed the problem for themselves, but inadvertently created another problem elsewhere. Sorting through all of these problems was hard to do.

But Hitz says, "Even if they fixed it entirely the wrong way, if they found the place where the problem went away, then they put a giant arrow on the problem." Eventually, enough arrows would provide someone with enough information to solve the problem correctly. Many of the new versions written by people may be lost to time, but that doesn't mean that they didn't have an important effect on the evolution of the Source.

"I think it's rarely the case that you get people who make a broad base of source code their life," he said. "There are just a whole bunch of people who are dilettantes. The message is, 'Don't underestimate the dilettantes.'"

How Free Software Can Be a Bazaar or a Cathedral

When Raymond wrote the essay, he was just trying to suss out the differences between several of the camps in the free source world. He noticed that people running free source projects had different ways of sharing. He wanted to explain which free source development method worked better than others. It was only later that the essay began to take on a more serious target when everyone began to realize that Microsoft was perhaps the biggest cathedral-like development team around.

Raymond said, "I think that like everyone else in the culture I wandered back and forth between the two modes as it seemed appropriate because I didn't have a theory or any consciousness."

He saw Richard Stallman and the early years of the GNU projects as an example of cathedral-style development. These teams would often labor for months if not years before sharing their tools with the world. Raymond himself said he behaved the same way with some of the early tools that he wrote and contributed to the GNU project.

Linus Torvalds changed his mind by increasing the speed of sharing, which Raymond characterized as the rule of "release early and often, delegate everything you can, be open to the point of promiscuity." Torvalds ran Linux as openly as possible, and this eventually attracted some good contributors. In the past, the FSF was much more careful about what it embraced and brought into the GNU project. Torvalds took many things into his distributions and they mutated as often as daily. Occasionally, new versions came out twice a day.

Of course, Stallman and Raymond have had tussles in the past. Raymond is careful to praise the man and say he values his friendship, but also tempers it by saying that Stallman is difficult to work with.

In Raymond's case, he says that he once wanted to rewrite much of the Lisp code that was built into GNU Emacs. Stallman's Emacs allowed any user to hook up their own software into Emacs by writing it in a special version of Lisp. Some had written mail readers. Others had added automatic comment-generating code. All of this was written in Lisp.

Raymond says that in 1992, "The Lisp libraries were in bad shape in a number of ways. They were poorly documented. There was a lot of work that had gone on outside the FSF and I wanted to tackle that project."

According to Raymond, Stallman didn't want him to do the work and refused to build it into the distribution. Stallman could do this because he controlled the Free Software Foundation and the distribution of the software. Raymond could have created his own version, but refused because it was too complicated and ultimately bad for everyone if two versions emerged.

For his part, Stallman explains that he was glad to accept parts of Raymond's work, but he didn't want to be forced into accepting them all. Stallman says, "Actually, I accepted a substantial amount of work that Eric had done. He had a number of ideas I liked, but he also had some ideas I thought were mistaken. I was happy to accept his help, as long as I could judge his ideas one by one, accepting some and declining some.

"But subsequently he asked me to make a blanket arrangement in which he would take over the development of a large part of Emacs, operating independently. I felt I should continue to judge his ideas individually, so I said no."

Raymond mixed this experience with his time watching Torvalds's team push the Linux kernel and used them as the basis for his essay on distributing the Source. "Mostly I was trying to pull some factors that I had observed as unconscious folklore so people could take them out and reason about them," he said.

Raymond says, "Somebody pointed out that there's a parallel of politics. Rigid political and social institutions tend to change violently if they change at all, while ones with more play in them tend to change peacefully."

There is a good empirical reason for the faith in the strength of free source. After all, a group of folks who rarely saw each other had assembled a great pile of source code that was kicking Microsoft's butt in some corners of the computer world. Linux servers were common on the Internet and growing more common every day. The desktop was waiting to be conquered. They had done this without stock options, without corporate jets, without secret contracts, and without potentially illegal alliances with computer manufacturers. The success of the software from the GNU and Linux world was really quite impressive.

Of course, myths can be taken too far. Programming computers is hard work and often frustrating. Sharing the source code doesn't make bugs or problems go away—it just makes it a bit easier for someone else to dig into a program to see what's going wrong. The source code may just be a list of instructions written in a programming language that is designed to be readable by humans, but that doesn't mean that it is easy to understand. In fact, most humans won't figure out most source code because programming languages are designed to be understood by other programmers, not the general population.

To make matters worse, programmers themselves have a hard time understanding source code. Computer programs are often quite complicated and it can take days, weeks, and even months to understand what a strange piece of source code is telling a computer to do. Learning what is happening in a program can be a complicated job for even the best programmers, and it is not something that is taken lightly.

While many programmers and members of the open source world are quick to praise the movement, they will also be able to cite problems with the myth of the Source. It isn't that the Source doesn't work, they'll say, it's just that it rarely works anywhere near as well as the hype implies. The blooms are rarely as vigorous and the free markets in improvements are rarely as liquid.

Larry McVoy, an avid programmer, proto-academic, and developer of the BitKeeper toolkit, likes to find fault with the model. It isn't that he doesn't like sharing source code, it's just that he isn't wealthy enough to take on free software projects. "We need to find a way for people to develop free software and pay their mortgages and raise a family," he says.

"If you look closely," he says, "there really isn't a bazaar. At the top it's always a one-person cathedral. It's either Linus, Stallman, or someone else." That is, the myth of a bazaar as a wide-open, free-for-all of competition isn't exactly true. Sure, everyone can download the source code, diddle with it, and make suggestions, but at the end of the day it matters what Torvalds, Stallman, or someone else says. There is always a great architect of Chartres lording it over his domain.

Part of this problem is the success of Raymond's metaphor. He said he just wanted to give the community some tools to understand the success of Linux and reason about it. But his two visions of a cathedral and a bazaar had such a clarity that people concentrated more on dividing the world into cathedrals and bazaars. In reality, there's a great deal of blending in between. The most efficient bazaars today are the suburban malls that have one management company building the site, leasing the stores, and creating a unified experience. Downtown shopping areas often failed because there was always one shop owner who could ruin an entire block by putting in a store that sold pornography. On the other side, religion has always been something of a bazaar. Martin Luther effectively split apart Christianity by introducing competition. Even within denominations, different parishes fight for the hearts and souls of people.

The same blurring holds true for the world of open source software. The Linux kernel, for instance, contains many thousands of lines of source code. Some put the number at 500,000. A few talented folks like Alan Cox or Linus Torvalds know all of it, but most are only familiar with the corners of it that they need to know. These folks, who may number in the thousands, are far outnumbered by the millions who use the Linux OS daily.

It's interesting to wonder if the ratio of technically anointed to blithe users in the free source world is comparable to the ratio in Microsoft's dominion. After all, Microsoft will share its source code with close partners after they sign some nondisclosure forms.[2] While Microsoft is careful about what it tells its partners, it will reveal information only when there's something to gain. Other companies have already jumped right in and started offering source code to all users who want to look at it.

Answering this question is impossible for two different reasons. First, no one knows what Microsoft reveals to its partners because it keeps all of this information secret, by reflex. Contracts are usually negotiated under nondisclosure, and the company has not been shy about exploiting the power that comes from the lack of information.

Second, no one really knows who reads the Linux source code for the opposite reason. The GNU/Linux source is widely available and frequently downloaded, but that doesn't mean it's read or studied. The Red Hat CDs come with one CD full of precompiled binaries and the second full of source code. Who knows whoever pops the second CD-ROM in their computer? Everyone is free to do so in the privacy of their own cubicle, so no records are kept.

If I were to bet, I would guess that the ratios of cognoscenti to uninformed users in the Linux and Microsoft worlds are pretty close. Reading the Source just takes too much time and too much effort for many in the Linux world to take advantage of the huge river of information available to them.

If this is true or at least close to true, then why has the free source world been able to move so much more quickly than the Microsoft world? The answer isn't that everyone in the free source world is using the Source, it's that everyone is free to use it. When one person needs to ask a question or scratch an itch, the Source is available with no questions asked and no lawyers consulted. Even at 3:00 A.M., a person can read the Source. At Microsoft and other corporations, they often need to wait for the person running that division or section to give them permission to access the source code.

There are other advantages. The free source world spends a large amount of time keeping the source code clean and accessible. A programmer who tries to get away with sloppy workmanship and bad doc-

---

[2]At this writing, Microsoft has not released its source code, but the company is widely known to be examining the option as part of its settlement with the Department of Justice.

umentation will pay for it later as others come along and ask thousands of questions.

Corporate developers, on the other hand, have layers of secrecy and bureaucracy to isolate them from questions and comments. It is often hard to find the right programmer in the rabbit warren of cubicles who has the source code in the first place. One Microsoft programmer was quoted as saying, "A developer at Microsoft working on the OS can't scratch an itch he's got with Excel, neither can the Excel developer scratch his itch with the OS—it would take him months to figure out how to build and debug and install, and he probably couldn't get proper source access anyway."

This problem is endemic to corporations. The customers are buying the binary version, not the source code, so there is no reason to dress up the backstage wings of the theater. After some time, though, people change cubicles, move to other corporations, and information disappears. While companies try to keep source code databases to synchronize development, the efforts often fall apart. After Apple canceled development of their Newton handheld, many Newton users were livid. They had based big projects on the platform and they didn't want to restart their work. Many asked whether Apple could simply give away the OS's source code instead of leaving it to rot on some hard disk. Apple dodged these requests, and this made some people even more cynical. One outside developer speculated, "It probably would not be possible to re-create the OS. The developers are all gone. All of them went to Palm, and they probably couldn't just put it back together again if they wanted to."

Of course, corporations try to fight this rot by getting their programmers to do a good job at the beginning and write plenty of documentation. In practice, this slips a bit because it is not rewarded by the culture of secrecy. I know one programmer who worked for a project at MIT. The boss thought he was being clever by requiring comments on each procedure and actually enforcing it with an automated text-scanning robot that would look over the source code and count the comments. My friend turned around and hooked up one version of the popular artificial intelligence chatterbots like Eliza and funneled the responses into the comment field. Then everyone was happy. The chatterbot filled the comment field, the automated comment police found something vaguely intelligent, and the programmer got to spend his free time doing other things. The boss never discovered the problem.

Programmers are the same the world over, and joining the free source world doesn't make them better people or destroy their impudence. But it does penalize them if others come along and try to use their code. If it's inscrutable, sloppy, or hard to understand, then others will either ignore it or pummel them with questions. That is a strong incentive to do it right.

Open Source and Lightbulbs

The limitations to the power of open source might be summarized in the answer to the question "How many open source developers does it take to change a lightbulb?" The answer is: 17. Seventeen to argue about the license; 17 to argue about the brain-deadedness of the lightbulb architecture; 17 to argue about a new model that encompasses all models of illumination and makes it simple to replace candles, campfires, pilot lights, and skylights with the same easy-to-extend mechanism; 17 to speculate about the secretive industrial conspiracy that ensures that lightbulbs will burn out frequently; 1 to finally change the bulb; and 16 who decide that this solution is good enough for the time being.

The open source development model is a great way for very creative people to produce fascinating software that breaks paradigms and establishes new standards for excellence. It may not be the best way, however, to finish boring jobs like fine-tuning a graphical interface, or making sure that the scheduling software used by executives is as bulletproof as possible.

While the open development model has successfully tackled the problem of creating some great tools, of building a strong OS, and of building very flexible appliance applications like web browsers, it is a long way from winning the battle for the desktop. Some free source people say the desktop applications for average users are just around the corner and the next stop on the Free Software Express. Others aren't so sure.

David Henkel-Wallace is one of the founders of the free software company Cygnus. This company built its success around supporting the development tools created by Stallman's Free Software Foundation. They would sign contracts with companies to answer any questions they had about using the free software tools. At first companies would balk at paying for support until they realized that it was cheaper than hiring in-house technical staff to do the work. John Gilmore, one of the co-founders, liked to say, "We make free software affordable."

The company grew by helping chip manufacturers tune the FSF compiler, GCC, for their chip. This was often a difficult and arduous task, but it was very valuable to the chip manufacturer because potential customers knew they could get a good compiler to produce software for the chip. While Intel continued to dominate the desktop, the market for embedded chips to go into products like stoves, microwave ovens, VCRs, or other smart boxes boomed as manufacturers rolled out new chips to make it cheaper and easier to add smart features to formerly dumb boxes. The engineers at the companies were often thrilled to discover that they could continue to use GCC to write software for a new chip, and this made it easier to sell the chip.

Cygnus always distributed to the Source their modifications to GCC as the GNU General Public License demanded. This wasn't a big deal because the chip manufacturers wanted the software to be free and easy for everyone to use. This made Cygnus one of the clearinghouses for much of the information on how GCC worked and how to make it faster.

Henkel-Wallace is quick to praise the power of publicly available source code for Cygnus's customers. They were all programmers, after all. If they saw something they didn't like with GCC, they knew how to poke around on the insides and fix it. That was their job.

"[GCC] is a compiler tool and it was used by developers so they were smart enough. When something bothered someone, we fixed it. There was a very tight coupling," he said.

He openly wonders, though, whether the average word processor or basic tool user will be able to do anything. He says, "The downside is that it's hard to transfer that knowledge with a user who isn't a developer. Let's say Quicken has a special feature for lawyers. You need to have a more formal model because the lawyers aren't developers. (We're fortunate in that regard.)"

That is, lawyers aren't schooled enough in the guts of computer development to complain in the right way. A programmer could say, "GCC is optimizing away too much dead code that isn't really dead." Other folks in the GCC community would know what is going on and be able to fix it. A lawyer might just say, "Quicken screwed up my billing and had me billing twenty-six hours in a day." This wouldn't pinpoint the problem enough for people to solve it. The lawyer doesn't understand the inside of the software like the programmer.

In situations like this, Henkel-Wallace believes that a corporate-style team may be the only one that can study the problems thoroughly enough to find solutions. Intuit, the manufacturer of Quicken, is well known for videotaping many standard users who use their product for the first time. This allows them to pinpoint rough spots in the program and identify places where it could be improved. This relentless smoothing and polishing has made the product one of the best-known and widely used tools on desktops. It isn't clear that nonprogrammers could have accomplished the same quality by working together with the Source at their disposal.

The Source and the Language that We Speak

There are deeper, more philosophical currents to the open source world. The personal computer industry is only a few decades old. While it has advanced rapidly and solved many problems, there is still very little understanding of the field and what it takes to make a computer easy to use. This has been the great struggle, and the free source world may be an essential part of this trip.

Tim O'Reilly, the publisher of many books and a vocal proponent of the open source world, says, "We've gone through this period of thinking of programs as artifacts. A binary object is a thing. Open source is part of thinking of computers as a process." In other words, we've done a good job of creating computers you can buy off the shelf and software that can be bought in shrink-wrapped boxes, but we haven't done a good job of making it possible for people to talk to the machines.

To a large extent, the process has been a search for a good language to use to communicate with the computer. Most of the recent development followed the work at Xerox PARC that created some of the first graphical user interfaces. Apple followed their lead and Microsoft followed Apple. Each bought into the notion that creating a neat picture representing the files on a screen would make a neat metaphor that could make it easier for people to interact with the computers. Dragging a file to the trash was somehow easier for people to do than typing a cryptic command like "rm."

In the 1980s, that sort of graphical thinking was considered brilliant. Pictures were prettier than words, so it was easy to look at the clean, pretty Macintosh screen and think it was easier to use just because it was easier to look at.

But the pretty features merely hid a massive amount of complexity, and it was still hard to work with the machines. Don Norman, a human/computer interface engineer at Apple, once wrote a fascinating discussion of the company's design of their computer's on-off switch. He pointed out that the switch couldn't be a simple power switch that could cut the power on and off because the computer needed to orchestrate the start-up and shutdown procedure. It needed to close up files, store data safely, and make sure everything was ready to start up again.

The design of the power switch was made even more complicated by the fact that it was supposed to work even when the computer crashed. That is, if bad programming jumbles the memory and screws up the central processor, the power switch is still supposed to shut down the machine. Of course, the computer couldn't even add two numbers together after it crashed, so it couldn't even begin to move through all the clerical work necessary to shut down the machine. The Macintosh on which I wrote this book can crash so badly that the power switch doesn't work, and I can only reset it by sticking a paper clip into a hidden hole.

Norman's work shows how hard it can be to come up with a simple language that allows humans and computers to communicate about a task that used to be solved with a two-position light switch. This problem can be seen throughout the industry. One computer tutor told me, "I am so tired of telling people to shut down their computers by pushing the 'Start' button." Microsoft Windows places all of the features on a menu tree that grows out of one button labeled "Start." This may have been a great way to capture the potential to do new things that they felt they were selling, but it continues to be confusing to all new users of the machines. Why should they push start to stop it?

The quest for this Source-level control can take many strange turns. By the middle of the 1980s, programmers at Apple realized that they had gone a bit too far when they simplified the Mac's interface. The visual language of pointing and clicking at icons may have been great for new users, but it was beginning to thwart sophisticated users who wanted to automate what they did. Many graphics designers would find themselves repeatedly doing the same steps to image files, and it was boring. They wondered, why couldn't the computer just repeat all their instructions and save them all that pointing and clicking?

In a sense, the sophisticated Mac users were looking for the Source. They wanted to be able to write and modify simple programs that controlled their software. The problem was that the graphical display on the Mac wasn't really suited to the task. How do you describe moving the mouse and clicking on a button? How do you come up with a language that means "cut out this sample and paste it over here"? The actions were so visual that there weren't any words or language to describe them.

This problem confounded Apple for the next 10 years, and the company is slowly finishing its solution, known as AppleScript. The task has not been simple, but it has been rewarding for many who use their Macintoshes as important chains in data production lines. Apple included instructions for moving icons to locations, uploading files, changing the color of icons, and starting up programs with others.

The nicest extension was a trick that made the AppleScript "recordable." That is, you could turn on a recorder before stepping through the different jobs. The Mac would keep track of your actions and generate a program that would allow you to repeat what you were doing. Still, the results were far from simple to understand or use. Here's a simple snippet of AppleScript code that will select all files in one directory with the word "Speckle" in their title and open them up with another application:

```
tell application "Finder"
    set theFiles to every file in folder (rootPlus) whose
    name contains "Speckle"

    with timeout of 600 seconds
        repeat with aFile in theFiles
            open (aFile) using (file "Macintosh HD: Make
            GIF (16 colors, Web)")
        end repeat
    end timeout
end tell
```

This Source can then be run again and again to finish a task. Making this tool available to users has been a challenge for Apple because it forces them to make programming easier. Many people learn AppleScript by turning on the recording feature and watching what happens when they do what they would normally do. Then they learn how to insert a few more commands to accomplish the task successfully. In the end, they become programmers manipulating the Source without realizing it.

O'Reilly and others believe that the open source effort is just an extension of this need. As computers become more and more complex, the developers need to make the internal workings more and more open to users. This is the only way users can solve their problems and use the computers effectively.

"The cutting edge of the computer industry is in infoware. There's not all that much juice in the kind of apps we wrote in the eighties and nineties. As we get speech recognition, we'll go even more in the direction of open source," he says.

"There are more and more recipes that are written down. These are going to migrate into lower and lower layers of software and the computer is going to get a bigger and bigger vocabulary."

That is, more and more of the Source is going to need to become transparent to the users. It's not just a political battle of Microsoft versus the world. It's not just a programmer's struggle to poke a nose into every corner of a device. It's about usability. More and more people need to write programs to teach computers to do what they need to do. Access to the Source is the only way to accomplish it.

In other words, computers are becoming a bigger and bigger part of our lives. Their language is becoming more readily understandable by humans, and humans are doing a better job of speaking the language of computers. We're converging. The more we do so, the more important the Source will be. There's nothing that Microsoft or corporate America can do about this. They're going to have to go along. They're going to have to give us access to the Source.

• • •

10. PEOPLE

When I was in college, a friend of mine in a singing group would often tweak his audience by making them recite Steve Martin's "Individualist's Creed" in unison. Everyone would proclaim that they were different, unique, and wonderfully eccentric individuals together with everyone else in the audience. The gag played well because all the individualists were also deeply committed to living a life filled with irony.

The free source world is sort of a Club Med for these kinds of individualists. Richard Stallman managed to organize a group of highly employable people and get them to donate their $50+-per-hour time to a movement by promising complete freedom. Everyone who showed up valued freedom much more than the money they could be making working for big companies. It's not a bit surprising that all of the free thinkers are also coming up with the same answers to life. Great minds think alike, right?

This large collection of dedicated individualists is predisposed to moments of easy irony. Black is by far their favorite color. Long hair and beards are common. T-shirts and shorts are the rule when it gets warm, and T-shirts and jeans dominate when the weather turns cold. No one wears suits or anything so traditional. That would be silly because they're not as comfortable as T-shirts and jeans. Fitting in with the free thinkers isn't hard.

The group is not particularly republican or democrat, but libertarian politics are easily understood and widely supported. Gun control is usually considered to be wrong, if only because the federal government will move on to controlling something else when they're finished with guns.[1] Taxes are bad, and some in the group like to dream of when they'll be driven away by the free-flowing, frictionless economy of the Internet. Folks like to say things like "Governments are just speed bumps on the information superhighway."

The first amendment is very popular and many are sure that practically everything they do with a computer is a form of speech or expression. The government shouldn't have the right to control a website's content because they'll surely come to abuse that power in the future. Some even rage against private plans to rate websites for their content because they're certain that these tools will eventually be controlled by those in power. To the most extreme, merely creating a list of sites with information unsuitable for kids is setting up the infrastructure for the future Nazis to start burning websites.

Virtually everyone believes that strong codes and cryptography are essential for protecting a person's privacy online. The U.S. government's attempt to control the technology by regulating its export is widely seen as a silly example of how governments are trying to grab power at the expense of their citizens. The criminals already have the secret codes; why shouldn't the honest people be able to protect their data?

Pornography or references to sex in the discussions are rare, if only because the world of the libido is off the main topic. It's not that sex isn't on the minds of the free software community, it's just that the images are so freely available that they're uninteresting. Anyone can go to www.playboy.com, but not everyone can write a recursively descending code optimizer. People also rarely swear. While four-letter words are common on Wall Street and other highly charged environments, they're rare in the technology world.

Much of the community are boys and men, or perhaps more correctly "guys." While there are some older programmers who continue to dig the excitement and tussle of the free source world, many are high school and college guys with plenty of extra time on their hands. Many of them are too smart for school, and writing neat software is a challenge for them. Older people usually get bogged down with a job and mort-

---

[1]In fact, the federal government already considers encryption software to be a munition and often tries to regulate it as such.

gage payments. It's hard for them to take advantage of the freedom that comes with the source code. Still, the older ones who survive are often the best. They have both deep knowledge and experience.

The average population, however, is aging quickly. As the software becomes better, it is easier for working stiffs to bring it into the corporate environments. Many folks brag about sneaking Linux into their office and replacing Microsoft on some hidden server. As more and more users find a way to make money with the free software, more and more older people (i.e., over 25) are able to devote some time to the revolution.

I suppose I would like to report that there's a healthy contingent of women taking part in the free source world, but I can't. It would be nice to isolate the free software community from the criticism that usually finds any group of men. By some definition or legal reasoning, these guys must be practicing some de facto discrimination. Somebody will probably try to sue someone someday. Still, the women are scarce and it's impossible to use many of the standard explanations. The software is, after all, free. It runs well on machines that are several generations old and available from corporate scrap heaps for several hundred dollars. Torvalds started writing Linux because he couldn't afford a real version of UNIX. Lack of money or the parsimony of evil, gender-nasty parents who refuse to buy their daughters a computer can hardly be blamed.

In fact, many of the people online don't even know the gender of the person on the other end. Oblique nicknames like "303," "nomad," "CmdrTaco," or "Hemos" are common. No one knows if you're a boy or a girl online. It's almost like the ideal of a gender-free existence proposed by the unisex dreamers who wrote such stuff as "Free to Be You and Me," trying to convince children that they were free to pursue any dream they wanted. Despite the prevalence of these gender-free visions, the folks who ended up dreaming of a world where all the software was free turned out to be almost entirely men.

Most of the men would like to have a few more women show up. They need dates as much as any guy. If anything, the crown of Evil Discriminator might be placed on the heads of the girls who scorn the guys who are geeks, dweebs, and nerds. A girl couldn't find a better ratio of men if she tried.

This may change in the future if organizations like LinuxChix (www.linuxchix.org) have their way. They run a site devoted to celebrating women who enjoy the open source world, and they've been trying to start up chapters around the world. The site gives members a chance to post their names and biographical details. Of course, several of the members are men and one is a man turning into a woman. The member writes, "I'm transsexual (male-to-female, pre-op), and at the moment still legally married to my wife, which means that if we stay together we'll eventually have a legal same-sex marriage."

Still, there's not much point in digging into this too deeply because the free source world rarely debates this topic. Everyone is free to use the software and contribute what they want. If the women want to come, they can. If they don't, they don't have to do so to fulfill some mandate from society. No one is sitting around debating whether having it all as a woman includes having all of the source code. It's all about freedom to use software, not dating, mating, or debating sexual roles in society.

Racial politics, however, are more complicated. Much of the Linux community is spread out throughout the globe. While many members come from the United States, major contributors can be found in most countries. Linus Torvalds, of course, came from Finland, one of the more technically advanced countries in the world. Miguel de Icaza, the lead developer of the GNOME desktop, comes from Mexico, a country perceived as technically underdeveloped by many in the United States.

Jon Hall, often called maddog, is one of the first members of corporate America to recognize that neat things were going on throughout the world of open source software. He met Torvalds at a conference and shipped him a Digital computer built around the Alpha chip when he found out that Torvalds wanted to experiment with porting his software to a 64-bit architecture. Hall loves to speculate about the spread of free software throughout the globe and says, "Who knows where the next great mind will come from? It could be Spain, Brazil, India, Singapore, or dare I say Finland?"

In general, the free source revolution is worldwide and rarely encumbered by racial and national barricades. Europe is just as filled with Linux developers as America, and the Third World is rapidly skipping over costly Microsoft and into inexpensive Linux. Interest in Linux is booming in China and India. English is, of course, the default language, but other languages continue to live thanks to automatic translation mechanisms like Babelfish.

This border-free existence can only help the spread of free source software. Many countries, claiming national pride, would rather use software developed by local people. Many countries explicitly distrust software coming from the United States because it is well known that the U.S. government tries to restrict security software like encryption at the request of its intelligence-gathering agencies. In November 1999, the German government's Federal Ministry of Finance and Technology announced a grant for the GNU Privacy Guard project. Why would a country want to send all of its money to Redmond, Washington, when it could bolster a local group of hackers by embracing a free OS? For everyone but the United States, installing a free OS may even be a patriotic gesture.

Icons

The archetypes are often defined by prominent people, and no one is more central to the free source world than Richard Stallman. Some follow the man like a disciple, others say that his strong views color the movement and scare away normal people. Everyone goes out of their way to praise the man and tell you how much they respect what he's done. Almost everyone will turn around and follow the compliment with a veiled complaint like, "He can be difficult to work with." Stallman is known for being a very unreasonable man in the sense that George Bernard Shaw used the word when he said, "The Reasonable man adapts to nature. The unreasonable man seeks to adapt nature to himself. Therefore it is only through the actions of unreasonable men that civilization advances." The reasonable man would still be waiting on hold as the tech support folks in MegaSoft played with their Nerf footballs and joked about the weenies who needed help using their proprietary software.

I often think that only someone as obsessed and brilliant as Stallman could have dreamed up the GNU Public License. Only he could have realized that it was possible to insist that everyone give away the source code *and* allow them to charge for it at the same time if they want. Most of us would have locked our brains if we found ourselves with a dream of a world of unencumbered source code but hobbled by the reality that we needed money to live. Stallman found himself in that place in the early days of the Free Software Foundation and then found a way to squeeze his way out of the dilemma by charging for CD-ROMs and printed manuals. The fact that others could still freely copy the information they got meant that he wasn't compromising his core dream.

If Stallman is a product of MIT, then one opposite of him is the group of hackers that emerged from Berkeley and produced the other free software known as FreeBSD, NetBSD, and OpenBSD. Berkeley's computer science department always had a tight bond with AT&T and Sun and shared much of the early UNIX code with both.

While there were many individuals at Berkeley who are well known among developers and hackers, no one stands out like Richard Stallman. This is because Stallman is such a strong iconoclast, not because Berkeley is the home of ne'er-do-wells who don't measure up. In fact, the pragmatism of some of the leaders to emerge from the university is almost as great as Stallman's idealism, and this pragmatism is one of the virtues celebrated by Berkeley's circle of coders. For instance, Bill Joy helped develop much of the early versions of the BSD before he went off to take a strong leadership role at Sun Microsystems.

Sun has a contentious relationship with the free software world. It's far from a free software company like Red Hat, but it has contributed a fair number of lines of software to the open source community. Still, Sun guards its intellectual property rights to some packages fiercely and refuses to distribute the source with an official open source license. Instead, it calls their approach the "community source license" and insists that it's good enough for almost everyone. Users can read the source code, but they can't run off with it and start their own distribution.

Many others from Berkeley followed Joy's path to Sun. John Ousterhout left his position as a professor at Berkeley in 1994 to move to Sun. Ousterhout was known for developing a fairly simple but powerful scripting tool known as TCL/Tk. One part of it, the Tool Control

Language (TCL), was a straightforward English-like language that made it pretty easy for people to knit together different modules of code. The user didn't have to be a great programmer to work with the code because the language was designed to be straightforward. There were no complicated data structures or pointers. Everything was a string of ASCII text.

The second part, the Tool kit (Tk), contained a variety of visual widgets that could be used to get input for and output from a program. The simplest ones were buttons, sliders, or menus, but many people wrote complicated ones that served their particular needs.

The TCL/Tk project at Berkeley attracted a great deal of attention from the Net. Ousterhout, like most academics, freely distributed his code and did a good job helping others use the software. He and his students rewrote and extended the code a number of times, and this constant support helped create even more fans. The software scratched an itch for many academics who were smart enough to program the machines in their lab, but burdened by more important jobs like actually doing the research they set out to do. TCL/Tk picked up a wide following because it was easy for people to learn a small amount quickly. Languages like C required a semester or more to master. TCL could be picked up in an afternoon.

Many see the pragmatism of the BSD-style license as a way for the Berkeley hackers to ease their trip into corporate software production. The folks would develop the way-out, unproven ideas using public money before releasing it with the BSD license. Then companies like Sun would start to resell it.

The supporters of the BSD licenses, of course, don't see corporate development as a bad thing. They just see it as a way for people to pay for the extra bells and whistles that a dedicated, market-driven team can add to software.

Ousterhout's decision to move to Sun worried many people because they thought it might lead to a commercialization of the language. Ousterhout answered these with an e-mail message that said TCL/Tk would remain free, but Sun would try to make some money on the project by selling development tools.

"Future enhancements made to Tcl and Tk by my group at Sun, including the ports to Macs and PCs, will be made freely available to anyone to use for any purpose. My view, and that of the people I report to at Sun, is that it wouldn't work for Sun to try to take Tcl and Tk proprietary anyway: someone (probably me, in a new job) would just pick up the last free release and start an independent development path. This would be a terrible thing for everyone since it would result in incompatible versions.

"Of course, Sun does need to make money from the work of my team or else they won't be able to continue to support us. Our current plan is to charge for development tools and interesting extensions and applications. Balancing the public and the profitable will be an ongoing challenge for us, but it is very important both to me and to Sun to keep the support of the existing Tcl community," he wrote.

In some respects, Ousterhout's pragmatism was entirely different from Stallman's. He openly acknowledged the need to make money and also admitted that Sun was leaving TCL/Tk free because it might be practically impossible to make it proprietary. The depth of interest in the community made it likely that a free version would continue to evolve. Stallman would never cut such a deal with a company shipping proprietary software.

In other respects, many of the differences are only at the level of rhetoric. Ousterhout worked on producing a compromise that would leave TCL/Tk free while the sales of development tools paid the bills. Stallman did the same thing when he figured out a way to charge people for CD-ROMs and manuals. Ousterhout's work at Sun was spun off into a company called Scriptics that is surprisingly like many of the other free software vendors. The core of the product, TCL/Tk 8.1 at this time, is governed by a BSD-style license. The source code can be downloaded from the site. The company itself, on the other hand, sells a more enhanced product known as TCLPro.

In many ways, the real opposite to Richard Stallman is not Bill Joy or John Ousterhout, it's Linus Benedict Torvalds. While Stallman, Joy, and Ousterhout are products of the U.S. academic system, Torvalds is very much an outsider who found himself trying to program in Europe without access to a decent OS. While the folks at Berkeley, MIT, and many U.S. universities were able to get access to UNIX thanks to carefully constructed licenses produced by the OS's then-owner, AT&T, students in Finland like Torvalds were frozen out.

"I didn't have many alternatives. I had the commercial alternative [UNIX], which was way too expensive. It was really out of reach for a normal human being, and not only out of reach in a monetary sense, but because years ago commercial UNIX vendors weren't interested in selling to individuals. They were interested in selling to large corporations and banks. So for a normal person, there was no choice," he told *VAR Business*.

When Linux began to take off, Torvalds moved to Silicon Valley and took a job with the supersecret research firm Transmeta. At Comdex in November 1999, Torvalds announced that Transmeta was working on a low-power computing chip with the nickname "Crusoe."

There are, of course, some conspiracy theories. Transmeta is funded by a number of big investors including Microsoft cofounder Paul Allen. The fact that they chose to employ Torvalds may be part of a plan, some think, to distract him from Linux development. After all, version 2.2 of the kernel took longer than many expected, although it may have been because its goals were too ambitious. When Microsoft needed a coherent threat to offer up to the Department of Justice, Transmeta courteously made Torvalds available to the world. Few seriously believe this theory, but it is constantly whispered as a nervous joke.

Flames

The fights and flamefests of the Internet are legendary, and the open source world is one of the most contentious corners of the Net. People frequently use strong words like "brain dead," "loser," "lame," "gross," and "stoooopid" to describe one another's ideas. If words are the only way to communicate, then the battle for mindshare means that those who wield the best words win.

In fact, most of the best hackers and members of the free source world are also great writers. Spending days, weeks, months, and years of your life communicating by e-mail and newsgroups teaches people how to write well and get to the point quickly. The Internet is very textual, and the hard-core computer programmers have plenty of experience spitting out text. As every programmer knows, you're supposed to send e-mail to the person next to you if you want to schedule lunch. That person might be in the middle of something.

Of course, there's a danger to making a sweeping generalization implying that the free source world is filled with great writers. The fact is that we might not have heard from the not-so-great writers who sit lurking on the Net. While some of the students who led the revolutions of 1968 were quite articulate, many of the tie-dyed masses were also in the picture. You couldn't miss them. On the Internet, the silent person is invisible.

Some argue that the free software world has burgeoned because the silent folks embraced the freely available source code. Anyone could download the source code and play with it without asking permission or spending money. That meant that 13-year-old kids could start using the software without asking their parents for money. SCO Unix and Windows NT cost big bucks.

This freedom also extended to programmers at work. In many companies, the computer managers are doctrinaire and officious. They often quickly develop knee-jerk reactions to technologies and use these stereotypes to make technical decisions. Free software like Linux was frequently rejected out of hand by the gatekeepers, who thought something must be wrong with the software if no one was charging for it. These attitudes couldn't stop the engineers who wanted to experiment with the free software, however, because it had no purchase order that needed approval.

The invisible-man quality is an important part of the free software world. While I've described the bodies and faces of some of the better-known free source poster boys, it is impossible to say much about many of the others. The community is spread out over the Internet throughout the world. Many people who work closely on projects never meet each other. The physical world with all of its ways of encoding a position in a hierarchy are gone. No one can tell how rich you are by your shoes. The color of your skin doesn't register. It's all about technology and technological ideas.

In fact, there is a certain degree of Emily Dickinson in the world. Just as that soul selected her own society and shut the door on the rest of the world, the free software world frequently splits and resplits into smaller groups. While there is some cross-pollination, many are happy to live in their own corners. OpenBSD, FreeBSD, and NetBSD are more separate countries than partners in crime. They evolve on their own, occasionally stealing ideas and source code to bridge the gap.

Many writers have described some of their problems with making hay of the Silicon Valley world. Screenwriters and television producers often start up projects to tap into the rich texture of nerdlands only to discover that there's nothing that compelling to film. It's just miles and miles of steel-frame buildings holding acres and acres of cubicles. Sure, there are some Ping-Pong tables and pinball machines, but the work is all in the mind. Eyes want physical action, and all of the excitement in a free source world is in the ideas.

But people are people. While there's no easy way to use the old standbys of race or clothes to discriminate, the technical world still develops ways to classify its members and place them in camps. The free software world has its own ways to distinguish between these camps.

The biggest distinction may be between folks who favor the GPL and those who use the BSD-style license to protect their software. This is probably the biggest decision a free software creator must make because it controls whether others will be able to build commercial versions of the software without contributing the new code back to the project.

People who embrace the GPL are more likely to embrace Richard Stallman, or at least less likely to curse him in public. They tend to be iconoclastic and individualistic. GPL projects tend to be more cultish and driven by a weird mixture of personality and ain't-it-cool hysteria.

The people on the side of BSD-style license, on the other hand, seem pragmatic, organized, and focused. There are three major free versions of BSD UNIX alone, and they're notable because they each have centrally administered collections of files. The GPL-protected Linux can be purchased from at least six major groups that bundle it together, and each of them includes packages and pieces of software they find all over the Net.

The BSD-license folks are also less cultish. The big poster boys, Torvalds and Stallman, are both GPL men. The free versions of BSD, which helped give Linux much of its foundation, are largely ignored by the press for all the wrong reasons. The BSD teams appear to be fragmented because they are all separate political organizations who have no formal ties. There are many contributors, which means that BSD has no major charismatic leader with a story as compelling as that of Linus Torvalds.

Many contributors could wear this mantle and many have created just as much code. But life, or at least the media's description of it, is far from fair.

The flagship of the BSD world may be the Apache web server group, which contributed greatly to the success of the platform. This core team has no person who stands out as a leader. Most of the people on the team are fully employed in the web business, and several members of the team said that the Apache team was just a good way for the people to advance their day jobs. It wasn't a crusade for them to free source code from jail.

The Apache web server is protected by a BSD-style license that permits commercial reuse of the software without sharing the source code. It is a separate program, however, and many Linux users run the software on Linux boxes. Of course, this devotion to business and relatively quiet disposition isn't always true. Theo de Raadt, the leader of the OpenBSD faction, is fond of making bold proclamations. In his interview with me, he dismissed the Free Software Foundation as terribly misnamed because you weren't truly free to do whatever you wanted with the software.

In fact, it's easy to take these stereotypes too far. Yes, GPL folks can be aggressive, outspoken, quick-thinking, driven, and tempestuous. Sure, BSD folks are organized, thorough, mainstream, dedicated, and precise. But there are always exceptions to these rules, and the people in each camp will be quick to spot them.

Someone might point out that Alan Cox, one of the steadfast keepers of the GPL-protected Linux kernels, is not particularly flashy nor given to writing long manifestos on the Net. Others might say that Brian Behlendorf has been a great defender of the Apache project. He certainly hasn't avoided defending the BSD license, although not in the way that Stallman might have liked. He was, after all, one of the members of the Apache team who helped convince IBM that they could use the Apache web server without danger.

After BSD versus GPL, the next greatest fault line is the choice of editor. Some use the relatively simple vi, which came out of Berkeley and the early versions of BSD. Others cleave to Stallman's Emacs, which is far more baroque and extreme. The vi camp loves the simplicity. The Emacs fans brag about how they've programmed their version of Emacs to break into the White House, snag secret pictures of people in compromising positions, route them through an anonymous re-mailer, and negotiate for a big tax refund all with one complicated control-meta-trans keystroke.

While this war is well known, it has little practical significance. People can choose for themselves, and their choices have no effect on others. GPL or BSD can affect millions; vi versus Emacs makes no big difference. It's just one of the endless gag controversies in the universe. If *Entertainment Tonight* were covering the free software world, they would spend hours cataloging which stars used vi and which used Emacs. Did Shirley MacLaine use vi or Emacs or even wordstar in a previous life?

Some of the other fault lines aren't so crisp, but end up being very important. The amount of order or lack of order is an important point of distinction for many free source people, and there is a wide spectrum of choices available. While the fact that all of the source code is freely redistributable makes the realm crazy, many groups try to control it with varying amounts of order. Some groups are fanatically organized. Others are more anarchic. Each has a particular temperament.

The three BSD projects are well known for keeping control of all the source code for all the software in the distribution. They're very cen-trally managed and brag about keeping all the source code together in one build tree. The Linux distributions, on the other hand, include soft-ware from many different sources. Some include the KDE desktop. Others choose GNOME. Many include both.

Some of the groups have carefully delineated jobs. The Debian group elects a president and puts individuals in charge of particular sections of the distribution. Or perhaps more correctly, the individuals nominate themselves for jobs they can accomplish. The group is as close to a gov-ernment as exists in the open software world. Many of the Open Source Initiative guidelines on what fits the definition of "open source" evolved from the earlier rules drafted by the Debian group to help define what could and couldn't be included in an official Debian distribution. The OpenBSD group, on the other hand, opens up much of the source tree to everyone on the team. Anyone can make changes. Core areas, on the other hand, are still controlled by leaders.

Some groups have become very effective marketing forces. Red Hat is a well-run company that has marketing teams selling people on upgrading their software as well as engineering teams with a job of writing improved code to include in future versions. Red Hat packages their distribution in boxes that are sold through normal sales channels like bookstores and catalogs. They have a big presence at trade shows like LinuxExpo, in part because they help organize them.

Other groups like Slackware only recently opened up a website. OpenBSD sells copies to help pay for its Internet bills, not to expand its marketing force. Some distributions are only available online.

In many cases, there is no clear spectrum defined between order and anarchy. The groups just have their own brands of order. OpenBSD brags about stopping security leaks and going two years without a root-level intrusion, but some of its artwork is a bit scruffy. Red Hat, on the other hand, has been carefully working to make Linux easy for everyone to use, but they're not as focused on security details.

Of course, this amount of order is always a bit of a relative term. None of these groups have strong lines of control. All of them depend upon the contributions of people. Problems only get solved if someone cares enough to do it.

This disorder is changing a bit now that serious companies like Red Hat and VA Linux are entering the arena. These companies pay full-time programmers to ensure that their products are bug free and easy to use. If their management does a good job, the open source software world may grow more ordered and actually anticipate more problems instead of waiting for the right person to come along with the time and the inclination to solve them.

These are just a few of the major fault lines. Practically every project comes with major technical distinctions that split the community. Is Java a good language or another attempt at corporate control? How should the basic Apache web server handle credit cards? What is the best way to handle 64-bit processors? There are thousands of differences, hundreds of fault lines, scores of architectural arguments, and dozens of licenses. But at least all of the individuals agree upon one thing: reading the source code is essential.

11. POLITICS

One of the great questions about the free source movement is its politics. The world loves to divide every issue into two sides and then start picking teams. You're either part of the problem or part of the solution. You're either for us or against us. You're either on the red team or the blue team.

The notion of giving software and source code away isn't really a radical concept. People give stuff away all the time. But when the process actually starts to work and folks start joining up, the stakes change. Suddenly it's not about random acts of kindness and isolated instances of charity—it's now a movement with emotional inertia and political heft. When things start working, people want to know what this group is going to do and how its actions are going to affect them. They want to know who gets the credit and who gets the blame.

The questions about the politics of the free source world usually boil down to a simple dilemma: some think it's a communist utopia and others think it's a free market nirvana. Normally, the two ideas sit on the opposite ends of the spectrum looking at each other with contempt and disdain. In the strange world of software, ideas aren't so easy to place. Anyone can duplicate software as many times as they want and it's still useful. The communist notion of sharing equally is much easier to achieve in this realm than in the world of, say, grain, which requires hard work in the sun to make it grow. On the other hand, the ease of exchange also means that people are able to swap and trade versions of software with little overhead or restriction. The well-greased marketplace in the free marketer's dreams is also easy to create. The act of giving a disk to a friend could either be a bona fide example of universal brotherhood or the vigorously competitive act of trying to win the hearts and minds of a software consumer. Take your pick.

The nature of software also mitigates many of the problems that naturally occur in each of these worlds. There is no scarcity, so there is no reason why sharing has to be so complicated or orchestrated from the central planning committees of the Soviets. People just give. On the other hand, the lack of scarcity also limits the differences between the rich and the poor. There's no reason why everyone can't have the same software as the rich because it's so easy to duplicate. Folks who are into economic competition for the ego gratification of having a bigger sport utility vehicle than everyone else on the street are going to be disappointed.

To some extent, the politics of the free source movement are such a conundrum that people simply project their wishes onto it. John Gilmore told me over dinner, "Well, it depends. Eric Raymond is sort of a libertarian but Richard Stallman is sort of a communist. I guess it's both." The freedom makes it possible for people to mold the movement to be what they want.

Raymond has no problem seeing his libertarian dreams acted out in the free software community. He looked at the various groups creating their own versions of free source code and saw a big bazaar where merchants competed to provide the best solutions to computer users everywhere. People wrote neat stuff and worked hard to make sure that others were happy. It was competition at its finest, and there was no money or costs of exchange to get in the way.

Most people quickly become keenly aware of this competition. Each of the different teams creating distributions flags theirs as the best, the most up-to-date, the easiest to install, and the most plush. The licenses mean that each group is free to grab stuff from the other, and this ensures that no one builds an unstoppable lead like Microsoft did in the proprietary OS world. Sure, Red Hat has a large chunk of the mindshare and people think their brand name is synonymous with Linux, but anyone can grab their latest distribution and start making improvements on it. It takes little time at all.

Stallman and his supposed communist impulse is a bit harder to characterize. He has made his peace with money and he's quick to insist that he's not a communist or an enemy of the capitalist state. He's perfectly happy when people charge for their work as programmers and he often does the same. But it's easy to see why people start to think he's something of a communist. One of his essays, which he insists is not strictly communist, is entitled "Why Software Should Not Have Owners."

Some of his basic instincts sure look Marxist. The source code to a program often acts like the means of production, and this is why the capitalists running the businesses try to control it. Stallman wanted to place these means of production in the hands of everyone so people could be free to do what they wanted. While Stallman didn't rail against the effects of money, he rejected the principle that intellectual capital, the source code, should be controlled.

Stallman stops well short of giving everything away to everyone. Copyrighting books is okay, he says, because it "restricts only the mass producers of copies. It did not take freedom away from readers of books. An ordinary reader, who did not own a printing press, could copy books only with pen and ink, and few readers were sued for that." In other words, the copyright rules in the age of printing only restricted the guy across town with a printing press who was trying to steal someone else's business. The emergence of the computer, however, changes everything. When people can copy freely, the shackles bind everyone.

Communism, of course, is the big loser of the 20th century, and so it's not surprising that Stallman tries to put some distance between the Soviet and the GNU empires. He notes puckishly that the draconian effects of the copyright laws in America are sort of similar to life in the Soviet Union, "where every copying machine had a guard to prevent forbidden copying, and where individuals had to copy information secretly and pass it from hand to hand as *samizdat*." He notes, however, that "There is of course a difference: the motive for information control in the Soviet Union was political; in the U.S. the motive is profit. But it is the actions that affect us, not the motive. Any attempt to block the sharing of information, no matter why, leads to the same methods and the same harshness."

Stallman has a point. The copyright rules restrict the ability of people to add, improve upon, or engage other people's work. The fair use rules that let a text author quote sections for comment don't really work in the software world, where it's pretty hard to copy anything but 100 percent of some source code. For programmers, the rules on source code can be pretty Soviet-like in practice.

He's also correct that some companies would think nothing of locking up the world. A consortium of megalithic content companies like Disney and the other studios got the U.S. Congress to pass a law restricting tools for making copies. Ostensibly it only applied to computer programs and other software used to pirate movies or other software, but the effect could be chilling on the marketplace. The home video enthusiast who loves to edit the tapes of his child's birthday party needs many of the same functions as the content pirate. Cutting and pasting is cutting and pasting. The rules are already getting a bit more Soviet-like in America.

But Stallman is right to distance himself from Soviet-style communism because there are few similarities. There's little central control in Stallman's empire. All Stallman can do to enforce the GNU General Public License is sue someone in court. He, like the Pope, has no great armies ready to keep people in line. None of the Linux companies have much power to force people to do anything. The GNU General Public License is like a vast disarmament treaty. Everyone is free to do what they want with the software, and there are no legal cudgels to stop them. The only way to violate the license is to publish the software and not release the source code.

Many people who approach the free software world for the first time see only communism. Bob Metcalfe, an entrepreneur, has proved himself several times over by starting companies like 3Com and inventing the Ethernet. Yet he looked at the free software world and condemned it with a derisive essay entitled "Linux's 60's technology, open-sores ideology won't beat W2K, but what will?"

Using the term "open sores" may be clever, but it belies a lack of understanding of some of the basic tenets. The bugs and problems in the software are open for everyone to see. Ideally, someone will fix them. Does he prefer the closed world of proprietary software where the bugs just magically appear? Does he prefer a hidden cancer to melanoma?

The essay makes more confounding points equating Richard Stallman to Karl Marx for his writing and Linus Torvalds to Vladimir Lenin because of his aim to dominate the software world with his OS. For grins, he compares Eric Raymond to "Trotsky waiting for The People's ice pick" for no clear reason. Before this gets out of hand, he backpedals a bit and claims, "OK, communism is too harsh on Linux. Lenin too harsh on Torvalds [sic]." Then he sets off comparing the world of open source to the tree-hugging, back-to-the-earth movement.

Of course, it's easy to see how the open source world is much different from the Soviet-style world of communism. That experiment failed because it placed the good of the many above the freedom of the individual. It was a dictatorship that did not shirk from state-sponsored terrorism or pervasive spying. It was no surprise, for instance, to discover that East German athletes were doped with performance-enhancing drugs without their knowledge. It was for the glory of Lenin or Marx or Stalin, or whoever held the reins. Does the country need someone to live in Siberia to mine for minerals? Does the country need land for vast collective farms? The state makes the call and people go.

The Soviet Union didn't really fail because it clung too deeply to the notion that no one should own property. It failed when it tried to enforce this by denying people the fruits of their labor. If someone wanted to build something neat, useful, or inventive, they had better do it for the glory of the Soviet state. That turned the place into a big cesspool of inactivity because everyone's hard work was immediately stolen away from them.

The free software world is quite different from that world. The GPL and the BSD licenses don't strip away someone's freedom and subjugate them to the state, it gives them the source code and a compiler to use with it. Yes, the GPL does restrict the freedom of people to take the free source code and sell their own proprietary additions, but this isn't the same as moving them to Siberia.

The Free Software State doesn't steal the fruits of someone's labor away from them. Once you develop the code, you can still use it. The GPL doesn't mean that only Torvalds can sit around his dacha and compile the code. You get to use it, too. In fact, one of the reasons that people cite for contributing to GPL projects is the legal assurance that the enhancements will never be taken away from them. The source will always remain open and accessible.

Metcalfe's point is that communism didn't work, so the free software world will fail, too. He makes his point a bit clearer when he starts comparing the free software folks to tree-hugging environmentalists.

"How about Linux as organic software grown in utopia by spiritualists?" he wonders. "If North America actually went back to the earth, close to 250 million people would die of starvation before you could say agribusiness. When they bring organic fruit to market, you pay extra for small apples with open sores—the Open Sores Movement."

The problem with this analogy is that no one is starving with open source software. Data is not a physical good. Pesticides and fertilizers can boost crop yields, but that doesn't matter with software. If anything, free software ends up in even more people's hands than proprietary software. Everyone in the free software world has a copy of the image editing tool, GIMP, but only the richest Americans have a copy of the very expensive Adobe Photoshop.

Of course, he has half a point about the polish of open source code. The programmers often spend more time adding neat features they like instead of making the code as accessible as possible. The tools are often designed for programmers by programmers. There isn't much of a quality assurance and human factors team trying to get them to engineer it so the other 95 percent of humanity can use it.

But this problem is going away. Companies like Red Hat and Caldera have a profit motive in making the software accessible to all. The tools look nicer, and they are often just as presentable as the tools from the proprietary firms. The programmers are also getting more sensitive to these problems. In the past, the free software world was sort of an alternative Eden where programmers went to escape from the rest of programmatically challenged society. Now the world is open to free software and the programmers are more open to taking everyone's needs into account.

The problem with all of Metcalfe's analogies is that he assumes the same rules that control the world of physical goods also govern the world of ideas. The software industry likes to pretend that this isn't true by packaging the software in big, empty boxes that look good on shelves. Swapping ideas is easy and costs little. Of course, the Soviet Union worried about the swapping of ideas and tried to control the press and all forms of expression. The free software movement is the exact opposite of this.

In fact, it is much easier to see the free software world as the libertarian ideal of strong competition and personal freedom if you remember that it exists in the realm of ideas. The landscape is similar to universities, which usually boast that they're just big melting pots where the marketplace of ideas stays open all night. The best ideas gradually push out the worst ones and society gradually moves toward a total understanding of the world.

Perhaps it's just not fair to characterize the politics of the open source or free software world at all. Terms like communism, libertarianism, liberalism, and Marxism all come from an age when large portions of society did not have easy access to ample supplies of food and housing.

Data and information are not limited goods that can only be consumed by a limited group. One person or one million people can read a computer file and the marginal costs aren't very different. Sharing is cheap, so it makes sense to use it to all of its advantages. We're just learning how to use the low cost of widespread cooperation.

Perhaps it's better to concentrate on the real political battles that rage inside the open source code community. It may be better to see the battle as one of GPL versus BSD instead of communist versus libertarian. The license debate is tuned to the Internet world. It sets out the debate in terms the computer user can understand.

12. CHARITY

The open source movement is filled with people who analyze software, look for bugs, and search for fixes. These quiet workhorses are the foundation of the movement's success. One member of this army is David Baron, an undergraduate student who started out at Harvard in the fall of 1998 and found, like most students, that he had a bit of spare time. Some students turn to theater, some to the newspaper, some to carousing, some to athletic teams, some to drinking, and most choose one or more of the above. A few students search out some charitable work for their spare time and volunteer at a homeless shelter or hospital. Law students love to work at the free legal clinic for the poor. Baron, however, is a bit of a nerd in all of the good senses of the word. He's been working on cleaning up Netscape's open source browser project known as Mozilla, and he thinks it's a great act of charity.

Baron spends his spare time poking around the Mozilla layout engine responsible for arranging the graphics, text, form slots, buttons, and whatnot in a consistent way. Graphic designers want all web browsers on the Net to behave in a consistent way and they've been agitating to try and get the browser companies (Netscape, Microsoft, iCab, WebTV, and Opera) to adhere to a set of standards developed by the W3C, the World Wide Web Consortium based at MIT. These standards spell out exactly how the browsers are supposed to handle complicated layout instructions like cascading style sheets.

Baron looked at these standards and thought they were a good idea. If all web browsers handled content in the same way, then little buttons saying "Best Viewed with Microsoft IE" or "Best Viewed by Netscape" would disappear. The browser companies would be able to compete on features, not on their ability to display weirder web pages. It would cut the web designers out of the battle between Microsoft and Netscape.

The standards also help users, especially users with different needs. He told me, "Standards (particularly CSS) encourage accessibility for users with all sorts of disabilities because they allow authors to use HTML as it was originally intended—as a structural markup language that can be interpreted by browsers that display things in nonvisual media or in very large fonts for users with poor vision. Changing the HTML on the web back to structural markup will also allow these browsers to produce sensible output."

Handling standards like this is always a bit of a political problem for companies. Every developer tries to stick their fingers in the wind and see which standards will be important and which ones will fall by the wayside. Microsoft, Netscape, iCab, WebTV, and Opera have all been wondering about the cascading style sheets because they're sort of a pain in the neck. Ideally, the graphics designers will be able to come up with graphics rules for a set of web pages and they'll be applied using the rules set out by the reader.

CSS is not about "total control by the author of the page," says Baron. "The basic idea of the cascade is that user preferences (through the browser's UI or possibly through a user CSS style sheet) and author suggestions (contained in CSS style sheets) combine to produce the formatting of the page."

A modern catalog conglomerate, for instance, may have two branches. One would be aimed at middle-aged men who dote on their cars by giving them endless wax jobs and cleaning them forever. Another might be aimed at young mothers who dote on their children, in part by keeping the home as clean as could be. Normally, the catalog company would use different designers to create very different-looking catalogs. One would come with retro, hard-edged graphics covered with racing stripes, and the other with floral prints. What happens when these catalogs head to the web? Normally two designers would give two different websites two different looks.

What if there is one cleaning product, say a car wheel cleaner, that appears in both catalogs? In the old days before cascading style sheets, both designers would have to do up each page separately. A well-designed system of cascading style sheets would let one web page for the product display correctly on both sites. It would pick up either the floral prints or the racing stripes automatically when either site called it up.

These standards are notoriously difficult to enforce. Armies around the world dream of turning out perfect privates that can be inserted into any conflict in any platoon without any retraining. Newspapers dream of having interchangeable reporters who can cover the White House or a cricket match in India. It's no wonder that the web industry wants the same thing.

Baron told me, "I got interested in Mozilla because I'm interested in web standards." He noticed that a group known as the Web Standards Project was running a political campaign to pressure the browser companies to lay out pages the same way (www.webstandards.org).

"A group of developers got together and said, 'The browsers aren't supporting the standards' and this makes it impossible to create pages," Baron explained. "If every browser supports the standards in a different way, then you have to design a different version of the site for each browser. Or, more realistically, web designers resort to hacks that make the page legible in all the 'major' browsers but not accessible to people with disabilities or people with older computers."

Of course, it's one thing for a web designer or a web master to take up this call. Baron, however, was just a college freshman who framed this as volunteer work. When he happened upon the Web Standards Project, he heard their message and saw an itch that he wanted to scratch.

"I want to see the standards supported correctly. Someone's got to do it," he told me. "I might as well be doing this instead of playing around and looking at websites all day. A lot of people do volunteer work, but not a lot of people get to do volunteer work at this level. It uses what I know pretty well. A lot of students who are very smart end up doing volunteer work which doesn't use their skills. When you can do volunteer work that uses what you know, it's even better."

So Baron would download the latest versions of the Mozilla layout engine known as Gecko and play with web pages. He would create weird web pages with strange style sheets, load them up, and watch where they broke. When things went wrong, he would write up detailed bug reports and mail them off to the folks doing the coding. He was part of a quality control team that included some Netscape employees and a wide variety of other users on the Net.

This community involvement was what Netscape wanted when it created Mozilla. They hoped that more people would take it upon themselves to test out the code and at least make complaints when things were going wrong. One hacker named James Clark, who isn't related to the founder of Netscape with the same name, actually kicked in a complete XML parser, a tool for taking apart the latest superset of HTML that is capturing the attention of software and web designers.

Baron is one of the few folks I met while writing this book who frames his work on an open source project as charity. Most devotees get into the projects because they offer them the freedom to mess with the source code. Most also cite the practical strengths of open source, like the relatively quick bug fixes and the stability of well-run projects. Most people like to distance themselves from the more political firebrands of the free software movement like Richard Stallman by pointing out that they're not really in it to bring about the second coming of the Communist Revolution. Few suggest that their work is sort of a gift of their time that might make the world a better place. Few compare their work to the folks cleaning up homeless shelters or hospitals. Most don't disagree when it is pointed out to them, but most free software hackers don't roll out the charitable rhetoric to explain what they're up to.

This may just be a class difference. Baron is a sophomore, as this is written, at Harvard and Harvard is, by definition, a finishing school for the upper crust. Even the vast sea of kids from middle-class families and public schools end up talking and acting as if they came out of Choate or Exeter by the end of their time at Harvard. They pick up the Kennedyesque noblesse oblige that somehow commands the rich and fortunate to be out helping the poor with very public acts of assistance. It just sort of seeps into all of those Harvard kids.

Most of the free software members, on the other hand, are kind of outcasts. The hackers come from all parts of the globe and from all corners of the social hierarchy, but few of them are from the beautiful people who glide through life on golden rails. The programmers usually have their heads in strange, obtuse mathematical clouds instead of the overstuffed clouds of Olympus. They're concerned with building neat software and spinning up wonderful abstract structures that interlock in endlessly repeating, elegant patterns. If they were interested in power or social prestige, they wouldn't be spending their nights in front of a terminal waiting for some code to compile.

But if the free software movement doesn't use the charitable card very often, it doesn't mean that the work is too different from that of the homeless shelters. In fact, so little money changes hands that there are not many reasons for people to take their donations off on their taxes. Donations of time don't count. Maybe a few companies could write it off their books, but that's about it.

In fact, Baron is right that work like his can make a difference for people. Software is a growing part of the cost of a computer today. In low-end PCs, the Microsoft OS may cost more than the processor or the memory. A free OS with a free web browser that works correctly can help the thousands of schools, homeless shelters, hospitals, and recreation centers get on the web at a cheaper cost.

The free software charity is often a bit cleaner. Bill Gates and many of the other Microsoft millionaires aren't shy about giving away real money to schools and other needy organizations. Melinda Gates, Bill's wife, runs a charitable foundation that is very generous. In 1999, for instance, the foundation made a very real gift of tuition money for minority students. The foundation has also given millions of dollars to help fund medical research throughout the globe.

Still, at other times, there has been a sly edge to the Gates benevolence. In some cases, the company gives away millions of dollars in Microsoft software. This helps get kids used to Microsoft products and acts like subtle advertising. Of course, there's nothing new about this kind of charity. Most corporations insist that they receive some publicity for their giving. It's how they justify the benevolence to their shareholders.

The value of giving copies of software away is a difficult act to measure. One million copies of Windows 95 might retail for about $100 million, but the cost to Microsoft is significantly lower. CD-ROMs cost less than one dollar to duplicate, and many schools probably received one CD-ROM for all of their machines. Giving the users support is an important cost, but it can be controlled and limited by restricting the number of employees dedicated to particular phone lines. Determining the value of all of the benevolence must be a tough job for the tax accountants. How Microsoft chose to account for its donations is a private matter between Gates, the Internal Revenue Service, and his God.

Consider the example of an imaginary proprietary software company called SoftSoft that gives away one million copies of its $50 WidgetWare product to schools and charities across the United States. This is, in many ways, generous because SoftSoft only sells 500,000 copies a year, giving them gross revenues of $25 million.

If SoftSoft values the gift at the full market value, they have a deduction of $50 million, which clearly puts them well in the red and beyond the reach of taxes for the year. They can probably carry the loss forward and wipe out next year's earnings, too.

The accountants may not choose to be so adventurous. The IRS might insist that they deduct the cost of the goods given, not their potentially inflated market price. Imagine that the company's cost for developing WidgetWare came to $21 million. If there were no gift, they would have a nice profit of $4 million. SoftSoft could split the development costs of $21 million between all of the 1.5 million units that are shipped. Instead of deducting the market value of the software, it would only deduct the costs allocated to it. Still, that means they get a $14 million deduction, which is still far from shabby.

More conservative companies may come up with smaller deductions based upon the cost of duplicating the additional copies and the cost of supporting the schools and charities. Strict accounting measures would be the most honest, but it's hard to know what companies do and what they should do.

Free software, of course, avoids all that paperwork and accounting. The software costs nothing, so giving it away generates no deduction. There's no need for complicated cost accounting or great press releases. It just sits on the web server and people download it.

Of course, it's possible to start counting up downloads and doing some multiplication to come up with outrageous numbers. Windows NT can sell for between $200 and $1,000. There are about 3.7 million web servers running Apache, according to the latest Netcraft poll. If 1 percent qualify as charitable sites, then 37,000 are served by Apache. Of course, not all sites sit on separate machines. To correct for this, assume that each server hosts 10 machines and there are only 3,700 machines using Apache. That's still about $3.7 million in donations.

But numbers like this can't really capture the depth of the gift. Linus Torvalds always likes to say that he started writing Linux because he couldn't afford a decent OS for his machine so he could do some experiments. Who knows how many kids, grown-ups, and even retired people are hacking Linux now and doing some sophisticated computer science experiments because they can? How do we count this beneficence?

Free software essentially removes the red tape and the institutional character of charity. There are no boards. There is no counting of gifts. There's no fawning or flattering. There are no new J. Henry P. Plutocrat Wings for the Franklin P. Moneysucker Museum of Philanthropy. It's just a pure gift with no overhead.

There is also a smooth efficiency to the world of free software charity. My economics professor used to joke that gifts were just very inefficient. Grandmas always bought unhip sweaters for their grandkids. Left on their own, children would give candy and stuffed animals to their parents on their birthdays and Christmas. All of these bad choices must be returned or thrown away, ruining the efficiency of the economy. The professor concluded by saying, "So, guys, when you go out on the date, don't bother with the flowers. Forget about the jewelry. Just give her cash."

Free source software, of course, doesn't fit into many of the standard models of economic theory. Giving the stuff away doesn't cost much money, and accepting it often requires a bit of work. The old rules of gift giving and charity don't really apply.

Imagine that some grandmother wrote some complicated software for computing the patterns for knitting sweaters. Some probably have. If they give the source code away, it ends up in the vast pool of free source code and other knitters may find it. It might not help any grandchildren, at least not for 20 or 30 years, but it will be moving to the place where it can do the most good with as little friction as possible. The software hacked by the kids, on the other hand, would flow from child to child without reaching the parents. The software tools for generating dumb jokes and sorting bubble gum cards would make a generation of kids happy, and they would be able to exchange it without their parents or grandparents getting in the way.

The inefficiencies of gift-giving can often affect charities, which have less freedom to be picky than grandchildren. Charities can't look a gift horse in the mouth. If a company wants to give a women's shelter 1,000 new men's raincoats, the shelter will probably take them. Refusing them can offend potential contributors who might give them something of value in the next quarter.

Free source code has none of these inefficiencies. Websites like *Slashdot, Freshmeat, Linux Weekly News, LinuxWorld, KernelTraffic*, and hundreds of other Linux or project-specific portals do a great job moving the software to the people who can use its value. People write the code and then other folks discover the value in it. Bad or unneeded code isn't foisted on anyone.

Free software also avoids being painted as a cynical tax scheme. It is not uncommon for drug manufacturers to donate some surplus pills to disaster relief operations. In some cases, the manufacturers clear their shelves of pills that are about to expire and thus about to be destroyed. They take a liability and turn it into a tax-deductible asset. This may be a good idea when the drugs are needed, but they are often superfluous. In many cases, the drugs just end up in a landfill. The relief organizations accept millions of dollars in drugs to get a few thousand dollars' worth of ones they really need.

Charitable Open Source Organizations

Of course, there are some open source charities. Richard Stallman's Free Software Foundation is a tax-exempt 501(c)(3) charity that raises money and solicits tax-deductible donations. This money is used to pay for computers, overhead, and the salaries of young programmers who have great ideas for free software. The Debian Project also has a charitable arm known as Software in the Public Interest that raises money and computer equipment to support the creation of more free software.

These organizations are certainly part of the world of tax deductions, fund-raisers, and the charity-industrial complex. The Free Software

Foundation, for instance, notes that you can arrange for all or part of your gift to the United Way to go to the Foundation.

But there are differences, too. Stallman, for instance, is proud of the fact that he accepts no salary or travel reimbursement from the Free Software Foundation. He works 2 months a year to support himself and then donates the other 10 months a year to raising money to support other programmers to work on Foundation projects.

Their budgets are pretty manageable as well. Perens notes that Debian's budget is about $10,000 a year, and this is spent largely on distributing the software. Servers that support plenty of traffic cost a fair amount of money, but the group does get donations of hardware and bandwidth. The group also presses a large number of CD-ROMs with the software.

The groups also make a point of insisting that good code is more valuable than money. The Free Software Foundation, for instance, lists projects that need work next to its call for money. Volunteers are needed to write documentation, test software, organize the office, and also write more code.

Jordan Hubbard, the director of the FreeBSD project, says that money is not always the best gift. "I'll take people over six-digit sums of donations almost any day," he says, and explains that FreeBSD is encouraging companies to donate some of the spare time of its employees. He suggests that companies assign a worker to the FreeBSD project for a month or two if there is time to spare.

"Employees also give us a window into what that company's needs are. All of those co-opted employees bring back the needs of their jobsite. Those are really valuable working relationships," he continues.

Hubbard has also found that money is often not the best motivator. Hardware, it turns out, often works well at extracting work out of programmers. He likes to ship a programmer one of the newest peripherals like a DVD drive or a joystick and ask him to write a driver for the technology in exchange. "It's so much more cost-effective to buy someone a $500 piece of hardware, which in turn motivates him to donate thousands of dollars worth of work, something we probably couldn't pay for anyway," he says.

Money is still important, however, to take care of all the jobs that can't be accomplished by piquing someone's curiosity. "The area we need the most contributions for are infrastructure. Secretarial things are no fun to do and you don't want to make volunteers do it," he says.

All of these charitable organizations are bound to grow in the next several years as the free software movement becomes more sophisticated. In some cases it will be because the hackers who loved playing with computers will discover that the tax system is just another pile of code filled with bugs looking to be hacked. In most cases, though, I think it will be because large companies with their sophisticated tax attorneys will become interested. I would not be surprised if a future version of this book includes a very cynical treatment of the tax habits of some open source organizations. Once an idea reaches a critical mass, it is impossible to shield it from the forces of minor and major corruption.

Gifts as a Cultural Imperative

Marcel Mauss was an anthropologist who studied the tribes of the northwestern corner of North America. His book *Gift: The Form and Reason for Exchange in Archaic Societies* explained how the tribes like the Chinook, the Tlinget, and the Kwakiutl would spend the months of the fall giving and going to huge feasts. Each year, the members in the tribe would take the bounty of the harvest and throw a feast for their friends. The folks who attended might have a good time, but they were then obligated to give a feast of equal or greater value next year.

Many anthropologists of the free software world like to draw parallels between these feasts, known as potlatches in one tribe, and the free-for-all world of free source software. The hackers are giving away source code in much the same way that the tribe members gave away salmon or deer meat.

The comparison does offer some insight into life in the free software community. Some conventions like LinuxExpo and the hundreds of install-fests are sort of like parties. One company at a LinuxExpo was serving beer in its booth to attract attention. Of course, Netscape celebrated its decision to launch the Mozilla project with a big party. They then threw another one at the project's first birthday.

But the giving goes beyond the parties and the conferences. Giving great software packages creates social standing in much the same way that giving a lavish feast will establish you as a major member of the tribe. There is a sort of pecking order, and the coders of great systems like Perl or Linux are near the top. The folks at the top of the pyramid often have better luck calling on other programmers for help, making it possible for them to get their jobs done a little better. Many managers justify letting their employees contribute to the free software community because they build up a social network that they can tap to finish their official jobs.

But there's a difference between tribal potlatch and free software. The potlatch feasts built very strong individual bonds between people in the same tribe who knew each other and worked together. The gifts flowed between people who were part of each other's small community.

The free source world, on the other hand, is a big free-for-all in both senses of the phrase. The code circulates for everyone to grab, and only those who need it dig in. There's no great connection between programmer and user. People grab software and take it without really knowing to whom they owe any debt. I only know a few of the big names who wrote the code running the Linux box on my desk, and I know that there are thousands of people who also contributed. It would be impossible for me to pay back any of these people because it's hard to keep them straight.

This vast mass of contributors often negates the value and prestige that comes from writing neat code. Since no one can keep track of it all, people tend to treat all requests from unknown people equally. The free source world tends to have many equals, just because there's no hierarchy to make it easy for us to suss out each other's place. Corporations have titles like executive vice president and super executive vice president. The military labels people as private, sergeant, or major. There are no guideposts in the free software world.

Still, good contributions pay off in good reputations. A bug fix here and a bug fix there might not build a name, but after a year or two they pay off. A good reputation opens doors, wins jobs, creates friendships, and makes it possible to interest people in new projects.

The free source world is also a strange mirror image of the hierarchies that emerge after a season of tribal potlatch ceremonies. In the tribes, those who receive great gifts are required to return the favor with even greater ones. So the skillful hunters and gatherers give good gifts and receive something better in return. The rich get richer by giving away their bounty. The less skillful end up at the bottom of the list. The free source world, on the other hand, spreads its riches out to everyone. There are many modest programmers who enjoy the source code of the great programmers, and there may be billions of nonprogrammers who also tag along. Many major websites run on free OSs alone. Who knows which cheap Internet tools will come along in the future? The poor get lifted along at no great cost to the economy. The charity is broadcast to everyone, not narrowcast to a few.

The efficiency goes deeper. There's a whole class of products for the home that are much fancier and sophisticated than what people need. One company near me sells perfectly usable nonstick pans for $2.95. A fancy department store sells hefty, industrial-grade pans that do the same thing for more than $100. Why? They make great gifts for people getting married. This wedding-industrial complex adds needless accoutrements, doodads, and schmaltz just to give products enough caché to make them great gifts.

The free source world, on the other hand, has no real incentive to generate phony, chrome-plated glitz to make its gifts acceptable or worthy enough of giving. People give away what they write for themselves, and they tend to write what they need. The result is a very efficient, usable collection of software that helps real people solve real problems. The inefficiency of the wedding-industrial complex, the Father's Day–industrial complex, the Christmas-industrial complex, and their need to create acceptable gifts are gone.

Of course, there's also a certain element of selfishness to the charity. The social prestige that comes from writing good free software is worth a fair amount in the job market. People like to list accomplishments like "wrote driver" or "contributed code to Linux Kernel 2.2" on their résumé. Giving to the right project is a badge of honor because serious folks doing serious work embraced the gift. That's often more valuable and more telling than a plaque or an award from a traditional boss.

Rob Newberry is a programmer at Group Logic, a small software house in northern Virginia where I once did some consulting. His official title is "Director of Fajita Technology," and he is sometimes known as "The Dude," a reference to a character in the movie *The Big*

Lebowski. Technically, his job is building and supporting their products, which are used to automate the prepress industry. One of their products, known as Mass Transit, will move files over the Internet and execute a number of automated programs to them before moving them on. Printers use them to take in new jobs, massage the data to their needs by performing tasks like color separation, and then send the jobs to the presses. This work requires great understanding of the various network protocols like FTP of NFS.

Newberry is also a Linux fan. He reads the Kernel list but rarely contributes much to it. He runs various versions of Linux around the house, and none of them were working as well as he wanted with his Macintosh. So he poked around in the software, fixed it, and sent his code off to Alan Cox, who watches over the part of the kernel where his fixes belonged.

"I contributed some changes to the Appletalk stack that's in the Linux Kernel that make it easier for a Linux machine to offer dial-in services for Macintosh users," he said in an article published in *Salon.* "As it stands, Mac users have always been able to dial into a Linux box and use IP protocols, but if they wanted to use Appletalk over PPP, the support wasn't really there."

Newberry, of course, is doing all of this on his own time because he enjoys it. But his boss, Derick Naef, still thinks it's pretty cool that he's spending some of his programming energy on a project that won't add anything immediately to the bottom line.

"He's plugged into that community and mailing lists a lot more," explains Naef. "There are other people here who are, too, but there are all these tools out there in the open source world. There's code out there that can be incorporated into our computer projects. It can cut your development costs if you can find stuff you can use."

Of course, all of this justification and rationalization aren't the main reason why Newberry spends so much of his time hacking on Linux. Sure, it may help his company's bottom line. Sure, it might beef up his résumé by letting him brag that he got some code in the Linux kernel. But he also sees this as a bit of charity.

"I get a certain amount of satisfaction from the work . . . but I get a certain amount of satisfaction out of helping people. Improving Linux and especially its integration with Macs has been a pet project of mine for some time," he says. Still, he sums up his real motivation by saying, "I write software because I just love doing it." Perhaps we're just lucky that so many people love writing open source software and giving it away.

13. LOVE

It's not hard to find bad stories about people who write good code. One person at a Linux conference told me, "The strange thing about Linus Torvalds is that he hasn't really offended everyone yet. All of the other leaders have managed to piss off someone at one time or another. It's hard to find someone who isn't hated by someone else." While he meant it as a compliment for Torvalds, he sounded as if he wouldn't be surprised if Torvalds did a snotty, selfish, petulant thing. It would just be par for the course.

There are thousands of examples of why people in the open source community hate each other and there are millions of examples of why they annoy each other. The group is filled with many strong-minded, independent individuals who aren't afraid to express their opinions. Flame wars spring up again and again as people try to decide technical questions like whether it makes more sense to use long integers or floating point numbers to hold a person's wealth in dollars.

Of course, hate is really too strong a word. If you manage to pin down some of the people and ask them, point blank, whether they really hate someone, they'll say, "No." They really just don't like a few of that person's technical decisions. These points of friction fester and turn into what might more commonly be called hate.

These technical debates are terrible tar pits for the community, and they eat up the energy. The debates turn frustrating because they have the strange distinction of being both technically important and utterly trivial. Everyone would like to just sail through life and not worry about tiny details like the type of integer used in a calculation. There are millions of these decisions that take up time that might be better spent

imagining grand dreams of a seamless information noosphere that provides the wisdom of the ages in a simple graphical interface. But every
programmer learns that it's the details that count. NASA lost a space-
craft when some programmer used English units instead of the metric
system. So the work needs to get done.

Occasionally, the fights get interesting. Eric Raymond and Bruce
Perens are both great contributors to the open source movement. In
fact, both worked together to try to define the meaning of the term.
Perens worked with the community that creates the Debian distribution of Linux to come up with a definition of what was acceptable for
the community. This definition morphed into a more official version
used by the Open Source Initiative. When they got a definition they
liked, they published it and tried to trademark the term "open source" in
order to make sure it was applied with some consistency. It should be
no surprise that all of that hard work brought them farther apart.

In early April 1999, soon after Apple Computer joined the free
source world by releasing some of the source code to their operating
system, Raymond and Perens found themselves at each other's throats.
Raymond had worked closely with Apple on developing their license
and blessed it soon after it emerged. Apple was so pleased that it put
Raymond's endorsement on their web page. The decision was a big
coup for the open source movement and strong proof that corporations
were embracing the movement. Big executives from big companies like
Apple were knocking on the open source movement's door. Raymond
thought the victory would bring more attention to the cause.

Others thought Raymond had given away the farm. Perens and
many others looked at the license and spotted a small clause that
seemed dangerous. The license for their open source code could be
withdrawn at a moment's notice. Someone pointed out that it would be
a real bummer to do lots of work on Apple's system and then find out
that some neb-nosed lawyer at Apple could just pull the license. No one
wanted to take that chance. Flame wars erupted and Perens started
publicly disagreeing with Raymond. To Perens, the Apple license just
wasn't open enough to be called "open source."

Raymond didn't take this too well. He had worked hard to build a
strong coalition. He had worked hard to convince corporations that

open source was much more than a way for teenagers to experiment with communism while they were living on their parents' dime. He wanted the open source world to be a smoothly running, suave machine that gracefully welcomed Apple into its fold. Now his buddy Bruce Perens was effectively aping Lloyd Bentsen's famous putdown of Dan Quayle: "I've known open source; I've worked with open source; and Eric, this license isn't open source." His whole announcement was supposed to unroll with the clockwork precision of great corporate PR, and now someone had lobbed a grenade.

Raymond fired back a terse e-mail that said, "If you ever again behave like that kind of disruptive asshole in public, insult me, and jeopardize the interests of our entire tribe, I'll take it just as personally—and I will find a way to make you regret it. Watch your step."

This note rattled Perens, so he started sending copies around the Net. Then he got serious and called the police. Officially, he was publicizing the disagreement to preserve his health because Raymond is quite vocal about his support for the second amendment. Therefore the phrase "Watch your step" should be taken as a veiled threat of violence.

Perens defended his decision to call the police and told me afterward, "When I don't like something, I write about it. Well, gee, maybe Eric was threatening to just write about me. In the signature at the bottom of the page was a Thomas Jefferson quote, which claimed the pistol was the best form of exercise. The next day, Perens decided that he was overreacting a bit and posted a new note: "Eric says he only meant to threaten me with 'defamation of character,' not with any kind of violence. Thus, I think I'll just let this issue drop now."

When I asked him about the matter several months later after tempers had cooled, Raymond said that the disagreement began several months before the Apple event when Perens and Raymond clashed over whether the book publisher O'Reilly should be allowed to use the term "open source" in the name of their conference. "He was *flaming*, and not the initiative itself but a critical supporter," says Raymond.

"Sometime back I had to accept Bruce's resignation from the OSI because he was flaming public allies on a mailing list. If you're going to go public, you can't run your mouth like a rabid attack dog. When the APSL [Apple Public Source License] came along, he convinced people that everybody should go mug Eric and the OSI," Raymond said. It caused more grief.

Perens, for his part, said, "I was disappointed in Eric because certainly open source is about freedom of speech. He should be able to tolerate a dissenting voice. The entire argument was about my not deferring to his leadership. He felt that my dissent was damaging. The actual result was that Apple took my criticism seriously and took all of the suggestions."

Raymond is still critical. He says, "Apple was more diplomatic to Bruce in public than they should have been. The truth is that his meddling got the people inside Apple who were pushing open source into considerable political trouble, and they considered him a disruptive asshole. Their bosses wanted to know, quite reasonably, why Apple should bother trying to do an open source license if all it meant was that they'd be attacked by every flake case with an agenda. By undermining OSI's status as trusted representatives of the whole community, Bruce nearly scuttled the whole process."

For now, the two work apart. Perens says he'll make up with Raymond, but doesn't see it happening too soon. Raymond is happy to focus on the future of open source and write more analysis of the movement. They've been separated, and the tempers are cool.

Giving away software seems like an entirely altruistic act. Writing code is hard work, and simply casting it onto the net with no restrictions is a pretty nice gift outright, especially if the code took months or years to write. This image of selflessness is so strong that many people assume that the free software world is inhabited by saints who are constantly doing nice things for each other. It seems like a big love-in.

But love is more than a many splendored thing. It's a strange commodity that binds us together emotionally in ways that run deeper than placid pools reflecting starry eyes. After the flush of infatuation, strong love lasts if and only if it answers everyone's needs. The hippie culture of free love lasted only a few years, but the institution of marriage continues to live on despite the battle scars and wounds that are almost mortal. Half may fail, but half succeed.

The free software community also flourishes by creating a strong, transcendent version of love and binding it with a legal document that sets out the rules of the compact. Stallman wrote his first copyleft virus more than

15 years before this book began, and the movement is just beginning to gain real strength. The free software world isn't just a groovy love nest, it's a good example of how strong fences, freedom, and mutual respect can build strong relationships.

The important thing to realize is that free software people aren't any closer to being saints than the folks in the proprietary software companies. They're just as given to emotion, greed, and the lust for power. It's just that the free software rules tend to restrain their worst instincts and prevent them from acting upon them.

The rules are often quite necessary. E-mail and the news services give people the ability to vent their anger quickly. Many of the programmers are very proficient writers, so they can tear each other apart with verbal scalpels. The free source world is cut up into hundreds if not thousands of political camps and many dislike each other immensely. One group begged with me not to ask them questions about another group because just hearing someone's name brought up terrible memories of pain and discord.

Despite these quick-raging arguments, despite the powerful disagreements, despite the personal animosities, the principles of the public licenses keep everything running smoothly. The people are just as human as the rats running around in the maze of the proprietary software business, but the license keeps them in line.

The various public licenses counter human behavior in two key ways. First, they encourage debate by making everyone a principal in the project. Everyone has a right to read, change, and of course make comments about the software. Making everything available opens the doors for discussion, and discussion usually leads to arguments.

But when the arguments come to blows, as they often do, the second effect of free source licenses kicks in and moderates the fallout by treating everyone equally. If Bob and John don't like each other, then there's still nothing they can do to stop each other from working on the project. The code is freely available to all and shutting off the distribution to your enemy just isn't allowed. You can't shut out anyone, even someone you hate.

Anyone familiar with corporate politics should immediately see the difference. Keeping rivals in the dark is just standard practice in a corporation. Information is a powerful commodity, and folks competing for the same budget will use it to the best of their ability. Bosses often move to keep their workers locked away from other groups to keep some control over the flow of information.

Retribution is also common in the corporate world. Many managers quickly develop enemies in the ranks, and the groups constantly spend time sabotaging projects. Requests will be answered quickly or slowly depending on who makes them. Work will be done or put off depending on which division is asking for it to be done. Managers will often complain that their job is keeping their underlings from killing each other and then turn around and start battling the other managers at their level.

The people in the free source world aren't any nicer than the people in the corporate cubicle farms, but their powers of secrecy and retribution are severely limited. The GNU General Public License requires that anyone who makes changes to a program and then releases the program must also release the source code to the world. No shutting off your enemies allowed.

This effect could be called a number of different things. It isn't much different from the mutual disarmament treaties signed by nations. Athletic teams strive for this sort of pure focus when they hire referees to make the tough calls and keep everyone playing by the same rules. The government sometimes tries to enforce some discipline in the free market through regulation.

Now, compare this disarmament with a story about the poor folks who stayed behind at the Hotmail website after Microsoft bought them. It's really just one of a million stories about corporate politics. The workers at Hotmail went from being supreme lords of their Hotmail domain to soldiers in the Microsoft army. Their decisions needed to further Microsoft's relentless growth in wealth, not the good of the Hotmail site. This probably didn't really bother the Hotmail people as much as the fact that the people at Microsoft couldn't decide what they wanted from Hotmail.

Robert X. Cringely described the situation in an article in *PBS Online,* and he quoted one Hotmail worker as saying, "They send a new top-level group down to see us every week, yet it really means nothing. The plan is constantly changing. Today Hotmail is primarily a way of shoveling new users into the MSN portal. We had for a short time a feature called Centerpoint for communicating directly with our users, but that was killed as a possible competitor with the MSN portal. No new features could be added because the Outlook Express team saw us as competition and sabotaged everything."

Cringely explained the corporate friction and gridlock this way: "What Hotmail learned is that at Microsoft almost anyone can say 'no,' but hardly anyone can say 'yes.' The way it specifically works at Microsoft is that everyone says 'no' to anyone below them on the organizational structure or on the same level, and 'yes' to anyone above. Since the vertical lines of authority are narrow this means people tend to agree only with their bosses and their boss's boss and try to kick and gouge everyone else."

The free software world, of course, removes these barriers. If the Hotmail folks had joined the Linux team instead of Microsoft, they would be free to do whatever they wanted with their website even if it annoyed Linus Torvalds, Richard Stallman, and the pope. They wouldn't be rich, but there's always a price.

Using the word "love" is a bit dangerous because the word manages to include the head-over-heels infatuation of teenagers and the affection people feel for a new car or a restaurant's food. The love that's embodied by the GPL, on the other hand, isn't anywhere near as much fun and it isn't particularly noteworthy. It just encompasses the mutual responsibility and respect that mature folks occasionally feel for each other. It's St. Paul's version of unconditional, everlasting love, not the pangs of desire that kept St. Augustine up late in his youth.

Anyone who has spent time in the trenches in a corporate cubicle farm knows how wasteful the battles between groups and divisions can be. While the competition can sometimes produce healthy rivalries, it often just promotes discord. Any veteran of these wars should see the immediate value of disarmament treaties like the GPL. They permit healthy rivalries to continue while preventing secrecy and selfishness from erupting. The free source movement may not have money to move mountains, but it does have this love.

This love also has a more traditional effect on the hackers who create the free source code. They do it because they love what they're doing. Many of the people in the free source movement are motivated by writing great software, and they judge their success by the recognition they get from equally talented peers. A "nice job" from the right person—like Richard Stallman, Alan Cox, or Linus Torvalds—can be worth more than $100,000 for some folks. It's a strange way to keep score, but for most of the programmers in the free source world it's more of a challenge than money. Any schmoe in Silicon Valley can make a couple of million dollars, but only a few select folks can rewrite the network interface code of the Linux kernel to improve the throughput of the Apache server by 20 percent.

Keeping score by counting the number of people who dig your work is a strange system, but one that offers the same incentives as business. A good store doesn't insult people who could be repeat customers. A good free software project doesn't insult people who have a choice of which package to use. A good businessman makes it easy for people to get to the store, park, and make a purchase. A good free software project makes it simple for people to download the code, compile it, modify it, understand it, and use it.

There's even some research to support the notion that rewards can diminish the creativity of people. Stallman likes to circulate a 1987 article from the *Boston Globe* that describes a number of different scientific experiments that show how people who get paid are less creative than those who produce things from their love of the art. The studies evaluated the success of poets, artists, and teachers who did their job for the fun of it and compared it with those who were rewarded for their efforts. In many cases, these were short-bounded exercises that could be evaluated fairly easily.

One scientist, Theresa Amabile, told the *Globe* that her work "definitely refutes the notion that creativity can be operantly conditioned." That is, you can't turn it on by just pouring some money on it. Many free software folks point out that this is why the free source movement is just as likely to succeed as a massively funded corporate juggernaut.

Many people don't need scientists to tell them that you can't throw money at many problems and expect them to go away. This is a hard lesson that managers and businesses learn quickly. But this doesn't mean that the lack of money means that the free source movement will beat the thousands of shackled programmers in their corporate rabbit hutches. These studies just measured "creativity" and found that the unpaid folks were more "creative." That's not necessarily a compliment. In fact, the word is often used as a euphemism for "strange," "weird," or just plain "bad." It's more often a measure of just how different something is instead of how good it is. Would you rather eat at the house of a creative chef or a good chef?

This love of creativity can be a problem for the free source world. Most people don't want to use a creative spreadsheet to do their accounting—it could get them in trouble with the SEC or the IRS. They want a solid team player for many of their jobs, not a way cool creative one.

The free source world is often seen as too artistic and temperamental to undertake the long, arduous task of creating good, solid software that solves the jobs of banks, pharmacies, airlines, and everyone else. Many of these tasks are both mind-numbingly boring and difficult to do. While they just involve adding a few numbers and matching up some data, the tasks have to be done right or airplanes will crash. The free source world can't rely on love or creativity to motivate people to take on these tasks. The only solution might be money.

Of course, it's important to recognize that even seemingly boring jobs can have very creative solutions. Stallman's GNU Emacs is a fascinating and over-the-top, creative solution to the simple job of manipulating text. Word processors and text editors might not be that exciting anymore, but finding creative ways to accomplish the task is still possible.

14. CORPORATIONS

Many movies about teenagers follow a time-proven formula: once the magic summer is over, the gang is going to split up and it will never be the same again. Bob's going to college; Rick is getting married; and Harry is going to be stuck in the old town forever. Right now, the free software world is playing out the same emotions and dramas as the greater world discovers open source software. In the fall, the corporations are coming and the old, cool world of late-night hackfests fueled by pizza and Jolt are in danger. Some people in the realm of free source software are going to grow up, get educated, and join the establishment; some will get married; and some will get left behind wondering why the old game isn't as cool anymore.

The free source world is suffering from an acute case of success. Many of the great projects like Apache and Sendmail are growing up and being taken over by corporations with balance sheets. Well, not exactly taken over, but the corporations will exist and they'll try to shepherd development. Other corporations like Apple, Sun, and Netscape are experimenting with open source licenses and trying to make money while sharing code. Some quaint open source companies like Red Hat are growing wealthy by floating IPOs to raise some money and maybe buy a few Porsches for their stakeholders. There's a lot of coming of age going on.

On the face of it, none of this rampant corporatization should scare the guys who built the free software world in their spare cycles. The corporations are coming to free source because it's a success. They want to grab some of the open software mojo and use it to drive their own companies. The suits on the plane are all tuning into Slashdot, buying

T-shirts, and reading Eric Raymond's essay "The Cathedral and the Bazaar" in the hopes of glomming on to a great idea. The suits have given up their usual quid pro quo: be a good nerd, keep the code running, and we'll let you wear a T-shirt in your basement office. Now they want to try to move in and live the life, too. If Eric Raymond were selling Kool-Aid, they would be fighting to drink it.

The talk is serious, and it's affecting many of the old-line companies as well. Netscape started the game by releasing the source code to a development version of their browser in March of 1998. Apple and Sun followed and began giving away the source code to part of their OS. Of course, Apple got part of the core of their OS from the open source world, but that's sort of beside the point. They're still sharing some of their new, Apple-only code. Some, not all. But that's a lot more than they shared before. Sun is even sharing the source code to their Java system. If you sign the right papers or click the right buttons, you can download the code right now. Its license is more restrictive, but they're joining the club, getting religion, and hopping on the bandwagon.

Most of the true devotees are nervous about all of this attention. The free software world was easy to understand when it was just late-night hackfests and endless railing against AT&T and UNIX. It was simple when it was just messing around with grungy code that did way cool things. It was a great, he-man, Windoze-hating clubhouse back then.

Well, the truth is that some of the free software world is going to go off to college, graduate with a business degree, and turn respectable. Eric Allman, for instance, is trying to build a commercial version of his popular free package Sendmail. The free version will still be free, but you can get a nicer interface and some cooler features for managing accounts if you buy in. If things work out, some of the folks with the free version will want all of the extra features he's tacking on and they'll pay him. No one knows what this will do to the long-term development of Sendmail, of course. Will he only make new improvements in the proprietary code? Will other folks stop contributing to the project because they see a company involved? There's some evidence that Allman's not the same guy who hung around the pizza joint. When I contacted him for an interview, he passed me along to his public relations expert, who wrote back wanting to "make sure this is a profitable way to spend Eric's time." For all we know, Eric may have even been wearing a suit when he hired a corporate PR team.

Some of the other free software folks are going to get married. The Apache group has leveraged its success with small server organizations into connections with the best companies selling high-powered products. IBM is now a firm supporter of Apache, and they run it on many of their systems. Brian Behlendorf still schedules his own appointments, jokes often, and speaks freely about his vision for Apache, but he's as serious as any married man with several kids to support. It's not just about serving up a few web pages filled with song lyrics or *Star Wars* trivia. People are using Apache for business—serious business. There can still be fun, but Apache needs to be even more certain that they're not screwing up.

And of course there are thousands of free software projects that are going to get left behind hanging out at the same old pizza joint. There were always going to be thousands left behind. People get excited about new projects, better protocols, and neater code all the time. The old code just sort of withers away. Occasionally someone rediscovers it, but it is usually just forgotten and superseded. But this natural evolution wasn't painful until the successful projects started ending up on the covers of magazines and generating million-dollar deals with venture capitalists. People will always be wondering why their project isn't as big as Linux.

There will also be thousands of almost great projects that just sail on being almost great. All of the distributions come with lots of programs that do some neat things. But there's no way that the spotlight can be bright enough to cover them all. There will be only one Torvalds and everyone is just going to be happy that he's so gracious when he reminds the adoring press that most of the work was done by thousands of other nameless folks.

Most of the teen movies don't bother trying to figure out what happens after that last fateful summer. It's just better to end the movie with a dramatic race or stage show that crystallizes all the unity and passion that built up among this group during their formative years. They sing, they dance, they win the big game, they go to the prom, and then cameras love to freeze the moment at the end of the film. The free software movement, on the other hand, is just too important and powerful to stop this book on a climactic note. It would be fun to just pause the book at the moment in time when Linus Torvalds and Bob Young were all over the magazines. Their big show was a success, but the real question is what will happen when some folks go to school, some folks get married, and some folks are left behind.

To some extent, the influx of money and corporations is old news. Very old news. Richard Stallman faced the same problem in the 1980s when he realized that he needed to find a way to live without a university paycheck. He came up with the clever notion that the software and the source must always be free, but that anyone could charge whatever the market would bear for the copies. The Free Software Foundation itself continues to fund much of its development by creating and selling both CD-ROMs and printed manuals.

This decision to welcome money into the fold didn't wreck free software. If anything, it made it possible for companies like Red Hat to emerge and sell easier-to-use versions of the free software. The companies competed to put out the best distributions and didn't use copyright and other intellectual property laws to constrain each other. This helped attract more good programmers to the realm because most folks would rather spend their time writing code than juggling drivers on their machine. Good distributions like Red Hat, Slackware, Debian, FreeBSD, and SuSE made it possible for everyone to get their machines up and running faster.

There's no reason why the latest push into the mainstream is going to be any different. Sure, Red Hat is charging more and creating better packages, but most of the distribution is still governed by the GPL. Whenever people complain that Red Hat costs too much, Bob Young just points people to the companies that rip off his CDs and charge only $2 or $3 per copy. The GPL keeps many people from straying too far from the ideal.

The source is also still available. Sure, the corporate suits can come in, cut deals, issue press releases, raise venture capital, and do some IPOs, but that doesn't change the fact that the source code is now widely distributed. Wasn't that the goal of Stallman's revolution? Didn't he want to be able to get at the guts of software and fix it? The source is now more omnipresent than ever. The corporations are practically begging folks to download it and send in bug fixes.

Of course, access to the source was only half of Stallman's battle. A cynic might growl that the corporations seem to be begging folks to do their research, testing, and development work for them. They're looking for free beers. Stallman wanted freedom to do whatever he wanted with the source and many of the companies aren't ready to throw away all of their control.

Apple sells its brand, and it was careful not to open up the source code to its classic desktop interface. They kept that locked away. Most of the source code that Apple released is from its next version of the operating system, Mac OS X, which came from the folks at NeXT when Apple acquired that company. Where did that code come from? Large portions came from the various free versions of BSD like NetBSD or Mach. It's easy to be generous when you only wrote a fraction of the code.

Ernest Prabhakar, the project manager for Apple's first open source effort known as Darwin, describes the tack he took to get Apple's management to embrace this small core version of the BSD operating system tuned to the Macintosh hardware platform.

"The first catalysts were the universities. There were a lot of universities like MIT and University of Michigan that had some specialized network infrastructure needs," he said.

"We realized that the pieces they're most interested in are the most commoditized. There wasn't really any proprietary technology added that we had to worry about them copying. There are people who know them better than we do like the BSD community. We started making the case, if we really want to partner with the universities we should just open the source code and release it as a complete BSD-style operating system.

"We wanted people to use this in classes, really embed it in the whole educational process without constraining teaching to fit some corporate model," he finishes.

Of course, Prabhakar suggests that there is some self-interest as well. Apple wants to be a full partner with the BSD community. It wants the code it shares to mingle and cross-pollinate with the code from the

BSD trees. In the long run, Apple's Darwin and the BSDs will grow closer together. In an ideal world, both groups will flourish as they avoid duplicating each other's efforts.

Prabhakar says, "This reduces our reintegration costs. The ability to take the standard version of FreeBSD and dump it into our OS was a big win. Prior to doing the open source, we had done a small scale of givebacks."

This view is echoed by other companies. IBM is a great hardware company and an even greater service company that's never had much luck selling software, at least in the same way that Microsoft sells software. Their OS/2 never got far off the ground. They've sold plenty of software to companies by bundling it with handholding and long-term service, but they've never had great success in the shrink-wrapped software business. Open source gives them the opportunity to cut software development costs and concentrate on providing service and hardware. They get free development help from everyone and the customers get more flexibility.

Sun's Community Source License is also not without some self-interest. The company would like to make sure that Java continues to be "Write Once, Run Anywhere," and that means carefully controlling the APIs and the code to make sure no idiosyncrasies or other glitches emerge. People and companies that want to be part of the community must abide by Sun's fairly generous, but not complete, gift to the world.

The company's web page points out the restriction Sun places on its source code fairly clearly. "Modified source code cannot be distributed without the express written permission of Sun" and "Binary programs built using modified Java 2 SDK source code may not be distributed, internally or externally, without meeting the compatibility and royalty requirements described in the License Agreement."

While some see this clause as a pair of manacles, Bill Joy explains that the Community Source License is closer to our definition of a real community. "It's a community in a stronger sense," he told an audience at Stanford. "If you make improvements, you can own them." After you negotiate a license with Sun, you can sell them. Joy also points out that Sun's license does require some of the GNU-like sharing by requiring everyone to report bugs.

Some customers may like a dictator demanding complete obeisance to Sun's definition of Java, but some users are chaffing a bit. The freedom to look at the code isn't enough. They want the freedom to add their own features that are best tuned to their own needs, a process that may start to Balkanize the realm by creating more and more slightly different versions of Java. Sun clearly worries that the benefits of all this tuning aren't worth living through the cacophony of having thousands of slightly different versions. Releasing the source code allows all of the users to see more information about the structure of Sun's Java and helps them work off the same page. This is still a great use of the source code, but it isn't as free as the use imagined by Stallman.

Alan Baratz, the former president of Sun's Java division, says that their Community Source License has been a large success. Sure, some folks would like the ability to take the code and fork off their own versions as they might be able to do with software protected by a BSD- or GNU-style license, but Java developers really want the assurance that it's all compatible. As many said, "Microsoft wanted to fork Java so it could destroy it."

Baratz said, "We now have forty thousand community source licensees. The developers and the systems builders and the users all want the branded Java technology. They want to know that all of the apps are going to be there. That's the number-one reason that developers are writing to the platform." Their more restrictive license may not make Stallman and other free software devotees happy, but at least Java will run everywhere.

Maybe in this case, the quality and strength of the unity Sun brings to the marketplace is more important than the complete freedom to do whatever you want. There are already several Java clones available, like Kaffe. They were created without the help of Sun, so their creators aren't bound by Sun's licenses. But they also go out of their way to avoid splitting with Sun. Tim Wilkinson, the CEO of Transvirtual, the creators of Kaffe, says that he plans to continue to make Kaffe 100 percent Java compatible without paying royalties or abiding by the Community Source License. If his project or other similar ones continue to thrive and grow, then people will know that the freedom of open source can be as important as blind allegiance to Sun.

These corporate efforts are largely welcomed by the open source world, but the welcome does not come with open arms or a great deal of warmth.

Source code with some restrictions is generally better than no source at all, but there is still a great deal of suspicion. Theo de Raadt, the leader of the OpenBSD project, says, "Is that free? We will not look at Apple source code because we'll have contaminated ourselves." De Raadt is probably overreacting, but he may have reason to worry. AT&T's USL tied up the BSD project for more than a year with a lawsuit that it eventually lost. Who knows what Apple could do to the folks at OpenBSD if there were a some debate over whether some code should be constrained by the Apple license? It's just easier for everyone at OpenBSD to avoid looking at the Apple code so they can be sure that the Apple license won't give some lawyers a toehold on OpenBSD's code base.

Richard Stallman says, "Sun wants to be thought of as having joined our club, without paying the dues or complying with the public service requirements. They want the users to settle for the fragments of freedom Sun will let them have."

He continues, "Sun has intentionally rejected the free software community by using a license that is much too restrictive. You are not allowed to redistribute modified versions of Sun's Java software. It is not free software."

Fat Cats and Alley Cats

The corporations could also sow discord and grief by creating two different classes: the haves and the have-nots. The people who work at the company and draw a salary would get paid for working on the software while others would get a cheery grin and some thanks. Everyone's code would still be free, but some of the contributors might get much more than others. In the past, everyone was just hanging out on the Net and adding their contributions because it was fun.

This split is already growing. Red Hat software employs some of the major Linux contributors like Alan Cox. They get a salary while the rest of the contributors get nothing. Sun, Apple, and IBM employees get salaries, but folks who work on Apache or the open versions of BSD get nothing but the opportunity to hack cool code.

One employee from Microsoft, who spoke on background, predicted complete and utter disaster. "Those folks are going to see the guys from

Red Hat driving around in the Porsches and they're just going to quit writing code. Why help someone else get rich?" he said. I pointed out that jealousy wasn't just a problem for free software projects. Didn't many contract employees from Microsoft gather together and sue to receive stock options? Weren't they locked out, too?

Still, he raises an interesting point. Getting people to join together for the sake of a group is easy to do when no one is getting rich. What will happen when more money starts pouring into some folks' pockets? Will people defect? Will they stop contributing?

Naysayers are quick to point to experiments like Netscape's Mozilla project, which distributed the source code to the next generation of its browser. The project received plenty of hype because it was the first big open source project created by a major company. They set up their own website and built serious tools for keeping track of bugs. Still, the project has not generated any great browser that would allow it to be deemed a success. At this writing, about 15 months after the release, they're still circulating better and better beta versions, but none are as complete or feature-rich as the regular version of Netscape, which remains proprietary.[1]

The naysayers like to point out that Netscape never really got much outside help on the Mozilla project. Many of the project's core group were Netscape employees and most of the work was done by Netscape employees. There were some shining examples like Jim Clark (no relation to the founder of Netscape with the same name), who contributed an entire XML parser to the project. David Baron began hacking and testing the Mozilla code when he was a freshman at Harvard. But beyond that, there was no great groundswell of enthusiasm. The masses didn't rise up and write hundreds of thousands of lines of code and save Netscape.

But it's just as easy to cast the project as a success. Mozilla was the first big corporate-sponsored project. Nothing came before it, so it isn't possible to compare it with anything. It is both the best and the worst example. The civilian devotees could just as well be said to have broken the world

---

[1]At this writing, version M13 of Mozilla looks very impressive. It's getting quite close to the proprietary version of Netscape.

record for source code contributed to a semi-commercial project. Yes, most of the work was officially done by Netscape employees, but how do you measure work? Many programmers think a good bug report is more valuable than a thousand lines of code. Sure, some folks like Baron spend most of their time testing the source code and looking for incompatibilities, but that's still very valuable. He might not have added new code himself, but his insight may be worth much more to the folks who eventually rely on the product to be bug-free.

It's also important to measure the scope of the project. Mozilla set out to rewrite most of the Netscape code. In the early days, Netscape grew by leaps and bounds as the company struggled to add more and more features to keep ahead of Microsoft. The company often didn't have the time to rebuild and reengineer the product, and many of the new features were not added in the best possible way. The Mozilla team started off by trying to rebuild the code and put it on a stable foundation for the future. This hard-core, structural work often isn't as dramatic. Casual observers just note that the Mozilla browser doesn't have as many features as plain old Netscape. They don't realize that it's completely redesigned inside.

Jeff Bates, an editor at *Slashdot,* says that Mozilla may have suffered because Netscape was so successful. The Netscape browser was already available for free for Linux. "There wasn't a big itch to scratch," he says. "We already had Netscape, which was fine for most people. This project interested a smaller group than if we'd not had Netscape–hence why it didn't get as much attention."

The experiences at other companies like Apple and Sun have been more muted. These two companies also released the source code to their major products, but they did not frame the releases as big barn-raising projects where all of the users would rise up and do the development work for the company. Some people portrayed the Mozilla project as a bit of a failure because Netscape employees continued to do the bulk of code writing. Apple and Sun have done a better job emphasizing the value of having the source available while avoiding the impossible dream of getting the folks who buy the computers to write the OS, too.

Not all interactions between open source projects and corporations involve corporations releasing their source code under a new open source license. Much more code flows from the open source community into corporations. Free things are just as tempting to companies as to people.

In most cases, the flow is not particularly novel. The companies just choose FreeBSD or some version of Linux for their machines like any normal human being. Many web companies use a free OS like Linux or FreeBSD because they're both cheap and reliable. This is going to grow much more common as companies realize they can save a substantial amount of money over buying seat licenses from companies like Microsoft.

In some cases, the interactions between the open source realm and the corporate cubicle farm become fairly novel. When the Apache web server grew popular, the developers at IBM recognized that they had an interesting opportunity at hand. If IBM could get the Apache server to work on its platforms, it might sell more machines. Apache was growing more common, and common software often sold machines. When people came looking for a new web server, the IBM salesmen thought it might be nice to offer something that was well known.

Apache's license is pretty loose. IBM could have taken the Apache code, added some modifications, and simply released it under their own name. The license only required that IBM give some credit by saying the version was derived from Apache itself. This isn't hard to do when you're getting something for free.

Other companies have done the same thing. Brian Behlendorf, one of the Apache core group, says, "There's a company that's taken the Apache code and ported it to Mac. They didn't contribute anything back to the Apache group, but it didn't really hurt us to do that." He suggested that the karma came back to haunt them because Apple began releasing their own version of Apache with the new OS, effectively limiting the company's market.

IBM is, of course, an old master at creating smooth relationships with customers and suppliers. They chose to build a deeper relationship with Apache by hiring one of the core developers, Ken Coar, and paying him to keep everyone happy.

"My job is multifaceted," says Coar. "I don't work on the IBM added-value stuff. I work on the base Apache code on whatever platforms are available to me. I serve as a liaison between IBM and the Apache group, basically advising IBM on whether the things that they want to do are appropriate. It's an interesting yet unique role. All of my code makes it back into the base Apache code."

Coar ended up with the job because he helped IBM and Apache negotiate the original relationship. He said there was a considerable amount of uncertainty on both sides. IBM wondered how they could get something without paying for it, and Apache wondered whether IBM would come in and simply absorb Apache.

"There were questions about it from the Apache side that any sort of IBM partnership would make it seem as if IBM had acquired Apache. It was something that Apache didn't want to see happen or seem to see happen," Coar said.

Today, Coar says IBM tries to participate in the Apache project as a peer. Some of the code IBM develops will flow into the group and other bits may remain proprietary. When the Apache group incorporated, Coar and another IBM employee, Ken Stoddard, were members. This sort of long-term involvement can help ensure that the Apache group doesn't start developing the server in ways that will hurt its performance on IBM's machine. If you pay several guys who contribute frequently to the project, you can be certain that your needs will be heard by the group. It doesn't guarantee anything, but it can buy a substantial amount of goodwill.

Of course, it's important to realize that the Apache group was always fairly business-oriented. Many of the original developers ran web servers and wanted access to the source code. They made money by selling the service of maintaining a website to the customers, not a shrink-wrapped copy of Apache itself. The deal with IBM didn't mean that Apache changed many of its ways; it just started working with some bigger fish.

At first glance, each of these examples doesn't really suggest that the coming of the corporations is going to change much in the free source world. Many of the changes were made long ago when people realized that some money flowing around made the free software world a much better place. The strongest principles still survive: (1) hackers thrive when the source code is available, and (2) people can create their own versions at will.

The arrival of companies like IBM doesn't change this. The core Apache code is still available and still running smoothly. The modules still plug in and work well. There's no code that requires IBM hardware to run and the committee seems determined to make sure that any IBM takeover doesn't occur. In fact, it still seems to be in everyone's best interest to keep the old development model. The marketplace loves standards, and IBM could sell many machines just offering a standard version of Apache. When the customers walk in looking for a web server, IBM's sales force can just say "This little baby handles X billion hits a day and it runs the industry-leading Apache server." IBM's arrival isn't much different from the arrival of a straightlaced, no-nonsense guy who strolls in from the Net and wants to contribute to Apache so he can get ahead in his job as a web-master. In this case, it's just a corporation, not a person.

Many suggest that IBM will gradually try to absorb more and more control over Apache because that's what corporations do. They generate inscrutable contracts and unleash armies of lawyers. This view is short-sighted because it ignores how much IBM gains by maintaining an arm's-length relationship. If Apache is a general program used on machines throughout the industry, then IBM doesn't need to educate customers on how to use it. Many of them learned in college or in their spare time on their home machines. Many of them read books published by third parties, and some took courses offered by others. IBM is effectively offloading much of its education and support costs onto a marketplace of third-party providers.

Would IBM be happier if Apache was both the leading product in the market and completely owned by IBM? Sure, but that's not how it turned out. IBM designed the PC, but they couldn't push OS/2 on everyone. They can make great computers, however, and that's not a bad business to be in. At least Apache isn't controlled by anyone else, and that makes the compromise pretty easy on the ego.

Some worry that there's a greater question left unanswered by the arrival of corporations. In the past, there was a general link between the creator of a product and the consumer. If the creator didn't do a good job, then the consumer could punish the creator by not buying another version. This marketplace would ensure that only the best survived.

Patrick Reilly writes, "In a free market, identifiable manufacturers own the product. They are responsible for product performance, and they can be held liable for inexcusable flaws."

What happens if a bug emerges in some version of the Linux kernel and it makes it into several distributions? It's not really the fault of the distribution creators, because they were just shipping the latest version of the kernel. And it's not really the kernel creators' fault, because they weren't marketing the kernel as ready for everyone to run. They were just floating some cool software on the Net for free. Who's responsible for the bug? Who gets sued?

Reilly takes the scenario even further. Imagine that one clever distribution company finds a fix for the bug and puts it into their distribution. They get no long-term reward because any of the other distribution companies can come along and grab the bug fix.

He writes, "Consumers concerned about software compatibility would probably purchase the standard versions. But companies would lose profit as other consumers would freely download improved versions of the software from the Internet. Eventually the companies would suffer from widespread confusion over the wide variety of software versions of each product, including standard versions pirated by profiteers."

There's no doubt that Reilly points toward a true breakdown in the feedback loop that is supposed to keep free markets honest and efficient. Brand names are important, and the free source world is a pretty confusing stew of brand names.

But he also overestimates the quality of the software emerging from proprietary companies that can supposedly be punished by the marketplace. Many users complain frequently about bugs that never get fixed in proprietary code, in part because the proprietary companies are frantically trying to glom on more features so they can convince more people to buy another version of the software. Bugs don't always get fixed in the proprietary model, either.

Richard Stallman understands Reilly's point, but he suggests that the facts don't bear him out. If this feedback loop is so important, why do so many people brag about free software's reliability?

Stallman says, "He has pointed out a theoretical problem, but if you look at the empirical facts, we do not have a real problem. So it is only a problem *for the theory*, not a problem *for the users*. Economists may have a challenge explaining why we DO produce such reliable software, but users have no reason to worry."

The Return of the Hardware Kings

The biggest effect of the free software revolution may be to shift the power between the hardware and software companies. The biggest corporate proponents of open source are IBM, Apple, Netscape/AOL, Sun, and Hewlett-Packard. All except Netscape are major hardware companies that watched Microsoft turn the PC world into a software monopoly that ruled a commodity hardware business.

Free source code changes the equation and shifts power away from software companies like Microsoft. IBM and Hewlett-Packard are no longer as beholden to Microsoft if they can ship machines running a free OS. Apple is borrowing open source software and using it for the core of their new OS. These companies know that the customers come to them looking for a computer that works nicely when it comes from the factory. Who cares whether the software is free or not? If it does what the customer wants, then they can make their money on hardware.

The free software movement pushes software into the public realm, and this makes it easier for the hardware companies to operate. Car companies don't sit around and argue about who owns the locations of the pedals or the position of the dials on the dashboard. Those notions and design solutions are freely available to all car companies equally. The lawyers don't need to get involved in that level of car creation.

Of course, the free software movement could lead to more consolidation in the hardware business. The car business coalesced over the years because the large companies were able to use their economies of scale to push out the small companies. No one had dominion over the idea of putting four wheels on a car or building an engine with pistons, so the most efficient companies grew big.

This is also a threat for the computer business. Microsoft licensed their OS to all companies, big or small, that were willing to prostrate

themselves before the master. It was in Microsoft's best interests to foster free competition between the computer companies. Free software
takes this one step further. If no company has control over the domi-
nant OS, then competition will shift to the most efficient producers.
The same forces that brought GM to the center of the car industry
could help aggregate the hardware business.

This vision would be more worrisome if it hadn't happened already.
Intel dominates the market for CPU chips and takes home the lion's
share of the price of a PC. The marketplace already chose a winner of
that battle. Now, free software could unshackle Intel from its need to
maintain a partnership with Microsoft by making Intel stronger.

Of course, the free OSs could also weaken Intel by opening it up to
competition. Windows 3.1, 95, and 98 always ran only on Intel platforms. This made it easier for Intel to dominate the PC world because
the OS that was most in demand would only run on Intel or Intel-
compatible chips. Microsoft made some attempt to break out of this
tight partnership by creating versions of Windows NT that ran on the
Alpha chip, but these were never an important part of the market.

The free OS also puts Intel's lion's share up for grabs. Linux runs well
on Intel chips, but it also runs on chips made by IBM, Motorola,
Compaq, and many others. The NetBSD team loves to brag that its software runs on almost all platforms available and is dedicated to porting it
to as many as possible. Someone using Linux or NetBSD doesn't care who
made the chip inside because the OS behaves similarly on all of them.

Free source code also threatens one of the traditional ways computer
manufacturers differentiated their products. The Apple Macintosh lost
market share and potential customers because it was said that there
wasn't much software available for it. The software written for the PC
would run on the Mac only using a slow program that converted it.
Now, if everyone has access to the source code, they can convert the
software to run on their machine. In many cases, it's as simple as just
recompiling it, a step that takes less than a minute. Someone using an
Amiga version of NetBSD could take software running on an Intel chip
version and recompile it.

This threat shows that the emergence of the free OSs ensures that
hardware companies will also face increased competitive pressure. Sure,

they may be able to get Microsoft off their back, but Linux may make things a bit worse.

In the end, the coming of age of free software may be just as big a threat to the old way of life for corporations as it is to the free software community. Sure, the hackers will lose the easy camaraderie of swapping code with others, but the corporations will need to learn to live without complete control. Software companies will be under increasing pressure from free versions, and hardware companies will be shocked to discover that their product will become more of a commodity than it was before. Everyone is going to have to find a way to compete and pay the rent when much of the intellectual property is free.

These are big changes that affect big players. But what will the changes mean to the programmers who stay up late spinning mountains of code? Will they be disenfranchised? Will they quit in despair? Will they move on to open source experiments on the human genome?

"The money flowing in won't turn people off or break up the community, and here's why," says Eric Raymond. "The demand for programmers has been so high for the last decade that anyone who really cared about money is already gone. We've been selected for artistic passion."

15. MONEY

Everyone who's made it past high school knows that money changes everything. Jobs disappear, love crumbles, and wars begin when money gets tight. Of course, a good number of free source believers aren't out of high school, but they'll figure this out soon enough. Money is just the way that we pay for things we need like food, clothing, housing, and of course newer, bigger, and faster computers.

The concept of money has always been the Achilles heel of the free software world. Everyone quickly realizes the advantages of sharing the source code with everyone else. As they say in the software business, "It's a no-brainer." But figuring out a way to keep the fridge stocked with Jolt Cola confounds some of the best advocates for free software.

Stallman carefully tried to spell out his solution in the GNU Manifesto. He wrote, "There's nothing wrong with wanting pay for work, or seeking to maximize one's income, as long as one does not use means that are destructive. But the means customary in the field of software today are based on destruction.

"Extracting money from users of a program by restricting their use of it is destructive because the restrictions reduce the amount and the way that the program can be used. This reduces the amount of wealth that humanity derives from the program. When there is a deliberate choice to restrict, the harmful consequences are deliberate destruction."

At first glance, Richard Stallman doesn't have to worry too much about making ends meet. MIT gave him an office. He got a genius grant from the MacArthur Foundation. Companies pay him to help port his free software to their platforms. His golden reputation combined with a frugal lifestyle means that he can support himself with two months of paid work a year. The rest of the time he donates to the Free Software Foundation. It's not in the same league as running Microsoft, but he gets by.

Still, Stallman's existence is far from certain. He had to work hard to develop the funding lines he has. In order to avoid any conflicts of interest, the Free Software Foundation doesn't pay Stallman a salary or cover his travel expenses. He says that getting paid by corporations to port software helped make ends meet, but it didn't help create new software. Stallman works hard to raise new funds for the FSF, and the money goes right out the door to pay programmers on new projects. This daily struggle for *some* form of income is one of the greatest challenges in the free source world today.

Many other free software folks are following Stallman's tack by selling the services, not the software. Many of the members of the Apache Webserver Core, for instance, make their money by running websites. They get paid because their customers are able to type in www.website.com and see something pop up. The customer doesn't care whether it is free software or something from Microsoft that is juggling the requests. They just want the graphics and text to keep moving.

Some consultants are following in the same footsteps. Several now offer discounts of something like 25 percent if the customer agrees to release the source code from the project as free software. If there's no great proprietary information in the project, then customers often take the deal. At first glance, the consultant looks like he's cutting his rates by 25 percent, but at second glance, he might be just making things a bit more efficient for all of his customers. He can reuse the software his clients release, and no one knows it better than he does. In time, all of his clients share code and enjoy lower development costs.

The model of selling services instead of source code works well for many people, but it is still far from perfect. Software that is sold as part of a shrink-wrapped license is easy for people to understand and budget. If you pay the price, you get the software. Services are often billed by the hour and they're often very open-ended. Managing these relationships can be just as difficult as raising some capital to write the software and then marketing it as shrink-wrapped code.

Cygnus—One Company that
Grew Rich on Free Software

There have been a number of different success stories of companies built around selling free software. One of the better-known examples is Cygnus, a company that specializes in maintaining and porting the GNU C Compiler. The company originally began by selling support contracts for the free software before realizing that there was a great demand for compiler development.

The philosophy in the beginning was simple. John Gilmore, one of the founders, said, "We make free software affordable." They felt that free software offered many great tools that people needed and wanted, but realized that the software did not come with guaranteed support. Cygnus would sell people contracts that would pay for an engineer who would learn the source code inside and out while waiting to answer questions. The engineer could also rewrite code and help out.

David Henkel-Wallace, one of the other founders, says, "We started in 1989 technically, 1990 really. Our first offices were in my house on University Avenue [in Palo Alto]. We didn't have a garage, we had a carport. It was an apartment complex. We got another apartment and etherneted them together. By the time we left, we had six apartments."

While the Bay Area was very technically sophisticated, the Internet was mainly used at that time by universities and research labs. Commercial hookups were rare and only found in special corners like the corporate research playpen, Xerox PARC. In order to get Net service, Cygnus came up with a novel plan to wire the apartment complex and sell off some of the extra bandwidth to their neighbors. Henkel-Wallace says, "We started our own ISP [Internet Service Provider] as a cooperative because there weren't those things in those days. Then people moved into those apartments because they were on the Internet."

At the beginning, the company hoped that the free software would allow them to offer something the major manufacturers didn't: cross-platform consistency. The GNU software would perform the same on a DEC Alpha, a Sun SPARC, and even a Microsoft box. The manufacturers, on the other hand, were locked up in their proprietary worlds where there was little cross-pollination. Each company developed its own editors, compilers, and source code tools, and each took slightly different approaches.

One of the other founders, Michael Tiemann, writes of the time: "When it came to tools for programmers in 1989, proprietary software was in a dismal state. First, the tools were primitive in the features they offered. Second, the features, when available, often had built-in limitations that tended to break when projects started to get complicated. Third, support from proprietary vendors was terrible . . . finally, every vendor implemented their own proprietary extensions, so that when you did use the meager features of one platform, you became, imperceptibly at first, then more obviously later, inextricably tied to that platform."

The solution was to clean up the GNU tools, add some features, and sell the package to people who had shops filled with different machines. Henkel-Wallace said, "We were going to have two products: compiler tools and shell tools. Open systems people will buy a bunch of SGIs, a bunch of HPs, a bunch of Unix machines. Well, we thought people who have the same environment would want to have the same tools."

This vision didn't work out. They sold no contracts that offered that kind of support. They did find, however, that people wanted them to move the compiler to other platforms. "The compilers people got from the vendors weren't as good and the compiler side of the business was making money from day one," says Henkel-Wallace.

The company began to specialize in porting GCC, the GNU compiler written first by Richard Stallman, to new chips that came along. While much of the visible world of computers was frantically standardizing on Intel chips running Microsoft operating systems, an invisible world was fragmenting as competition for the embedded systems blossomed. Everyone was making different chips to run the guts of microwave ovens, cell phones, laser printers, network routers, and other devices. These manufacturers didn't care whether a chip ran the latest MS software, they just wanted it to run. The appliance makers would set up the chip makers to compete against each other to provide the best solution with the cheapest price, and the chip manufacturers responded by churning out a stream of new, smaller, faster, and cheaper chips.

Cygnus began porting the GCC to each of these new chips, usually after being paid by the manufacturer. In the past, the chip companies would write or license their own proprietary compilers in the hope of generating something unique that would attract sales. Cygnus undercut this idea by offering something standard and significantly cheaper. The chip companies would save themselves the trouble of coming up with their own compiler tools and also get something that was fairly familiar to their customers. Folks who used GCC on Motorola's chip last year were open to trying out National Semiconductor's new chip if it also ran GCC. Supporting free software may not have found many takers, but Cygnus found more than enough people who wanted standard systems for their embedded processors.

Selling processor manufacturers on the conversion contracts was also a bit easier. Businesses wondered what they were doing paying good money for free software. It just didn't compute. The chip manufacturers stopped worrying about this when they realized that the free compilers were just incentives to get people to use their chips. The companies spent millions buying pens, T-shirts, and other doodads that they gave away to market the chips. What was different about buying software? If it made the customers happy, great. The chip companies didn't worry as much about losing a competitive advantage by giving away their work. It was just lagniappe.

Cygnus, of course, had to worry about competition. There was usually some guy who worked at the chip company or knew someone who worked at the chip company who would say, "Hey, I know compilers as well as those guys at Cygnus. I can download GCC too and underbid them."

Henkel-Wallace says, "Cygnus was rarely the lowest bidder. People who cared about price more than anyone else were often the hardest customers anyway. We did deals on a fair price and I think people were happy with the result. We rarely competed on price. What really matters to you? Getting a working tool set or a cheap price?"

How the GPL Built Cygnus's Monopoly

The GNU General Public License was also a bit of a secret weapon for Cygnus. When their competitors won a contract, they had to release the source code for their version when they were done with it. All of the new features and insights developed by competitors would flow directly back to Cygnus.

Michael Tiemann sounds surprisingly like Bill Gates when he speaks about this power: "Fortunately, the open source model comes to the rescue again. Unless and until a competitor can match the one hundred-plus engineers we have on staff today, most of whom are primary authors or maintainers of the software we support, they cannot displace us from our position as the 'true GNU' source. The best they can hope to do is add incremental features that their customers might pay them to add. But because the software is open source, whatever value they add comes back to Cygnus. . . ."

Seeing these effects is something that only a truely devoted fan of free software can do. Most people rarely get beyond identifying the problems with giving up the source code to a project. They don't realize that the GPL affects all users and also hobbles the potential competitors. It's like a mutual disarmament or mutual armament treaty that fixes the rules for all comers and disarmament treaties are often favored by the most powerful.

The money Cygnus makes by selling this support has been quite outstanding. The company continues to grow every year, and it has been listed as one of the largest and fastest-growing private software companies. The operation was also a bootstrap business where the company used the funds from existing contracts to fund the research and development of new tools. They didn't take funding from outside venture capital firms until 1995. This let the founders and the workers keep a large portion of the company, one of the dreams of every Silicon Valley start-up. In 1999, Red Hot merged with Cygnus to "create an open source powerhouse."

The success of Cygnus doesn't mean that others have found ways of duplicating the model. While Cygnus has found some success and venture capital, Gilmore says, "The free software business gives many MBAs the willies." Many programmers have found that free software is just a free gift for others. They haven't found an easy way to charge for their work.

Snitchware

Larry McVoy is one programmer who looks at the free source world and cringes. He's an old hand from the UNIX world who is now trying to build a new system for storing the source code. To him, giving away source code is a one-way train to no money. Sure, companies like Cygnus and Red Hat can make money by adding some extra service, but the competition means that the price of this value will steadily go to zero. There are no regulatory or large capital costs to restrain entry, so he feels that the free software world will eventually push out all but the independently wealthy and the precollege teens who can live at home. "We need to find a sustainable method. People need to write code and raise families, pay mortgages, and all of that stuff," he says.

McVoy's solution is a strange license that some call "snitchware." He's developing a product known as BitKeeper and he's giving it away, with several very different hooks attached. He approached this philosophically. He says, "In order to make money, I need to find something that the free software guys don't value that the businesspeople do value. Then I take it away from the free software guys. The thing I found is your privacy."

BitKeeper is an interesting type of product that became essential as software projects grew larger and more unwieldy. In the beginning, programmers wrote a program that was just one coherent file with a beginning, a middle, some digressions, and then an end. These were very self-contained and easily managed by one person.

When more than one programmer started working on a project together, however, everyone needed to work on coordinating their work with each other. One person couldn't start tearing apart the menus because another might be trying to hook up the menus to a new file system. If both started working on the same part, the changes would be difficult if not impossible to sort out when both were done. Once a team of programmers digs out from a major mess like that, they look for some software like BitKeeper to keep the source code organized.

BitKeeper is sophisticated and well-integrated with the Internet. Teams of programmers can be spread out throughout the world. At particular times, programmers can call each other up and synchronize their projects. Both tightly controlled, large corporate teams and loose and uncoordinated open source development teams can use the tool.

The synchronization creates change logs that summarize the differences between two versions of the project. These change logs are optimized to move the least amount of information. If two programmers don't do too much work, then synchronizing them doesn't take too long. The change logs build up a complete history of the project and make it possible to roll back the project to earlier points if it turns out that development took the wrong path.

McVoy's snitchware solution is to post the change logs of the people who don't buy a professional license. These logs include detailed information on how two programs are synchronized, and he figures that this information should be valuable enough for a commercial company to keep secret. They might say, "Moved auction control structure to Bob's version from Caroline's version. Moved new PostScript graphics engine to Caroline's version from Bob's."

McVoy says, "If you're Sun or Boeing, you don't want the Internet to be posting a message like 'I just added the bomb bay.' But for the free software guys, not only is that acceptable, but it's desirable. If you're doing open source, what do you have to hide?"

BitKeeper is free for anyone to use, revise, and extend as long as they don't mess with the part that tattles. If you don't care about the world reading your change logs, then it's not much different from the traditional open source license. The user has the same rights to extend, revise, and modify BitKeeper as they do GNU Emacs, with one small exception: you can't disable the snitch feature.

McVoy thinks this is an understandable trade-off. "From the business guys you can extract money. You can hope that they'll pay you. This is an important point I learned consulting at Schwab and Morgan Stanley. They insist that they pay for the software they get. They don't want to pay nothing. I used to think that they were idiots. Now I think they're very smart," he says.

The matter is simple economics, he explains. "They believe that if enough money is going to their supplier, it won't be a total disaster. I call this an insurance model of software."

Companies that pay for the privacy with BitKeeper will also be funding further development. The work won't be done in someone's spare time between exams and the homecoming game. It won't be done between keeping the network running and helping the new secretary learn Microsoft Word. It will be developed by folks who get paid to do the work.

"There's enough money going back to the corporation so it can be supported," McVoy says. "This is the crux of the problem with the open source model. It's possible to abuse the proprietary model, too. They get you in there, they lock you in, and then they rape you. This business of hoping that it will be okay is unacceptable. You need to have a lock. The MIS directors insist you have a lock."

He has a point. Linux is a lot of fun to play with and it is now a very stable OS, but it took a fair number of years to get to this point. Many folks in the free source world like to say things like, "It used to be that the most fun in Linux was just getting it to work." Companies like Morgan Stanley, Schwab, American Airlines, and most others live and die on the quality of their computer systems. They're quite willing to pay money if it helps ensure that things don't go wrong.

McVoy's solution hasn't rubbed everyone the right way. The Open Source Initiative doesn't include his snitchware license in a list of acceptable solutions. "The consensus of the license police is that my license is NOT open source," he says. "The consensus of my lawyer is that it is. But I don't call it open source anymore."

He's going his own way. "I made my own determination of what people value in the OS community: they have to be able to get the source, modify the source, and redistribute the source for no fee. All of the other crap is yeah, yeah whatever," he says.

"The problem with the GPL is the GPL has an ax to grind, and in order to grind that ax it takes away all of the rights of the person who wrote the code. It serves the need of everyone in the community except the person who wrote it."

McVoy has also considered a number of other alternatives. Instead of taking away something that the free software folks don't value, he considered putting in something that the businesses would pay to get rid of. The product could show ads it downloaded from a central location. This solution is already well known on the Internet, where companies give away e-mail, searching solutions, directories, and tons of information in order to sell ads. This solution, however, tends to wreck the usability of the software. Eudora, the popular e-mail program, is distributed with this option.

McVoy also considered finding a way to charge for changes and support to BitKeeper. "The Cygnus model isn't working well because it turns them into a contracting shop. That means you actually have to do something for every hour of work."

To him, writing software and charging for each version can generate money without work—that is, without doing further work. The support house has to have someone answering the phone every moment. A company that is selling shrinkwrapped software can collect money as people buy new copies. McVoy doesn't want this cash to spend tipping bartenders on cruise ships, although he doesn't rule it out. He wants the capital to reinvest in other neat ideas. He wants to have some cash coming in so he can start up development teams looking at new and bigger projects.

The Cygnus model is too constraining for him. He argues that a company relying on support contracts must look for a customer to fund each project. Cygnus, for instance, had to convince Intel that they could do a good job porting the GCC to the i960. They found few people interested in general support of GNU, so they ended up concentrating on GCC.

McVoy argues that it's the engineers who come up with the dreams first. The customers are often more conservative and less able to see how some new tool or piece of software could be really useful. Someone needs to hole up in a garage for a bit to create a convincing demonstration of the idea. Funding a dream takes capital.

To him, the absence of money in the free software world can be a real limitation because money is a way to store value. It's not just about affording a new Range Rover and balsamic vinegars that cost more than cocaine by weight. Money can be a nice way to store up effort and transport it across time. Someone can work like a dog for a six months, turn out a great product, and sell it for a pile of cash. Ten years later, the cash can be spent on something else. The work is effectively stored for the future.

Of course, this vision isn't exactly true. Cygnus has managed to charge enough for their contracts to fund the development of extra tools. Adding new features and rolling them out into the general distribution of some GNU tool is part of the job that the Cygnus team took on for themselves. These new features also mean that the users need more support. On one level, it's not much different from a traditional software development cycle. Cygnus is doing its work by subscription while a traditional house is creating its new features on spec.

In fact, Cygnus did so well over such a long period of time that it found it could raise capital. "Once Cygnus had a track record of making money and delivering on time, investors wanted a piece of it," says Gilmore.

Red Hat has managed to sell enough CD-ROM disks to fund the development of new projects. They've created a good selection of installation tools that make it relatively easy for people to use Linux. They also help pay salaries for people like Alan Cox who contribute a great deal to the evolution of the kernel. They do all of this while others are free to copy their distribution disks verbatim.

McVoy doesn't argue with these facts, but feels that they're just a temporary occurrence. The huge growth of interest in Linux means that many new folks are exploring the operating system. There's a great demand for the hand-holding and packaging that Red Hat offers. In time, though, everyone will figure out how to use the product and the revenue stream should disappear as competition drives out the ability to charge $50 for each disk.

Of course, the folks at Cygnus or Red Hat might not disagree with McVoy either. They know it's a competitive world and they figure that their only choice is to remain competitive by finding something that people will want to pay for. They've done it in the past and they should probably be able to do it in the future. There are always new features.

Bounties for Quicker Typer-Uppers

Some developers are starting to explore a third way of blending capital with open source development by trying to let companies and people put bounties out on source code. The concept is pretty simple and tuned to the open software world. Let's say you have an annoying habit of placing French *bon mots* in the middle of sentences. Although this looks *stupide* to your friends, you think it's quite *chic*. The problem is that your old word processor's spell checker isn't quite *à la mode* and it only operates *avec une seule langue*. The problem is that you've spent too much

time studying *français* and drinking *de café* and not enough time studying Java, the programming language. You're *très désolé* by your word
processor's inability to grok just how *BCBG* you can be and spell-check
in *deux* languages.

The bounty system could be your savior. You would post a message saying, "Attention! I will reward with a check for $100 anyone who creates a
two-language spell-checker." If you're lucky, someone who knows something about the spell-checker's source code will add the feature in a few
minutes. One hundred dollars for a few minutes' work isn't too shabby.

It is entirely possible that another person out there is having the
same problem getting their word processor to *verstehen* their needs.
They might chip in $50 to the pool. If the problem is truly *grande,* then
the pot could grow quite large.

This solution is blessed with the wide-open, free-market sensibility
that many people in the open software community like. The bounties
are posted in the open and anyone is free to try to claim the bounties by
going to work. Ideally, the most knowledgeable will be the first to complete the job and nab the payoff.

Several developers are trying to create a firm infrastructure for the
plan. Brian Behlendorf, one of the founding members of the Apache
web server development team, is working with Tim O'Reilly's company
to build a website known as SourceXchange. Another group known as
CoSource is led by Bernie Thompson and his wife, Laurie. Both will
work to create more software that is released with free source.

Of course, these projects are more than websites. They're really a
process, and how the process will work is still unclear right now. While
it is easy to circulate a notice that some guy will pay some money for
some software, it is another thing to actually make it work. Writing
software is a frustrating process and there are many chances for disagreement. The biggest question on every developer's mind is "How can
I be sure I'll be paid?" and the biggest question on every sugar daddy's
mind is "How can I be sure that the software works?"

These questions are part of any software development experience.
There is often a large gap between the expectations of the person com-
missioning the software and the person writing the code. In this
shadow are confusion, betrayal, and turmoil.

The normal solution is to break the project up into milestones and require payment after each milestone passes. If the coder is doing something unsatisfactory, the message is transmitted when payment doesn't arrive. Both SourceXchange and CoSource plan on carrying over the same structure to the world of bounty-hunting programmers. Each project might be broken into a number of different steps and a price for each step might be posted in advance.

Both systems try to alleviate the danger of nonpayment by requiring that someone step in and referee the end of the project. A peer reviewer must be able to look over the specs of the project and the final code and then determine whether money should be paid. Ideally, this person should be someone both sides respect.

A neutral party with the ability to make respectable decisions is something many programmers and consultants would welcome. In many normal situations, the contractors can only turn to the courts to solve disagreements, and the legal system is not really schooled in making these kinds of decisions. The company with the money is often able to dangle payment in front of the programmers and use this as a lever to extract more work. Many programmers have at least one horror story to tell about overly ambitious expectations.

Of course, the existence of a wise neutral party who can see deeply into the problems and provide a fair solution is close to a myth. Judging takes time. SourceXchange promises that these peer reviewers will be paid, and this money will probably have to come from the people offering the bounty. They're the only ones putting money into the system in the long run. Plus, the system must make the people offering bounties happy in the long run or it will fail.

The CoSource project suggests that the developers must come up with their own authority who will judge the end of the job and present this person with their bid. The sponsors then decide whether to trust the peer reviewer when they okay the job. The authorities will be judged like the developers, and summaries of their reputation will be posted on the site. While it isn't clear how the reviewers will be paid, it is not too much to expect that there will be some people out there who will do it just for the pleasure of having their finger in the stew. They might, for instance, want to offer the bounty themselves but be unable to put up much money. Acting as a reviewer would give them the chance to make sure the software did what they wanted without putting up much cash.

One of the most difficult questions is how to run the marketplace. A wide-open solution would let the sponsors pay when the job was done satisfactorily. The first person to the door with running code that met the specs would be the one to be paid. Any other team that showed up later would get nothing.

This approach would offer the greatest guarantees of creating well-running code as quickly as possible. The programmers would have a strong incentive to meet the specs quickly in order to win the cash. The downside is that the price would be driven up because the programmers would be taking on more risk. They would need to capitalize their own development and take the chance that someone might beat them to the door. Anxious sponsors who need some code quickly should be willing to pay the price.

Another solution is to award contracts before any work is done. Developers would essentially bid on the project and the sponsor would choose one to start work. The process would be fairly formal and favor the seasoned, connected programmers. A couple of kids working in their spare time might be able to win an open bounty, but they would be at a great disadvantage in this system. Both CoSource and SourceXchange say that they'll favor this sort of preliminary negotiation.

If the contracts are awarded before work begins, the bounty system looks less like a wild free-for-all and more like just a neutral market-place for contract programmers to make their deals. Companies like Cygnus already bid to be paid for jobs that produce open source. These marketplaces for bounties will need to provide some structure and effi-ciencies to make it worth people's time to use them.

One possible benefit of the bounty system is to aggregate the desires of many small groups. While some bounties will only serve the person who asks for them, many have the potential to help people who are willing to pay. An efficient system should be able to join these people together into one group and put their money into one pot.

CoSource says that it will try to put together the bounties of many small groups and allow people to pay them with credit cards. It uses the example of a group of Linux developers who would gather together to fund the creation of an open source version of their favorite game. They would each chip in $10, $20, or $50 and when the pot got big enough, someone would step forward. Creating a cohesive political group that could effectively offer a large bounty is a great job for these sites.

Of course, there are deeper questions about the flow of capital and the nature of risks in these bounty-based approaches. In traditional software development, one group pays for the creation of the software in the hope that they'll be able to sell it for more than it cost to create. Here, the programmer would be guaranteed a fixed payment if he accomplished the job. The developer's risk is not completely eliminated because the job might take longer than they expected, but there is little of the traditional risk of a start-up firm. It may not be a good idea to separate the risk-taking from the people doing the work. That is often the best way to keep people focused and devoted.

Each of these three systems shows how hard the free software industry is working at finding a way for people to pay their bills and share information successfully. Companies like Cygnus or BitKeeper are real efforts built by serious people who can't live off the largesse of a university or a steady stream of government grants. Their success shows that it is quite possible to make money and give the source code away for free, but it isn't easy.

Still, there is no way to know how well these companies will survive the brutal competition that comes from the free flow of the source code. There are no barriers to entry, so each corporation must be constantly on its toes. The business becomes one of service, not manufacturing, and that changes everything. There are no grand slam home runs in that world. There are no billion-dollar explosions. Service businesses grow by careful attention to detail and plenty of focused effort.

· · ·

16. FORK

A T-shirt once offered this wisdom to the world: "If you love someone, set them free. If they come back to you, it was meant to be. If they don't come back, hunt them down and kill them." The world of free software revolves around letting your source code go off into the world. If things go well, others will love the source code, shower it with bug fixes, and send all of this hard work flowing back to you. It will be a shining example of harmony and another reason why the free software world is great. But if things don't work out, someone might fork you and there's nothing you can do about it.

"Fork" is a UNIX command that allows you to split a job in half. UNIX is an operating system that allows several people to use the same computer to do different tasks, and the operating system pretends to run them simultaneously by quickly jumping from task to task. A typical UNIX computer has at least 100 different tasks running. Some watch the network for incoming data, some run programs for the user, some watch over the file system, and others do many menial tasks.

If you "fork a job," you arrange to split it into two parts that the computer treats as two separate jobs. This can be quite useful if both jobs are often interrupted, because one can continue while the other one stalls. This solution is great if two tasks, A and B, need to be accomplished independently of each other. If you use one task and try to accomplish A first, then B won't start until A finishes. This can be quite inefficient if A stalls. A better solution is to fork the job and treat A and B as two separate tasks.

Most programmers don't spend much time talking about these kinds of forks. They're mainly concerned about forks in the political process.

Programmers use "fork" to describe a similar process in the organization of a project, but the meaning is quite different. Forks of a team mean that the group splits and goes in different directions. One part might concentrate on adding support for buzzword Alpha while the other might aim for full buzzword Beta compatibility.

In some cases, there are deep divisions behind the decision to fork. One group thinks buzzword Alpha is a sloppy, brain-dead kludge job that's going to blow up in a few years. The other group hates buzzword Beta with a passion. Disputes like this happen all the time. They often get resolved peacefully when someone comes up with buzzword Gamma, which eclipses them both. When no Gamma arrives, people start talking about going their separate ways and forking the source. If the dust settles, two different versions start appearing on the Net competing with each other for the hearts and CPUs of the folks out there. Sometimes the differences between the versions are great and sometimes they're small. But there's now a fork in the evolution of the source code, and people have to start making choices.

The free software community has a strange attitude toward forks. On one hand, forking is the whole reason Stallman wrote the free software manifesto. He wanted the right and the ability to mess around with the software on his computer. He wanted to be free to change it, modify it, and tear it to shreds if he felt like doing it one afternoon. No one should be able to stop him from doing that. He wanted to be totally free.

On the other hand, forking can hurt the community by duplicating efforts, splitting alliances, and sowing confusion in the minds of users. If Bob starts writing and publishing his own version of Linux out of his house, then he's taking some energy away from the main version. People start wondering if the version they're running is the Missouri Synod version of Emacs or the Christian Baptist version. Where do they send bug fixes? Who's in charge? Distribution groups like Debian or Red Hat have to spend a few moments trying to decide whether they want to include one version or the other. If they include both, they have to choose one as the default. Sometimes they just throw up their hands and forget about both. It's a civil war, and those are always worse than a plain old war.

Some forks evolve out of personalities that just rub each other the wrong way. I've heard time and time again, "Oh, we had to kick him out of the group because he was offending people." Many members of the community consider this kind of forking bad. They use the same tone of voice to describe a fork of the source code as they use to describe the breakup of two lovers. It is sad, unfortunate, unpleasant, and something we'll never really understand because we weren't there. Sometimes people take sides because they have a strong opinion about who is right. They'll usually go off and start contributing to that code fork. In other cases, people don't know which to pick and they just close their eyes and join the one with the cutest logo.

Forks and the Threat of Disunity

Eric Raymond once got in a big fight with Richard Stallman about the structure of Emacs Lisp. Raymond said, "The Lisp libraries were in bad shape in a number of ways. They were poorly documented. There was a lot of work that had gone on outside the FSF that should be integrated and I wanted to merge in the best work from outside."

The problem is that Stallman didn't want any part of Raymond's work. "He just said, 'I won't take those changes into the distribution.' That's his privilege to do," Raymond said.

That put Raymond in an awkward position. He could continue to do the work, create his own distribution of Emacs, and publicly break with Stallman. If he were right and the Lisp code really needed work, then he would probably find more than a few folks who would cheer his work. They might start following him by downloading his distribution and sending their bug fixes his way. Of course, if he were wrong, he would set up his own web server, do all the work, put his Lisp fixes out there, and find that no one would show up. He would be ignored because people found it easier to just download Stallman's version of Emacs, which everyone thought was sort of the official version, if one could be said to exist. They didn't use the Lisp feature too much so it wasn't worth thinking about how some guy in Pennsylvania had fixed it. They were getting the real thing from the big man himself.

Of course, something in between would probably happen. Some folks who cared about Lisp would make a point of downloading Raymond's version. The rest of the world would just go on using the regular version. In time, Stallman might soften and embrace the changes, but he might not. Perhaps someone would come along and create a third distribution that melded Raymond's changes with Stallman's into a harmonious version. That would be a great thing, except that it would force everyone to choose from among three different versions.

In the end, Raymond decided to forget about his improvements. "Emacs is too large and too complicated and forking is bad. There was in fact one group that got so fed up with working with him that they did fork Emacs. That's why X Emacs exists. But major forks like that are rare events and I didn't want to be part of perpetrating another one," he said. Someone else was going to have to start the civil war by firing those shots at Fort Sumter.

BSD's Garden of Forking Paths

Some forks aren't so bad. There often comes a time when people have legitimate reasons to go down different paths. What's legitimate and what's not is often decided after a big argument, but the standard reasons are the same ones that drive programming projects. A good fork should make a computer run software a gazillion times faster. Or it might make the code much easier to port to a new platform. Or it might make the code more secure. There are a thousand different reasons, and it's impossible to really measure which is the right one. The only true measure is the number of people who follow each branch of the fork. If a project has a number of good disciples and the bug fixes are coming quickly, then people tend to assume it is legitimate.

The various versions of the BSD software distribution are some of the more famous splits around. All are descended, in one way or another, from the original versions of UNIX that came out of Berkeley. Most of the current ones evolved from the 4.3BSD version and the Network Release 2 and some integrated code from the 4.4BSD release after it became free. All benefited from the work of the hundreds of folks who spent their free time cloning the features controlled by AT&T. All of them are controlled by the same loose BSD license that gives people the right to do pretty much anything they want to the code. All of them share the same cute daemon as a mascot.

That's where the similarities end. The FreeBSD project is arguably the most successful version. It gets a fairly wide distribution because its developers have a good deal with Walnut Creek CD-ROM Distributors, a company that packages up large bundles of freeware and shareware on the Net and then sells them on CD-ROM. The system is well known and widely used because the FreeBSD team concentrates on making the software easy to use and install on Intel computers. Lately, they've created an Alpha version, but most of the users run the software on x86 chips. Yahoo! uses FreeBSD.

FreeBSD, of course, began as a fork of an earlier project known as 386BSD, started by Bill Jolitz. This version of BSD was more of an academic example or a proof-of-concept than a big open source project designed to take over the world.

Jordan Hubbard, someone who would come along later to create a fork of 386BSD, said of Jolitz's decision to create a 386-based fork of BSD, "Bill's real contribution was working with the 386 port. He was kind of an outsider. No one else saw the 386 as interesting. Berkeley had a myopic attitude toward PCs. They were just toys. No one would support Intel. That was the climate at the time. No one really took PCs seriously. Bill's contribution was to realize that PCs were going places."

From the beginning, Hubbard and several others saw the genius in creating a 386 version of BSD that ran on the cheapest hardware available. They started adding features and gluing in bug fixes, which they distributed as a file that modified the main 386BSD distribution from Jolitz. This was practical at the beginning when the changes were few, but it continued out of respect for the original creator, even after the patches grew complicated.

Finally, a tussle flared up in 1993. Jordan Hubbard, one of the forkers, writes in his history of the project,

386BSD was Bill Jolitz's operating system, which had been up to that point suffering rather severely from almost a year's worth of neglect. As

*the patchkit swelled ever more uncomfortably with each passing day,
we were in unanimous agreement that something had to be done and
decided to try and assist Bill by providing this interim "cleanup"
snapshot. Those plans came to a rude halt when Bill Jolitz suddenly
decided to withdraw his sanction from the project and without any
clear indication of what would be done instead.*

The FreeBSD team pressed on despite the denial. They decided to
fork. Today, 386BSD is largely part of the history of computing while
FreeBSD is a living, current OS, at least at the time this book was
written. The FreeBSD team has done a good job distributing bug-free
versions, and they've been paid off in loyalty, disciples, and money and
computers from Walnut Creek. Forking can often be good for society
because it prevents one person or clique from thwarting another group.
The free software world is filled with many of the same stories of politics that float across the watercoolers of corporations, but the stories
don't have to end the same way. If one boss or group tries to shut down
a free software project, it really can't. The source code is freely available, and people are free to carry on. The FreeBSD project is one
example.

Of course, good software can have anti-forking effects. Linus
Torvalds said in one interview, "Actually, I have never even checked
386BSD out; when I started on Linux it wasn't available (although Bill
Jolitz's series on it in *Dr. Dobbs Journal* had started and were interesting), and when 386BSD finally came out, Linux was already in a state
where it was so usable that I never really thought about switching. If
386BSD had been available when I started on Linux, Linux would
probably never have happened." So if 386BSD had been easier to find
on the Net and better supported, Linux might never have begun.

Once someone starts forking BSD, one fork is rarely enough.
Another group known as NetBSD also grew fed up with the progress of
386BSD in 1993. This group, however, wanted to build a platform that
ran well on many different machines, not just the Intel 386. The
FreeBSD folks concentrated on doing a good job on Intel boxes, while
the NetBSD wanted to create a version that ran on many different
machines. Their slogan became "Of course it runs NetBSD."

NetBSD runs on practically every machine you can imagine, including older, less up-to-date machines like the Amiga and the Atari. It has also been embraced by companies like NeXT, which bundled parts of it into the version of the OS for the Macintosh known as Rhapsody. Of course, the most common chips like the Intel line and the Alpha are also well supported.

The NetBSD community emerged at the same time as the FreeBSD world. They didn't realize that each team was working on the same project at the same time. But once they started releasing their own versions, they stayed apart.

"The NetBSD group has always been the purest. They saw it as an OS research vehicle. That was what CSRG was doing. Their only mandate was to do interesting research," said Hubbard. "It's a very different set of goals than we concentrated on for the 386. The important thing for us was to polish it up. We put all of our efforts into polishing, not porting. This was part of our bringing BSD to the masses kind of thing. We're going for numbers. We're going for mass penetration."

This orientation meant that NetBSD never really achieved the same market domination as FreeBSD. The group only recently began shipping versions of NetBSD on CD-ROM. FreeBSD, on the other hand, has always excelled at attracting new and curious users thanks to their relationship with Walnut Creek. Many experimenters and open-minded users picked up one of the disks, and a few became excited enough to actually make some contributions. The Walnut Creek partnership also helped the FreeBSD team understand what it needed to do to make their distribution easier to install and simpler to use. That was Walnut Creek's business, after all.

Flames, Fights, and the Birth of OpenBSD

The forking did not stop with NetBSD. Soon one member of the NetBSD world, Theo de Raadt, began to rub some people the wrong way. One member of the OpenBSD team told me, "The reason for the split from NetBSD was that Theo got kicked out. I don't understand it completely. More or less they say he was treating users on the mailing list badly. He does tend to be short and terse, but there's nothing wrong with that. He was one of the founding members of NetBSD and they asked him to resign."

Now, four years after the split began in 1995, de Raadt is still a bit hurt by their decision. He says about his decision to fork BSD again, "I had no choice. I really like what I do. I really like working with a community. At the time it all happened, I was the second most active developer in their source tree. They took the second most active developer and kicked him off."

Well, they didn't kick him out completely, but they did take away his ability to "commit" changes to the source tree and make them permanent. After the split, de Raadt had to e-mail his contributions to a member of the team so they could check them in. This didn't sit well with de Raadt, who saw it as both a demotion and a real impediment to doing work.

The root of the split is easy to see. De Raadt is energetic. He thinks and speaks quickly about everything. He has a clear view about most free software and isn't afraid to share it. While some BSD members are charitable and conciliatory to Richard Stallman, de Raadt doesn't bother to hide his contempt for the organization. "The Free Software Foundation is one of the most misnamed organizations," he says, explaining that only BSD-style licensees have the true freedom to do whatever they want with the software. The GNU General Public License is a pair of handcuffs to him.

De Raadt lives in Calgary and dresses up his personal web page with a picture of himself on top of a mountain wearing a bandanna. If you want to send him a pizza for any reason, he's posted the phone number of his favorite local shop (403/531–3131). Unfortunately, he reports that they don't take foreign credit card numbers anymore.

He even manages to come up with strong opinions about simple things that he ostensibly loves. Mountain biking is a big obsession, but, he says, "I like mud and despise 'wooded back-alleys' (what most people call logging roads)." That's not the best way to make friends with less extreme folks who enjoy a Sunday ride down logging roads.

If you like cats, don't read what he had to say about his pets: "I own cats. Their names are Galileo and Kepler—they're still kittens. Kepler—

the little bitch—can apparently teleport through walls. Galileo is a rather cool monster. When they become full-grown cats I will make stew & soup out of them. (Kepler is only good for soup)."

Throwaway comments like this have strange effects on the Net, where text is the only way people can communicate. There are no facial gestures or tonal clues to tell people someone is joking around, and some people don't have well-developed scanners for irony or sarcasm. Some love the sniping and baiting, while others just get annoyed. They can't let snide comments slide off their back. Eventually, the good gentlefolk who feel that personal kindness and politeness should still count for something in this world get annoyed and start trying to do something.

It's easy to see how this affected the NetBSD folks, who conduct their business in a much more proper way. Charles Hannum, for instance, refused to talk to me about the schism unless I promised that he would be able to review the parts of the book that mentioned NetBSD. He also suggested that forks weren't particularly interesting and shouldn't be part of the book. Others begged off the questions with more polite letters saying that the split happened a long time ago and wasn't worth talking about anymore. Some pointed out that most of the members of the current NetBSD team weren't even around when the split happened.

While their silence may be quite prudent and a better way to spend a life, it certainly didn't help me get both sides of the story. I pointed out that they wouldn't accept code into the NetBSD tree if the author demanded the right to review the final distribution. I said they could issue a statement or conduct the interview by e-mail. One argued that there was no great problem if a few paragraphs had to be deleted from the book in the end. I pointed out that I couldn't give the hundreds of people I spoke with veto power over the manuscript. It would be impossible to complete. The book wasn't being written by a committee. No one at NetBSD budged.

De Raadt, on the other hand, spoke quite freely with no preconditions or limitations. He still keeps a log file with a good number of e-mail letters exchanged during the separation and makes it easy to read them on his personal website. That's about as open as you can get. The

NetBSD folks who refused to talk to me, on the other hand, seemed intent on keeping control of the story. Their silence came from a different world than the website offering the phone number of the local pizza place as a hint. They were *Dragnet;* de Raadt was *Politically Incorrect.*

When the NetBSD folks decided to do something, they took away de Raadt's access to the source tree. He couldn't just poke around code making changes as he went along. Well, he could poke around and make changes, but not to the official tree with the latest version. The project was open source, after all. He could download the latest release and start fiddling, but he couldn't make quasi-official decisions about what source was part of the latest official unreleased version.

De Raadt thought this was a real barrier to work. He couldn't view the latest version of the code because it was kept out of his view. He was stuck with the last release, which might be several months old. That put him at an extreme disadvantage because he might start working on a problem only to discover that someone had either fixed it or changed it.

Chris Demetriou found himself with the task of kicking de Raadt off of the team. His letter, which can still be found on the OpenBSD site, said that de Raadt's rough behavior and abusive messages had driven away people who might have contributed to the project. Demetriou also refused to talk about NetBSD unless he could review the sections of the book that contained his comments. He also threatened to take all possible action against anyone who even quoted his letters in a commercial book without his permission.

De Raadt collected this note from Demetriou and the firestorm that followed in a 300k file that he keeps on his website. The NetBSD core tried to be polite and firm, but the matter soon degenerated into a seven-month-long flame war. After some time, people started having meta-arguments, debating whether the real argument was more or less like the bickering of a husband and wife who happen to work at the same company. Husbands and wives should keep their personal fights out of the workplace, they argued. And so they bickered over whether de Raadt's nastygrams were part of his "job" or just part of his social time.

Through it all, de Raadt tried to get back his access to the source tree of NetBSD and the group tried to propose all sorts of mechanisms for making sure he was making a "positive" contribution and getting along with everyone. At one time, they offered him a letter to sign. These negotiations went nowhere, as de Raadt objected to being forced to make promises that other contributors didn't have to.

De Raadt wrote free software because he wanted to be free to make changes or write code the way he wanted to do it. If he had wanted to wear the happy-face of a positive contributor, he could have gotten a job at a corporation. Giving up the right to get in flame wars and speak at will may not be that much of a trade-off for normal people with full-time jobs. Normal folks swallow their pride daily. Normal people don't joke about turning their cats into soup. But de Raadt figured it was like losing a bit of his humanity and signing up willingly for a set of manacles. It just wasn't livable.

The argument lasted months. De Raadt felt that he tried and tried to rejoin the project without giving away his honor. The core NetBSD team argued that they just wanted to make sure he would be positive. They wanted to make sure he wouldn't drive away perfectly good contributors with brash antics. No one ever gained any ground in the negotiations and in the end, de Raadt was gone.

The good news is that the fork didn't end badly. De Raadt decided he wasn't going to take the demotion. He just couldn't do good work if he had to run all of his changes by one of the team that kicked him off the project. It took too long to ask "Mother, may I?" to fix every little bug. If he was going to have to run his own tree, he might as well go whole hog and start his own version of BSD. He called it OpenBSD. It was going to be completely open. There were going to be relatively few controls on the members. If the NetBSD core ran its world like the Puritan villagers in a Nathaniel Hawthorne story, then de Raadt was going to run his like Club Med.

OpenBSD struggled for several months as de Raadt tried to attract more designers and coders to his project. It was a battle for popularity in many ways, not unlike high school. When the cliques split, everyone had to pick and choose. De Raadt had to get some folks in his camp if he was going to make some lemonade.

The inspiration came to de Raadt one day when he discovered that the flame war archive on his web page was missing a few letters. He says that someone broke into his machine and made a few subtle deletions. Someone who had an intimate knowledge of the NetBSD system. Someone who cared about the image portrayed by the raw emotions in the supposedly private letters.

He clarifies his comments to make it clear that he's not sure it was someone from the NetBSD core. "I never pursued it. If it happens, it's your own fault. It's not their fault," he said. Of course, the folks from NetBSD refused to discuss this matter or answer questions unless they could review the chapter.

This break-in gave him a focus. De Raadt looked at NetBSD and decided that it was too insecure. He gathered a group of like-minded people and began to comb the code for potential insecurities.

"About the same time, I got involved with a company that wrote a network security scanner. Three of the people over there started playing with the source tree and searching for security holes. We started finding problems all over the place, so we started a comprehensive security audit. We started from the beginning. Our task load increased massively. At one time, I had five pieces of paper on my desk full of things to look for," he said.

Security holes in operating systems are strange beasts that usually appear by mistake when the programmer makes an unfounded assumption. One of the best-known holes is the buffer overflow, which became famous in 1988 after Robert Morris, then a graduate student at Cornell, unleashed a program that used the loophole to bring several important parts of the Internet to a crawl.

In this case, the programmer creates a buffer to hold all of the information that someone on the net might send. Web browsers, for instance, send requests like "GET http://www.nytimes.com" to ask for the home page of the *New York Times* website. The programmer must set aside some chunk of memory to hold this request, usually a block that is about 512 bytes long. The programmer chooses an amount that should be more than enough for all requests, including the strangest and most complicated.

Before the attack became well known, programmers would often ignore the length of the request and assume that 512 bytes was more than enough for anything. Who would ever type a URL that long?

Who had an e-mail address that long? Attackers soon figured out that they could send more than 512 bytes and started writing over the rest of the computer's memory. The program would dutifully take in 100,000 bytes and keep writing it to memory. An attacker could download any software and start it running. And attackers did this.

De Raadt and many others started combing the code for loopholes. They made sure every program that used a buffer included a bit of code that would check to ensure that no hacker was trying to sneak in more than the buffer could hold. They checked thousands of other possibilities. Every line was checked and changes were made even if there was no practical way for someone to get at the potential hole. Many buffers, for instance, only accept information from the person sitting at the terminal. The OpenBSD folks changed them, too.

This audit began soon after the fork in 1995 and continues to this day. Most of the major work is done and the group likes to brag that they haven't had a hole that could be exploited remotely to gain root access in over two years. The latest logo boasts the tag line "Sending kiddies to /dev/null since 1995." That is, any attacker is going to go nowhere with OpenBSD because all of the extra information from the attacks would be routed to /dev/null, a UNIX conceit for being erased, ignored, and forgotten.

The OpenBSD fork is a good example of how bad political battles can end up solving some important technical problems. Everyone fretted and worried when de Raadt announced that he was forking the BSD world one more time. This would further dilute the resources and sow confusion among users. The concentration on security, however, gave OpenBSD a brand identity, and the other BSD distributions keep at least one eye on the bug fixes distributed by the OpenBSD team. These often lead to surreptitious fixes in their own distribution.

The focus also helped him attract new coders who were interested in security. "Some of them used to be crackers and they were really cool people. When they become eighteen, it becomes a federal offense, you know," de Raadt says.

This fork may have made the BSD community stronger because it effectively elevated the focus on security and cryptography to the highest level. In the corporate world, it's like taking the leader of the development team responsible for security and promoting him from senior manager to senior executive vice president of a separate division. The autonomy also gave the OpenBSD team the ability to make bold technical decisions for their own reasons. If they saw a potential security problem that might hurt usability or portability, the OpenBSD team could make the change without worrying that other team members would complain. OpenBSD was about security. If you wanted to work on portability, go to NetBSD. If you cared about ease-of-use on Intel boxes, go to FreeBSD. Creating a separate OpenBSD world made it possible to give security a strong focus.

Temporary Forks

It's a mistake to see these forks as absolute splits that never intermingle again. While NetBSD and OpenBSD continue to glower at each other across the Internet ether, the groups share code frequently because the licenses prevent one group from freezing out another.

Jason Wright, one of the OpenBSD developers, says, "We do watch each other's source trees. One of the things I do for fun is take drivers out of FreeBSD and port them to OpenBSD. Then we have support for a new piece of hardware."

He says he often looks for drivers written by Bill Paul, because "I've gotten used to his style. So I know what to change when I receive his code. I can do it in about five to six hours. That is, at least a rough port to test if it works."

Still, the work is not always simple. He says some device drivers are much harder to handle because both groups have taken different approaches to the problem. "SCSI drivers are harder," he says. "There's been some divergence in the layering for SCSI. They're using something called CAM. We've got an older implementation that we've stuck to." That is, the FreeBSD has reworked the structure of the way that the SCSI information is shipped to the parts of the system asking for information. The OpenBSD hasn't adopted their changes, perhaps because of security reasons or perhaps because of inertia or perhaps because no one has gotten around to thinking about it. The intermingling isn't perfect.

Both NetBSD and FreeBSD work on security, too. They also watch the change logs of OpenBSD and note when security holes are fixed. They also discover their own holes, and OpenBSD may use them as an inspiration to plug their own code. The discoveries and plugs go both ways as the groups compete to make a perfect OS.

Kirk McKusick says, "The NetBSD and the OpenBSD have extremely strong personalities. Each one is absolutely terrified the other will gain an inch."

While the three forks of BSD may cooperate more than they compete, the Linux world still likes to look at the BSD world with a bit of contempt. All of the forks look somewhat messy, even if having the freedom to fork is what Stallman and GNU are ostensibly fighting to achieve. The Linux enthusiasts seem to think, "We've got our ducks in a single row. What's your problem?" It's sort of like the Army mentality. If it's green, uniform, and the same everywhere, then it must be good.

The BSD lacks the monomaniacal cohesion of Linux, and this seems to hurt their image. The BSD community has always felt that Linux is stealing the limelight that should be shared at least equally between the groups. Linux is really built around a cult of Linus Torvalds, and that makes great press. It's very easy for the press to take photos of one man and put him on the cover of a magazine. It's simple, clean, neat, and perfectly amenable to a 30-second sound bite. Explaining that there's FreeBSD, NetBSD, OpenBSD, and who knows what smaller versions waiting in the wings just isn't as manageable.

Eric Raymond, a true disciple of Linus Torvalds and Linux, sees it in technical terms. The BSD community is proud of the fact that each distribution is built out of one big source tree. They get all the source code for all the parts of the kernel, the utilities, the editors, and whatnot together in one place. Then they push the compile button and let people work. This is a crisp, effective, well-managed approach to the project.

The Linux groups, however, are not that coordinated at all. Torvalds only really worries about the kernel, which is his baby. Someone else worries about GCC. Everyone comes up with their own source trees for the parts. The distribution companies like Red Hat worry about gluing the mess together. It's not unusual to find version 2.0 of the kernel in one distribution while another is sporting version 2.2.

"In BSD, you can do a unified make. They're fairly proud of that," says Raymond. "But this creates rigidities that give people incentives to fork. The BSD things that are built that way develop new spin-off groups each week, while Linux, which is more loosely coupled, doesn't fork."

He elaborates, "Somebody pointed out that there's a parallel of politics. Rigid political and social institutions tend to change violently if they change at all, while ones with more play in them tend to change peacefully."

But this distinction may be semantic. Forking does occur in the Linux realm, but it happens as small diversions that get explained away with other words. Red Hat may choose to use GNOME, while another distribution like SuSE might choose KDE. The users will see a big difference because both tools create virtual desktop environments. You can't miss them. But people won't label this a fork. Both distributions are using the same Linux kernel and no one has gone off and said, "To hell with Linus, I'm going to build my own version of Linux." Everyone's technically still calling themselves Linux, even if they're building something that looks fairly different on the surface.

Jason Wright, one of the developers on the OpenBSD team, sees the organization as a good thing. "The one thing that all of the BSDs have over Linux is a unified source tree. We don't have Joe Blow's tree or Bob's tree," he says. In other words, when they fork, they do it officially, with great ceremony, and make sure the world knows of their separate creations. They make a clear break, and this makes it easier for developers.

Wright says that this single source tree made it much easier for them to turn OpenBSD into a very secure OS. "We've got the security over Linux. They've recently been doing a security audit for Linux, but they're going to have a lot more trouble. There's not one place to go for the source code."

To extend this to political terms, the Linux world is like the 1980s when Ronald Reagan ran the Republican party with the maxim that no one should ever criticize another Republican. Sure, people argued internally about taxes, abortion, crime, and the usual controversies, but they displayed a rare public cohesion. No one criticizes Torvalds, and everyone is careful to pay lip service to the importance of Linux cohesion even as they're essentially forking by choosing different packages.

The BSD world, on the other hand, is like the biblical realm in Monty Python's film *The Life of Brian*. In it, one character enumerates the various splinter groups opposing the occupation by the Romans. There is the People's Front of Judea, the Judean People's Front, the Front of Judean People, and several others. All are after the same thing and all are manifestly separate. The BSD world may share a fair amount of code; it may share the same goals, but it just presents it as coming from three different camps.

John Gilmore, one of the founders of the free software company Cygnus and a firm believer in the advantages of the GNU General Public License, says, "In Linux, each package has a maintainer, and patches from all distributions go back through that maintainer. There is a sense of cohesion. People at each distribution work to reduce their differences from the version released by the maintainer. In the BSD world, each tree thinks they own each program—they don't send changes back to a central place because that violates the ego model."

Jordan Hubbard, the leader of FreeBSD, is critical of Raymond's characterization of the BSD world. "I've always had a special place in my heart for that paper because he painted positions that didn't exist," Hubbard said of Raymond's piece "The Cathedral and the Bazaar." "You could point to just the Linux community and decide which part was cathedral-oriented and which part was bazaar-oriented.

"Every single OS has cathedral parts and bazaar parts. There are some aspects of development that you leave deliberately unfocused and you let people contribute at their own pace. It's sort of a bubble-up model and that's the bazaar part. Then you have the organizational part of every project. That's the cathedral part. They're the gatekeepers and the standards setters. They're necessary, too," he said.

When it comes right down to it, there's even plenty of forking going on about the definition of a fork. When some of the Linux team point at the BSD world and start making fun about the forks, the BSD team gets defensive. The BSD guys always get defensive because their founder isn't on the cover of all the magazines. The Linux team hints that maybe, if they weren't forking, they would have someone with a name in lights, too.

Hubbard is right. Linux forks just as much, they just call it a distribution or an experimental kernel or a patch kit. No one has the chutzpah to spin off their own rival political organization. No one has the political clout.

A Fork, a Split, and a Reunion

Now, after all of the nasty stories of backstabbing and bickering, it is important to realize that there are actually some happy stories of forks that merge back together. One of the best stories comes from the halls of an Internet security company, C2Net, that dealt with a fork in a very peaceful way.

C2Net is a Berkeley-based company run by some hard-core advocates of online privacy and anonymity. The company began by offering a remailing service that allowed people to send anonymous e-mails to one another. Their site would strip off the return address and pass it along to the recipient with no trace of who sent it. They aimed to fulfill the need of people like whistleblowers, leakers, and other people in positions of weakness who wanted to use anonymity to avoid reprisals.

The company soon took on a bigger goal when it decided to modify the popular Apache web server by adding strong encryption to make it possible for people to process credit cards over the web. The technology, known as SSL for "secure sockets layer," automatically arranged for all of the traffic between a remote web server and the user to be scrambled so that no one could eavesdrop. SSL is a very popular technology on the web today because many companies use it to scramble credit card numbers to defeat eavesdroppers.

C2Net drew a fair deal of attention when one of its founders, Sameer Parekh, appeared on the cover of *Forbes* magazine with a headline teasing that he wanted to "overthrow the government." In reality, C2Net wanted to move development operations overseas, where there were no regulations on the creation of cryptographically secure software. C2Net went where the talent was available and priced right.

In this case, C2Net chose a free version of SSL written by Eric Young known as SSLeay. Young's work is another of the open source success stories. He wrote the original version as a hobby and released it with a BSD-like license. Everyone liked his code, downloaded it, experimented with it, and used it to explore the boundaries of the protocol. Young was just swapping code with the Net and having a good time.

Parekh and C2Net saw an opportunity. They would merge two free products, the Apache web server and Young's SSLeay, and make a secure version so people could easily set up secure commerce sites for the Internet. They called this product Stronghold and put it on the market commercially.

C2Net's decision to charge for the software rubbed some folks the wrong way. They were taking two free software packages and making something commercial out of them. This wasn't just a fork, it seemed like robbery to some. Of course, these complaints weren't really fair. Both collections of code emerged with a BSD-style license that gave everyone the right to create and sell commercial additions to the product. There wasn't any GPL-like requirement that they give back to the community. If no one wanted a commercial version, they shouldn't have released the code with a very open license in the first place.

Parekh understands these objections and says that he has weathered plenty of criticism on the internal mailing lists. Still, he feels that the Stronghold product contributed a great deal to the strength of Apache by legitimizing it.

"I don't feel guilty about it. I don't think we've contributed a whole lot of source code, which is one of the key metrics that the people in the Apache group are using. In my perspective, the greatest contribution we've made is market acceptance," he said.

Parekh doesn't mean that he had to build market acceptance among web developers. The Apache group was doing a good job of accomplishing that through their guerrilla tactics, excellent product, and free price tag. But no one was sending a message to the higher levels of the computer industry, where long-term plans were being made and corporate deals were being cut. Parekh feels that he built first-class respectability for the Apache name by creating and supporting a first-class product that big corporations could use successfully. He made sure that everyone knew that Apache was at the core of Stronghold, and people took notice.

Parekh's first job was getting a patent license from RSA Data Security. Secure software like SSL relies on the RSA algorithm, an idea that was patented by three MIT professors in the 1970s. This patent is controlled by RSA Data Security. While the company publicized some of its licensing terms and went out of its way to market the technology, negotiating a license was not a trivial detail that could be handled by some free software team. Who's going to pay the license? Who's going to compute what some percentage of free is? Who's going to come up with the money? These questions are much easier to answer if you're a corporation charging customers to buy a product. C2Net was doing that. People who bought Stronghold got a license from RSA that ensured they could use the method without being sued.

The patent was only the first hurdle. SSL is a technology that tries to bring some security to web connections by encrypting the connections between the browser and the server. Netscape added one feature that allows a connection to be established only if the server has a digital certificate that identifies it. These certificates are only issued to a company after it pays a fee to a registered certificate agent like Verisign.

In the beginning, certificate agents like Verisign would issue the certificates only for servers created by big companies like Netscape or Microsoft. Apache was just an amorphous group on the Net. Verisign and the other authorities weren't paying attention to it.

Parekh went to them and convinced them to start issuing the certificates so he could start selling Stronghold.

"We became number three, right behind Microsoft and Netscape. Then they saw how much money they were making from us, so they started signing certificates for everyone," he said. Other Apache projects that used SSL found life much easier once Parekh showed Verisign that there was plenty of money to be made from folks using free software.

Parekh does not deny that C2Net has not made many contributions to the code base of Apache, but he doesn't feel that this is the best measure. The political and marketing work of establishing Apache as a worthwhile tool is something that he feels may have been more crucial to its long-term health. When he started putting money in the hands of Verisign, he got those folks to realize that Apache had a real market share. That cash talked.

The Stronghold fork, however, did not make everyone happy. SSL is an important tool and someone was going to start creating another free version. C2Net hired Eric Young and his collaborator Tim Hudson and paid them to do some work for Stronghold. The core version of Young's original SSLeay stayed open, and both continued to add bug fixes and other enhancements over time. Parekh felt comfortable with this relationship. Although Stronghold was paying the salaries of Young and

Hudson, they were also spending some of their spare time keeping their SSLeay toolkit up to date.

Still, the notion of a free version of SSL was a tempting project for someone to undertake. Many people wanted it. Secure digital commerce demanded it. There were plenty of economic incentives pushing for it to happen. Eventually, a German named Ralf S. Engelschall stepped up and wrote a new version he called mod_SSL. Engelschall is a well-regarded contributor to the Apache effort, and he has written or contributed to a number of different modules that could be added to Apache. He calls one the "all-dancing-all-singing mod_rewrite module" for handling URLs easily.

Suddenly, Engelschall's new version meant that there were dueling forks. One version came out of Australia, where the creators worked for a company selling a proprietary version of the code. C2Net distributed the Australian version and concentrated on making their product easy to install. The other came out of Europe, distributed for free by someone committed to an open source license. The interface may have been a bit rougher, but it didn't cost any money and it came with the source code. The potential for battle between SSLeay and mod_SSL could have been great.

The two sides reviewed their options. Parekh must have felt a bit frustrated and at a disadvantage. He had a company that was making a good product with repeat buyers. Then an open source solution came along. C2Net's Stronghold cost money and didn't come with source code, while Engelschall's mod_SSL cost nothing and came with code. Those were major negatives that he could combat only by increasing service. When Engelschall was asked whether his free version was pushing C2Net, he sent back the e-mail with the typed message, "[grin]."

In essence, C2Net faced the same situation as many major companies like Microsoft and Apple do today. The customers now had a viable open source solution to their problems. No one had to pay C2Net for the software. The users in the United States needed a patent license, but that would expire in late 2000. Luckily, Parekh is a true devotee to the open source world, even though he has been running a proprietary source company for the last several years. He looked at the problem and decided that the only way to stay alive was to join forces and mend the fork.

To make matters worse, Hudson and Young left C2Net to work for RSA Data Security. Parekh lost two important members of his team, and he faced intense competition. Luckily, his devotion to open source came to the rescue. Hudson and Young couldn't take back any of the work they did on SSLeay. It was open source and available to everyone.

Parekh, Engelschall, several C2Net employees, and several others sat down (via e-mail) and created a new project they called OpenSSL. This group would carry the torch of SSLeay and keep it up-to-date. Young and Hudson stopped contributing and devoted their time to creating a commercial version for RSA Data Security.

Parekh says of the time, "Even though it was a serious setback for C2Net to have RSA pirate our people, it was good for the public. Development really accelerated when we started OpenSSL. More people became involved and control became less centralized. It became more like the Apache group. It's a lot bigger than it was before and it's much easier for anyone to contribute."

Parekh also worked on mending fences with Engelschall. C2Net began to adopt some of the mod_SSL code and blend it into their latest version of Stronghold. To make this blending easier, C2Net began sending some of their formerly proprietary code back to Engelschall so he could mix it with mod_SSL by releasing it as open source. In essence, C2Net was averting a disastrous competition by making nice and sharing with this competitor. It is a surprising move that might not happen in regular business.

Parekh's decision seems open and beneficent, but it has a certain amount of self-interest behind it. He explains, "We just decided to contribute all of the features we had into mod_SSL so we could start using mod_SSL internally, because it makes our maintenance of that easier. We don't have to maintain our own proprietary version of mod_SSL. Granted, we've made the public version better, but those features weren't significant."

This mixing wasn't particularly complicated—most of it focused on the structure of the parts of the source code that handle the interface. Programmers call these the "hooks" or the "API." If Stronghold and mod_SSL use the same hook structure, then connecting them is a piece of cake. If Engelschall had changed the hook structure of mod_SSL, then the C2Net would have had to do more work.

The decision to contribute the code stopped Engelschall from doing the work himself in a way that might have caused more grief for C2Net. "He was actually planning on implementing them himself, so we were better off contributing ours to avoid compatibility issues," says Parekh. That is to say, Parekh was worried that Engelschall was going to go off and implement all the features C2Net used, and there was a very real danger that Engelschall would implement them in a way that was unusable to Parekh. Then there would be a more serious fork that would further split the two groups. C2Net wouldn't be able to borrow code from the free version of OpenSSL very easily. So it decided to contribute its own code. It was easier to give their code and guarantee that OpenSSL fit neatly into Stronghold. In essence, C2Net chose to give a little so it could continue to get all of the future improvements.

It's not much different from the car industry. There's nothing inherently better or worse about cars that have their steering wheel on the right-hand side. They're much easier to use in England. But if some free car engineering development team emerged in England, it might make sense for a U.S. company to donate work early to ensure that the final product could have the steering wheel on either side of the car without extensive redesign. If Ford just sat by and hoped to grab the final free product, it might find that the British engineers happily designed for the only roads they knew.

Engelschall is happy about this change. He wrote in an e-mail message, "They do the only reasonable approach: They base their server on mod_SSL because they know they cannot survive against the Open Source solution with their old proprietary code. And by contributing stuff to mod_SSL they implicitly make their own product better. This way both sides benefit."

Parekh and C2Net now have a challenge. They must continue to make the Stronghold package better than the free version to justify the cost people are paying.

Not all forks end with such a happy-faced story of mutual cooperation. Nor do all stories in the free software world end with the money-making corporation turning around and giving back their proprietary code to the general effort. But the C2Net/OpenSSL case illustrates how the nature of software development encourages companies and people to give and cooperate to satisfy their own selfish needs. Software can do a variety of wonderful things, but the structure often governs how easy it is for some of us to use. It makes sense to spend some extra time and make donations to a free software project if you want to make sure that the final product fits your specs.

The good news is that most people don't have much incentive to break off and fork their own project. If you stay on the same team, then you can easily use all the results produced by the other members. Cooperating is so much easier than fighting that people have a big incentive to stay together. If it weren't so selfish, it would be heartwarming.

17. CORE

Projects in corporations have managers who report to other managers who report to the CEO who reports to the board. It's all very simple in theory, although it never really works that way in practice. The lines of control get crossed as people form alliances and struggle to keep their bosses happy.

Projects in the world of open source software, on the other hand, give everyone a copy of the source code and let them be the master of the code running on their machine. Everyone gets to be the Board of Directors, the CEO, and the cubicle serfs rolled into one. If a free software user doesn't like something, then he has the power to change it. You don't like that icon? Boom, it's gone. You don't want KDE on your desktop? Whoosh, it's out of there. No vice president in charge of MSN marketing in Redmond is going to force you to have an icon for easy connection to the Microsoft Network on your desktop. No graphic designer at Apple is going to force you to look at that two-faced Picasso-esque MacOS logo every morning of your life just because their marketing studies show that they need to build a strong brand identity. You're the captain of your free software ship and you decide the menu, the course, the arrangement of the deck chairs, the placement of lookouts from which to watch for icebergs, the type of soap, and the number of toothpicks per passenger to order. In theory, you're the Lord High Master and Most Exalted Ruler of all Software Big and Small, Wild and Wonderful, and Interpreted and Compiled on your machine.

In practice, no one has the time to use all of that power. It's downright boring to worry about soap and toothpicks. It's exhausting to rebuild window systems when they fail to meet your caviar-grade tastes in software.

No one has the disk space to maintain an Imelda Marcos–like collection of screen savers, window managers, layout engines, and games for your computer. So you start hanging around with some friends who want similar things and the next thing you know, you've got a group. A group needs leadership, so the alpha dog emerges. Pretty soon, it all begins to look like a corporate development team. Well, kind of.

Many neophytes in the free software world are often surprised to discover that most of the best free source code out there comes from teams that look surprisingly like corporate development groups. While the licenses and the rhetoric promise the freedom to go your own way, groups coalesce for many of the same reasons that wagon trains and convoys emerge. There's power in numbers. Sometimes these groups even get so serious that they incorporate. The Apache group recently formed the Apache Foundation, which has the job of guiding and supporting the development of the Apache web server. It's all very official-looking. For all we know, they're putting cubicles in the foundation offices right now.

This instinct to work together is just as powerful a force in the free software world as the instinct to grab as much freedom as possible and use it every day. If anything, it's just an essential feature of human life. The founders of the United States of America created an entire constitution without mentioning political parties, but once they pushed the start button, the parties appeared out of nowhere.

These parties also emerged in the world of free source software. When projects grew larger than one person could safely handle, they usually evolved into development teams. The path for each group is somewhat different, and each one develops its own particular style. The strength of this organization is often the most important determinant of the strength of the software because if the people can work together well, then the problems in the software will be well fixed.

The most prevalent form of government in these communities is the benign dictatorship. Richard Stallman wrote some of the most important code in the GNU pantheon, and he continues to write new code and help maintain the old software. The world of the Linux kernel is dominated by Linus Torvalds. The original founders always seem to hold a strong sway over the group. Most of the code in the Linux kernel is written by others and checked out by a tight circle of friends, but Torvalds still has the final word on many changes.

The two of them are, of course, benign dictators, and the two of them don't really have any other choice. Both have a seemingly absolute amount of power, but this power is based on a mixture of personal affection and technical respect. There are no legal bounds that keep all of the developers in line. There are no rules about intellectual property or nondisclosure. Anyone can grab all of the Linux kernel or GNU source code, run off, and start making whatever changes they want. They could rename it FU, Bobux, Fredux, or Meganux and no one could stop them. The old threats of lawyers, guns, and money aren't anywhere to be seen.

Debian's Core Team

The Debian group has a wonderful pedigree and many praise it as the purest version of Linux around, but it began as a bunch of outlaws who cried mutiny and tossed Richard Stallman overboard. Well, it wasn't really so dramatic. In fact, "mutiny" isn't really the right word when everyone is free to use the source code however they want.

Bruce Perens remembers the split occurred less than a year after the project began and says, "Debian had already started. The FSF had been funding Ian Murdock for a few months. Richard at that time wanted us to make all of the executables unstripped."

When programmers compile software and convert it from human-readable source code into machine-readable binary code, they often leave in some human readable information to help debug the program. Another way to say this is that the programmers don't strip the debugging tags out of the code. These tags are just the names of the variables used in the software, and a programmer can use them to analyze what each variable held when the software started going berserk.

Perens continued, "His idea was if there was a problem, someone can send a stacktrace back without having to recompile a program and then making it break again. The problem with this was distributing executables unstripped makes them four times as large. It was a lot of extra expense and trouble. And our software didn't dump core anyway. That was really the bottom line. That sort of bug did not come up so often that it was necessary for us to distribute things that way anyways."

Still, Stallman insisted it was a good idea. Debian resisted and said it took up too much space and raised duplication costs. Eventually, the debate ended as the Debian group went their own way. Although Stallman paid Murdock and wrote much of the GNU code on the disk, the GPL prevented him from doing much. The project continued. The source code lived on. And the Debian disks kept shipping. Stallman was no longer titular leader of Debian.

The rift between the group has largely healed. Perens now praises Stallman and says that the two of them are still very close philosophically on the most important issues in the free software world. Stallman, for his part, uses Debian on his machines because he feels the closest kinship with it.

Perens says, "Richard's actually grown up a lot in the last few years. He's learned a lot more about what to do to a volunteer because obviously we're free to walk away at any time."

Stallman himself remembers the argument rather eloquently. "The fact is, I wanted to influence them, but I did not want to force them. Forcing them would go against my moral beliefs. I believe that people are entitled to freedom in these matters, which means that I cannot tell them what to do," he told me. "I wrote the GPL to give everyone freedom from domination by authors of software, and that includes me on both sides."

There's much debate over the best way to be a benign dictator. Eric Raymond and many others feel that Torvalds's greatest claim to success was creating a good development model. Torvalds released new versions of his kernel often and he tried to share the news about the development as openly as possible. Most of this news travels through a mailing list that is open to all and archived on a website. The mailing list is sort of like a perpetual congress where people debate the technical issues behind the latest changes to the kernel. It's often much better than the real United States Congress because the debate floor is open to all and there are no glaring special interests who try to steer the debate in their direction. After some period of debate, eventually Torvalds makes a decision and this becomes final. Usually he doesn't need to do anything. The answer is pretty obvious to everyone who's followed the discussion.

This army is a diverse bunch. At a recent Linux conference, Jeff Bates, one of the editors of the influential website Slashdot (www.slashdot.org), pointed me toward the Debian booth, which was next to theirs. "If you look in the booth, you can see that map. They put a pushpin in the board for every developer and project leader they have around the world. China, Netherlands, Somalia, there are people coming from all over."

James LewisMoss is one of the members, who just happened to be in the Debian booth next door. He lives in Asheville, North Carolina, which is four hours west of the Convention Center in downtown Raleigh. The Debian group normally relies upon local volunteers to staff the booth, answer questions, distribute CD-ROMs, and keep people interested in the project.

LewisMoss is officially in charge of maintaining several packages, including the X Emacs, a program that is used to edit text files, read e-mail and news, and do a number of other tasks. A package is the official name for a bundle of smaller programs, files, data, and documentation. These parts are normally installed together because the software won't work without all of its component parts.

The packager's job is to download the latest software from the programmer and make sure that it runs well with the latest version of the other software to go in the Debian distribution. This crucial task is why groups like Debian are so necessary. If LewisMoss does his job well, someone who installs Debian on his computer will not have any trouble using X Emacs.

LewisMoss's job isn't exactly programming, but it's close. He has to download the source code, compile the program, run it, and make sure that the latest version of the source works correctly with the latest version of the Linux kernel and the other parts of the OS that keep a system running. The packager must also ensure that the program works well with the Debian-specific tools that make installation easier. If there are obvious bugs, he'll fix them himself. Otherwise, he'll work with the author on tracking down and fixing the problems.

He's quite modest about this effort and says, "Most Debian developers don't write a whole lot of code for Debian. We just test things to make sure it works well together. It would be offensive to some of the actual programmers to hear that some of the Debian folks are writing the programs when they're actually not."

He added that many of the packagers are also programmers in other projects. In his case, he writes Java programs during the day for a company that makes point-of-sale terminals for stores.

LewisMoss ended up with this job in the time-honored tradition of committees and volunteer organizations everywhere. "I reported a bug in X Emacs to Debian. The guy who had the package at that time said, 'I don't want this anymore. Do you want it?' I guess it was random. It was sort of an accident. I didn't intend to become involved in it, but it was something I was interested in. I figured 'Hell, might as well.'"

The Linux development effort moves slowly forward with thousands of stories like LewisMoss's. Folks come along, check out the code, and toss in a few contributions that make it a bit better for themselves. The mailing list debates some of the changes if they're controversial or if they'll affect many people. It's a very efficient system in many ways, if you can stand the heat of the debates.

Most Americans are pretty divorced from the heated arguments that boil through the corridors of Washington. The view of the House and Senate floor is largely just for show because most members don't attend the debates. The real decisions are made in back rooms.

The mailing lists that form the core of the different free software projects take all of this debate and pipe it right through to the members. While some discussions occur in private letters and even in the occasional phone call, much of the problem and controversy is dissected for everyone to read. This is crucial because most of the decisions are made largely by consensus.

"Most of the decisions are technical and most of them will have the right answer or the best possible one at the moment," says LewisMoss. "Often things back down to who is willing to do the work. If you're willing to do the work and the person on the other side isn't willing, then yours is the right one by definition."

While the mailing list looks like an idealized notion of a congress for the Linux kernel development, it is not as perfect as it may seem. Not all comments are taken equally because friendships and political alliances have evolved through time. The Debian group elected a president to make crucial decisions that can't be made by deep argument and consensus. The president doesn't have many other powers in other cases.

While the Linux and GNU worlds are dominated by their one great Sun King, many other open source projects have adopted a more modern government structure that is more like Debian. The groups are still fairly ad hoc and unofficial, but they are more democratic. There's less idolatry and less dependence on one person.

The Debian group is a good example of a very loose-knit structure with less reliance on the central leader. In the beginning, Ian Murdock started the distribution and did much of the coordination. In time, the mailing list grew and attracted other developers like Bruce Perens. As Murdock grew busier, he started handing off work to others. Eventually, he handed off central control to Perens, who slowly delegated more of the control until there was no key maintainer left. If someone dies in a bus crash, the group will live on.

Now a large group of people act as maintainers for the different packages. Anyone who wants to work on the project can take responsibility for a particular package. This might be a small tool like a game or a bigger tool like the C compiler. In most cases, the maintainer isn't the author of the software or even a hard-core programmer. The maintainer's job is to make sure that the particular package continues to work with all the rest. In many cases, this is a pretty easy job. Most changes in the system don't affect simple programs. But in some cases it's a real challenge and the maintainer must act as a liaison between Debian and the original programmer. Sometimes the maintainers fix the bugs themselves. Sometimes they just report them. But in either case, the maintainer must make sure that the code works.

Every once and a bit, Debian takes the latest stable kernel from Torvalds's team and mixes it together with all of the other packages. The maintainers check out their packages and when everything works well, Debian presses another CD-ROM and places the pile of code on the net. This is a stable "freeze" that the Debian group does to make sure they've got a stable platform that people can always turn to.

"Making a whole OS with just a crew of volunteers and no money is a pretty big achievement. You can never discount that. It's easy for Red Hat to do it. They're all getting paid. The fact is that Debian makes a good system and still continues to do so. I don't think that there've been that many unpaid, collaborative projects that complex before," says Perens.

When Perens took over at Debian he brought about two major changes. The first was to create a nonprofit corporation called Software in the Public Interest and arrange for the IRS to recognize it as a bona fide charitable organization. People and companies who donate money and equipment can take them off their taxes.

Perens says that the group's budget is about $10,000 a year. "We pay for hardware sometimes. Although a lot of our hardware is donated. We fly people to conferences so they can promote Debian. We have a trade show booth. In general we get the trade show space from the show for free or severely discounted. We also have the conventional PO boxes, accounting, phone calls. The project doesn't have a ton of money, but it doesn't spend a lot, either."

The Debian group also wrote the first guidelines for acceptable open source software during Perens's time in charge. These eventually mutated to become the definition endorsed by the Open Source Initiative. This isn't too surprising, since Perens was one of the founders of the Open Source Initiative.

Debian's success has inspired many others. Red Hat, for instance, borrowed a significant amount of work done by Debian when they put together their distribution, and Debian borrows some of Red Hat's tools. When Red Hat went public, it arranged for Debian members to get a chance to buy some of the company's stock reserved for friends and family members. They recognized that Debian's team of package maintainers helped get their job done.

Debian's constitution and strong political structure have also inspired Sun, which is trying to unite its Java and Jini customers into a community. The company is framing its efforts to support customers as the creation of a community that's protected by a constitution. The old paradigm of customer support is being replaced by a more active world of customer participation and representation.

Of course, Sun is keeping a close hand on all of these changes. They protect their source code with a Community Source License that places crucial restrictions on the ability of these community members to stray. There's no real freedom to fork. Sun's not willing to embrace Debian's lead on that point, in part because they say they're afraid that Microsoft will use that freedom to scuttle Java.

Apache's Corporate Core

The Apache group is one of the more businesslike development teams in the free source world. It emerged in the mid-1990s when the World Wide Web was just blossoming. In the early years, many sites relied on web servers like the free version that came from the NCSA, the super-computer center at the University of Illinois that helped spark the web revolution by writing a server and a browser. This code was great, but it rarely served all of the purposes of the new webmasters who were starting new sites and building new tools as quickly as they could.

Brian Behlendorf, one of the founders of the Apache group, remembers the time. "It wasn't just a hobbyist kind of thing. We had need for commercial-quality software and this was before Netscape released its software. We had developed our own set of patches that we traded like baseball cards. Finally we said, 'We had so many paths that overlap. Why don't we create our own version and continue on our own.'"

These developers then coalesced into a core group and set up a structure for the code. They chose the basic, BSD-style license for their software, which allowed anyone to use the code for whatever purpose without distributing the source code to any changes. Many of the group lived in Berkeley then and still live in the area today. Of course, the BSD-style license also made sense for many of the developers who were involved in businesses and often didn't want to jump into the open source world with what they saw as Stallman's absolutist fervor. Businesses could adopt the Apache code without fear that some license would force them to reveal their source code later. The only catch was that they couldn't call the product Apache unless it was an unmodified copy of something approved by the Apache group.

Several members of the group went off and formed their own companies and used the code as the basis for their products. Sameer Parekh based the Stronghold server product on Apache after his company added the encryption tools used to protect credit card information. Others just used versions of Apache to serve up websites and billed others for the cost of development.

In 1999, the group decided to formalize its membership and create a not-for-profit corporation that was devoted to advancing the Apache server source code and the open source world in general. New members can apply to join the corporation, and they must be approved by a majority of the current members. This membership gets together and votes on a board of directors who make the substantive decisions about the group.

This world isn't much different from the world before the corporation. A mailing list still carries debate and acts as the social glue for the group. But now the decision-making process is formalized. Before, the members of the core group would assign responsibility to different people but the decisions could only be made by rough consensus. This mechanism could be bruising and fractious if the consensus was not easy. This forced the board to work hard to develop potential compromises, but pushed them to shy away from tougher decisions. Now the board can vote and a pure majority can win.

This seriousness and corporatization are probably the only possible steps that the Apache group could take. They've always been devoted to advancing the members' interests. Many of the other open source projects like Linux were hobbies that became serious. The Apache project was always filled with people who were in the business of building the web. While some might miss the small-town kind of feel of the early years, the corporate structure is bringing more certainty and predictability to the realm. The people don't have to wear suits now that it's a corporation. It just ensures that tough decisions will be made at a predictable pace.

Still, the formalism adds plenty of rigidity to the structure. An excited newcomer can join the mailing lists, write plenty of code, and move mountains for the Apache group, but he won't be a full member before he is voted in. In the past, an energetic outsider could easily convert hard work into political clout in the organization. Now, a majority of the current members could keep interlopers out of the inner circle. This bureaucracy doesn't have to be a problem, but it has the potential to fragment the community by creating an institution where some people are more equal than others. Keeping the organization open in practice will be a real challenge for the new corporation.

18. T-SHIRTS

If there's a pantheon for marketing geniuses, then it must include the guy who realized people would pay $1 for several cents' worth of sugar water if it came in a shapely bottle blessed by the brand name Coca-Cola. It might also include the guy who first figured out that adding new blue crystals to detergent would increase sales. It is a rare breed that understands how to get people to spend money they don't need to spend.

The next induction ceremony for this pantheon should include Robert Young, the CEO of Red Hat Software, who helped the Linux and the open source world immeasurably by finding a way to charge people for something they could get for free. This discovery made the man rich, which isn't exactly what the free software world is supposed to do. But his company also contributed a sense of stability and certainty to the Linux marketplace, and that was sorely needed. Many hard-core programmers, who know enough to get all of the software for free, are willing to pay $70 to Red Hat just because it is easier. While some may be forever jealous of the millions of dollars in Young's pocket, everyone should realize that bringing Linux to a larger world of computer illiterates requires good packaging and hand-holding. Free software wouldn't be anywhere if someone couldn't find a good way to charge for it.

The best way to understand why Young ranks with the folks who discovered how to sell sugar water is to go to a conference like LinuxExpo. In the center of the floor is the booth manned by Red Hat Software, the company Young started in Raleigh, North Carolina, after he got through working in the computer-leasing business. Young is in his fifties now and manages to survive despite the fact that most of his company's devotees are much closer to 13. Red Hat bundles together some of the free software made by the community and distributed over the Net and puts it on one relatively easy-to-use CD-ROM. Anyone who wants to install Linux or some of its packages can simply buy a disk from Red Hat and push a bunch of keys. All of the information is on one CD-ROM, and it's relatively tested and pretty much ready to go. If things go wrong, Red Hat promises to answer questions by e-mail or telephone to help people get the product working.

Red Hat sells their disk at prices that range from $29.95 to $149.95. That buys the user a pretty box, three CD-ROMs including some demonstration versions of other software, all of the source code, a manual, and some telephone or e-mail support. That is pretty much like the same stuff that comes in software boxes from a normal company. The manual isn't as nice as the manuals produced by Apple or Microsoft, but it's not too bad.

The big difference is that no one needs to buy the CD-ROM from Red Hat. Anyone can download all of the software from the Net. A friend of mine, Hal Skinner, did it yesterday and told me, "I just plugged it in and the software downloaded everything from the Net. I got everything in the Red Hat 6.0 distribution, and it didn't cost me anything."

Of course, Red Hat isn't hurt too much by folks who grab copies without paying for them. In fact, the company maintains a website that makes it relatively easy for people to do just that. Red Hat didn't write most of the code. They also just grabbed it from various authors throughout the Net who published it under the GNU General Public License. They grabbed it without paying for it, so they're not really put out if someone grabs from them.

The ability to snag GPL'ed software from around the Net keeps their development costs much lower than Sun, Apple, or Microsoft. They never paid most of the authors of the code they ship. They just package it up. Anyone else can just go find it on the Net and grab it themselves. This pretty much guarantees that Red Hat will be in a commodity business.

To make matters worse for Red Hat, the potential competitors don't have to go out onto the Net and reassemble the collection of software for themselves. The GPL specifically forbids people from placing limitations on redistributing the source code. That means that a potential competitor doesn't have to do much more than buy a copy of Red Hat's disk and send it off to the CD-ROM pressing plant. People do this all the time. One company at the exposition was selling copies of all the major Linux distributions like Red Hat, Slackware, and OpenBSD for about $3 per disk. If you bought in bulk, you could get 11 disks for $25. Not a bad deal if you're a consumer.

So, on one side of the floor, Young had a flashy booth filled with workers talking about what you could get if you paid $50 or more for Red Hat's version 6.0 with new enhancements like GNOME. Just a few hundred feet away, a company was selling ripoff copies of the same CDs for $3. Any company that is able to stay in business in a climate like that must be doing something right.

It's not much different from the supermarket. Someone can pay $1 or more for two liters of Coca-Cola, or they can walk over a few aisles and buy Kool-Aid and raw sugar. It may be much cheaper to buy the raw ingredients, but many people don't.

Young is also smart enough to use the competition from other cheap disk vendors to his advantage. He can't do anything about the GPL restrictions that force him to share with knockoff competitors, so he makes the best of them. "When people complain about how much we're charging for free software, I tell them to just go to CheapBytes.com," he said at the Expo. This is just one of the companies that regularly duplicates the CDs of Red Hat and resells them. Red Hat often gets some heat from people saying that the company is merely profiting off the hard work of others who've shared their software with the GPL. What gives them the right to charge so much for other people's software? But Young points out that people can get the software for $3. There must be a rational reason why they're buying Red Hat.

Of course, the two packages aren't exactly equal. Both the original and the knockoff CD-ROM may have exactly the same contents, but the extras are different. The Red Hat package comes with "support," a rather amorphous concept in the software business. In theory, Red Hat has a team of people sitting around their offices diligently waiting to answer the questions of customers who can't get Red Hat software to do the right thing.

In practice, the questions are often so hard or nebulous that even the support team can't answer them. When I first tried to get Red Hat to run on an old PC, the support team could only tell me that they never promised that their package would run on my funky, slightly obscure Cyrix MediaGX chip. That wasn't much help. Others probably have had better luck because they were using a more standard computer. Of course, I had no trouble installing Red Hat on my latest machine, and I didn't even need to contact tech support.

The Red Hat packages also come with a book that tries to answer some of the questions in advance. This manual describes the basic installation procedure, but it doesn't go into any detail about the software included in the distribution. If you want to know how to run the database package, you need to dig into the online support provided by the database's developers.

Many people enjoy buying these extra packages like the manual and the support, even if they never use them. Red Hat has blossomed by providing some hand-holding. Sure, some programmers could download the software from the Internet on their own, but most people don't want to spend the time needed to develop the expertise.

When I say "Red Hat software," I really mean free source software that Red Hat picked up from the Net and knit into a coherent set of packages that should be, in theory, pretty bug free, tested, and ready for use. Red Hat is selling some hand-holding and filtering for the average user who doesn't want to spend time poking around the Net, checking out the different versions of the software, and ensuring that they work well together. Red Hat programmers have spent some time examining the software on the CD-ROM. They've tested it and occasionally improved it by adding new code to make it run better.

Red Hat also added a custom installation utility to make life easier for people who want to add Red Hat to their computer.[1] They could have made this package installation tool proprietary. After all, Red Hat programmers wrote the tool on company time. But Young released it with the GNU General Public License, recognizing that the political

---

[1] Er, I mean to say "add Linux" or "add GNU/Linux." "Red Hat" is now one of the synonyms for free software.

value of giving something back was worth much more than the price they could charge for the tool.

This is part of a deliberate political strategy to build goodwill among the programmers who distribute their software. Many Linux users compare the different companies putting together free source software CD-ROMs and test their commitment to the free software ideals. Debian, for instance, is very popular because it is a largely volunteer project that is careful to only include certified free source software on their CD-ROMs. Debian, however, isn't run like a business and it doesn't have the same attitude. This volunteer effort and enlightened pursuit of the essence of free software make the Debian distribution popular among the purists.

Distributors like Caldera, on the other hand, include nonfree software with their disk. You pay $29.95 to $149.95 for a CD-ROM and get some nonfree software like a word processor tossed in as a bonus. This is a great deal if you're only going to install the software once, but the copyright on the nonfree software prevents you from distributing the CD-ROM to friends. Caldera is hoping that the extras it throws in will steer people toward its disk and get them to choose Caldera's version of Linux. Many of the purists, like Richard Stallman, hate this practice and think it is just a not very subtle way to privatize the free software. If the average user isn't free to redistribute all the code, then there's something evil afoot. Of course, Stallman or any of the other software authors can't do anything about this because they made their software freely distributable.

Young is trying to walk the line between these two approaches. Red Hat is very much in the business of selling CD-ROMs. The company has a payroll with more than a handful of programmers who are drawing nonvolunteer salaries to keep the distributions fresh and the code clean. But he's avoided the temptation of adding not-so-free code to his disks. This gives him more credibility with the programmers who create the software and give it away. In theory, Young doesn't need to ingratiate himself to the various authors of GPL-protected software packages. They've already given the code away. Their power is gone. In practice, he gains plenty of political goodwill by playing the game by their rules.

Several companies are already making PCs with Linux software installed at the factory. While they could simply download the software from the Net themselves and create their own package, several have chosen to bundle Red Hat's version with their machines. Sam Ockman, the president of Penguin Computing, runs one of those companies.

Ockman is a recent Stanford graduate in his early twenties and a strong devotee of the Linux and GPL world. He says he started his company to prove that Linux could deliver solid, dependable servers that could compete with the best that Sun and Microsoft have to offer.

Ockman has mixed feelings about life at Stanford. While he fondly remembers the "golf course–like campus," he says the classes were too easy. He graduated with two majors despite spending plenty of time playing around with the Linux kernel. He says that the computer science department's hobbled curriculum drove him to Linux. "Their whole CS community is using a stupid compiler for C on the Macintosh," he says. "Why don't they start you off on Linux? By the time you get to [course] 248, you could hack on the Linux kernel or your own replacement kernel. It's just a tragedy that you're sitting there writing virtual kernels on a Sun system that you're not allowed to reboot."

In essence, the computer science department was keeping their kids penned up in the shallow end of the pool instead of taking them out into the ocean. Ockman found the ocean on his own time and started writing GPL-protected code and contributing to the political emergence of free software.

When Ockman had to choose a version of Linux for his Penguin computers, he chose Red Hat. Bob Young's company made the sale because it was playing by the rules of the game and giving software back with a GPL. Ockman says, "We actually buy the box set for every single one. Partially because the customers like to get the books, but also to support Red Hat. That's also why we picked Red Hat. They're the most free of all of the distributions."

Debian, Ockman concedes, is also very free and politically interesting, but says that his company is too small to support multiple distributions. "We only do Red Hat. That was a very strategic decision on our part. All of the distributions are pretty much the same, but there are slight differences in this and that. We could have a twelve-person Debian group, but it would just be a nightmare for us to support all of these different versions of Linux."

Of course, Penguin Computing could have just bought one Red Hat CD-ROM and installed their software on all of the machines going out the door. That would have let them cut their costs by about $50. The GPL lets anyone install the software as often as they wish. But this wouldn't be pure savings because Ockman is also offloading some of his own work when he bundles a Red Hat package with his computers. He adds, "Technically the box set I include allows customers to call Red Hat, but no one ever does, nor do we expect them or want them to call anyone but us." In essence, his company is adding some extra support with the Red Hat box.

The support is an important add-on that Young is selling, but he realized long ago that much more was on sale. Red Hat was selling an image, the sense of belonging, and the indeterminant essence of cool. Soda manufacturers realized that anyone could put sugar and water in a bottle, but only the best could rise above the humdrum nature of life by employing the best artists in the land to give their sugar water the right hip feeling. So Young invested in image. His T-shirts and packages have always been some of the most graphically sophisticated on the market. While some folks would get girlfriends or neighbors to draw the images that covered their books and CDs, Red Hat used a talented team to develop their packaging.

Young jokes about this. He said he was at a trade show talking to a small software company that was trying to give him one of their free promotional T-shirts. He said, "Why don't you try giving away the source code and selling the T-shirts?"

At the LinuxExpo, Red Hat was selling T-shirts, too. One slick number retailing for $19 just said "The Revolution of Choice" in Red Hat's signature old typewriter font. Others for sale at the company's site routinely run for $15 or more. They sucked me in. When I ordered my first Red Hat disk from them, I bought an extra T-shirt to go with the mix.

The technology folks at Red Hat may be working with some cutting-edge software that makes the software easy to install, but the marketing group was stealing its plays from Nike, Pepsi, and Disney. They weren't selling running shoes, sugar water, or a ride on a roller coaster—they were selling an experience. Red Hat wasn't repackaging some hacker's science project from the Net, it was offering folks a ticket to a revolution. If the old 1960s radicals had realized this, they might have been able to fund their movement without borrowing money from their square parents. Selling enough groovy, tie-died T-shirts would have been enough.[2]

Many of the other groups are part of the game. The OpenBSD project sold out of their very fashionable T-shirts with wireframe versions of its little daemon logo soon after the beginning of the LinuxExpo. They continue to sell more T-shirts from their website. Users can also buy CD-ROMs from OpenBSD.

Several attendees wear yellow copyleft shirts that hold an upside-down copyright logo (⊚) arranged so the open side points to the left.

The most expensive T-shirt at the show came with a logo that imitated one of the early marketing images of the first *Star Wars* movie. The shirt showed Torvalds and Stallman instead of Han Solo and Luke Skywalker under a banner headline of "OS Wars." The shirt cost only $100, but "came with free admission to the upcoming Linux convention in Atlanta."

The corporate suits, of course, have adjusted as best they can. The IBM folks at the show wore identical khaki outfits with nicely cut and relatively expensive polo shirts with IBM logos. A regular suit would probably stick out less than the crisp, clean attempt to split the difference between casual cool and button-down business droid.

Of course, the T-shirts weren't just about pretty packaging and slick images. The shirts also conveyed some information about someone's political affiliations in the community and showed something about the person's technical tastes. Sure, someone could wear an OpenBSD shirt because they liked the cute little daemon logo, but also because they wanted to show that they cared about security. The OpenBSD project began because some users wanted to build a version of UNIX that was much more secure. The group prides itself on fixing bugs early and well. Wearing an OpenBSD shirt proclaims a certain alliance with this

---

[2]Apple is an old hand at the T-shirt game, and internal projects create T-shirts to celebrate milestones in development. These images were collected in a book, which may be as good a technical history of Apple as might exist. Many projects, including ones that failed, are part of the record.

team's commitment to security. After all, some of the profits from the shirts went to pay for the development of the software. Wearing the right T-shirt meant choosing an alliance. It meant joining a tribe.

Young is keenly aware that much of his target market is 13-year-old boys who are flexing their minds and independence for the first time. The same images of rebellion that brought James Dean his stardom are painted on the T-shirts. Some wear shirts proclaiming TOTAL WORLD DOMINATION SOON. Raging against Microsoft is a cliché that is avoided as much as it is still used. The shirts are a mixture of parody, bluster, wit, and confidence. Of course, they're usually black. Everyone wears black.

Ockman looks at this market competition for T-shirts and sees a genius. He says, "I think Bob Young's absolutely brilliant. Suddenly he realized that there's no future in releasing mainframes. He made a jump after finding college kids in Carolina [using Linux]. For him to make that jump is just amazing. He's a marketing guy. He sat down and figured it out.

"Every time I hear him talk," Ockman says about Young, "he tells a different story about ketchup. If you take people who've never had ketchup before in their life and you blindly feed them ketchup, they have no taste for ketchup. They don't like it." If you feed them ketchup over time, they begin to demand it on their hamburgers.

"No one who's never had Coca-Cola before would like it," Ockman continues. "These things are purely a branding issue. It has to be branded for cool in order for people to sit down and learn everything they have to know."

In essence, Young looked around and saw that a bunch of scruffy kids were creating an OS that was just as good, if not better, than the major OSs costing major sums of money. This OS was, best of all, free for all comers. The OS had a problem, though. The scruffy kids never marketed their software. The deeply intelligent, free-thinking hackers picked up on how cool it was, but the rest of society couldn't make the jump. The scruffy kids didn't bother to try to market it to the rest of society. They were artists.

Most people who looked at such a situation would have concluded that this strange clan of techno-outsiders was doomed to inhabit the periphery of society forever. There was no marketing of the product because there was no money in the budget and there would never be money in the budget because the software was free. Young recognized that you could still market the software without owning it. You could still slap on a veneer of cool without writing the code yourself. Sugar water costs practically nothing, too.

Young's plan to brand the OS with a veneer of cool produced more success than anyone could imagine. Red Hat is by far the market leader in providing Linux to the masses, despite the fact that many can and do "steal" a low-cost version. Of course, "steal" isn't the right word, because Red Hat did the same thing. "Borrow" isn't right, "grab" is a bit casual, and "join in everlasting communion with the great free software contin-uum" is just too enthusiastic to be cool.

In August 1999, Red Hat completed an initial public offering of the shares of its stock, the common benchmark for success in the cash-driven world of Silicon Valley. Many of the principals at Red Hat got rich when the stock opened at $14 a share on August 11 and closed the day at $52. Bob Young, the CEO of Red Hat, started the day with a bit more than 9 million shares or 15 percent of the company. Technically, not all of this was his because he had distributed some (3,222,746 shares, to be exact) to his wife, Nancy, and put some more (1,418,160) in various trusts for his children. Still, this cut adds up to about $468 million. Marc Ewing, executive vice president and chief technology officer, also ended up with a similar amount of money divided between trusts and his own pocket. Matthew Sulzik, the president, who joined in November 1998, got a bit less (2,736,248 shares) in his pot, but he was a relative newcomer. The big investors, Greylock IX Limited Partnership, Benchmark Capital Partners II, and Intel, split up the big part of the rest of the shares.

Now, what happened to the boys who wrote the code? Did Richard Stallman get any of it? Did Linus Torvalds? Some of the major devel-opers like Alan Cox and David Miller already work for Red Hat, so they probably drew shares out of the employee pool. There are thou-sands of names, however, who aren't on anyone's radar screen. They've written many lines of code for naught.

Red Hat tried to alleviate some of the trouble by allocating 800,000 shares to "directors, officers and employees of Red Hat and to open source software developers and other persons that Red Hat believes have contributed to the success of the open source software community and the growth of Red Hat." This group, occasionally known as the "friends and family," was a way to reward buddies. Red Hat drew up a list of major contributors to the open source distribution and sent out invitations.

"Dear open source community member," began the e-mail letter that Red Hat sent to about 1,000 people.

```
In appreciation of your contribution to the open source
community, Red Hat is pleased to offer you this personal,
non-transferable, opportunity. . . . Red Hat couldn't have
grown this far without the ongoing help and support of the
open source community, therefore, we have reserved a
portion of the stock in our offering for distribution
online to certain members of the open source community. We
invite you to participate.
```

Many programmers and developers were touched by the thoughtfulness. The list probably wasn't long enough or inclusive enough to pull everyone into the circle, but it did do a good job of spreading the wealth around. The plan began to backfire, however, when E*Trade began to parcel out the shares. Everyone who made it onto the list filled out a form listing their net worth, and E*Trade attempted to decide who was a sophisticated investor and who wasn't. Some folks who had little money (perhaps because they spent too much time writing free software) were locked out.

One contributor, C. Scott Ananian, wrote about his rejection in *Salon* magazine, "I filled out the eligibility questionnaire myself. I knew they were trying to weed out inexperienced investors, so on every question that related to experience, I asserted the maximum possible. I knew what I was doing. And it was my money, anyway—I had a God-given right to risk it on as foolhardy a venture as I liked."

The article drew plenty of flack and murmurs of a class action lawsuit from the disenfranchised. A discussion broke out on Slashdot, the hardcore site for nerds. Some defended E*Trade and pointed out that a Red Hat IPO was not a lock or a guarantee of wealth. Too many grandmothers had been burned by slick-talking stock salesmen in the past. E*Trade had to block out the little guys for their own protection. Stock can go down as well as up.

Steve Gilliard, a "media operative" at the website NetSlaves, wrote, "If the Red Hat friends and family group were judged by normal standards, there is no brokerage in the U.S. which would let many of them buy into an IPO. In many cases, they would be denied a brokerage account. Poor people are usually encouraged to make other investments, like paying off Visa and Master Card."

Others saw it as a trick to weed out the pool and make sure that E*Trade could allocate the shares to its buddies. The more the small guys were excluded, the more the big guys would get for their funds. In the end, the complaints reached some ears. More people were able to sneak in, but the circle was never big enough for all.

World Domination Pretty Soon?

Red Hat's big pool of money created more than jealousy in the hearts and minds of the open source world. Jealousy was an emotional response. Fear of a new Microsoft was the rational response that came from the mind. Red Hat's pool of cash was unprecedented in the open source community. People saw what the pile of money and the stock options did to Bill Gates. Everyone began to wonder if the same would happen to Red Hat.

On the face of it, most open source developers have little to worry about. All the code on the Red Hat disk is covered with a General Protection License and isn't going to become proprietary. Robert Young has been very open about his promise to make sure that everything Red Hat ships falls under the GPL. That includes the distribution tools it writes in-house.

The GPL is a powerful force that prevents Red Hat from making many unilateral decisions. There are plenty of distributions that would like to take over the mantle of the most popular version of Linux. It's not hard. The source code is all there.

But more savvy insiders whisper about a velvet-gloved version of Microsoft's "embrace and extend." The company first gains control by stroking the egos and padding the wallets of the most important developers.

In time, other Red Hat employees will gradually become the most important developers. They're paid to work on open source projects all day. They'll gradually supplant the people who have day jobs. They'll pick up mindshare. Such a silent coup could guarantee that Red Hat will continue to receive large influxes of cash from people who buy the CD-ROMs.

There are parts of this conspiracy theory that are already true. Red Hat does dominate the United States market for Linux and it controls a great deal of the mindshare. Their careful growth supported by an influx of cash ensured a strong position in the marketplace.

In November 1999, Red Hat purchased Cygnus Solutions, the other major commercial developer of GPL-protected software, which specialized in maintaining and extending the compiler, GCC. Red Hat had 235 employees at the time and Cygnus Solutions had 181. That's a huge fraction of the open source developers under one roof. The Cygnus press release came with the headline, RED HAT TO ACQUIRE CYGNUS AND CREATE OPEN SOURCE POWERHOUSE.

To make matters worse, one of the founders of Cygnus, Michael Tiemann, likes to brag that the open source software prevents competitors from rising up to threaten Cygnus. The GPL guarantees that the competitors will also have to publish their source, giving Cygnus a chance to stay ahead. In this model, any company with the money and stamina to achieve market dominance isn't going to be knocked down by some kids in a garage.

Those are scary confluences. Let's imagine that the conspiracy theory is completely borne out. Let's imagine that all of the other distributions wither away as corporate and consumer clients rush head over heels to put Red Hat on their machines. Red Hat becomes the default in much the same way that Microsoft is the default today. Will Red Hat have the power that Microsoft has today?

Will they be able to force everyone to have a Red Hat Network logon button on their desktop? Perhaps. Many people are going to trust Red Hat to create a good default installation. Getting software to be loaded by default will give them some power.

Can they squeeze their partners by charging different rates for Linux? Microsoft is known to offer lower Windows prices to their friends. This is unlikely. Anyone can just buy a single Red Hat CD-ROM from a duplicator like CheapBytes. This power play won't work.

Can they duplicate the code of a rival and give it away in much the same way that Microsoft created Internet Explorer and "integrated" it into their browser? You bet they can. They're going to take the best ideas they can get. If they're open source, they'll get sucked into the Red Hat orbit. If they're not, then they'll get someone to clone them.

Can they force people to pay a "Red Hat tax" just to upgrade to the latest software? Not likely. Red Hat is going to be a service company, and they're going to compete on having the best service for their customers. Their real competitor will be companies that sell support contracts like LinuxCare. Service industries are hard work. Every customer needs perfect care or they'll go somewhere else next time. Red Hat's honeymoon with the IPO cash will only last so long. Eventually, they're going to have to earn the money to get a return on the investment. They're going to be answering a lot of phone calls and e-mails.

• • •

19. NEW

Most of this book frames the entire free source movement as something new and novel. The notion of giving away free source code is something that seems strange and counterintuitive. But despite all of the gloss and excitement about serious folks doing serious work and then just *giving it away* like great philanthropists, it's pretty easy to argue that this has all been done before. The software world is just rediscovering secrets that the rest of the world learned long ago.

Giving things away isn't a radical idea. People have been generous since, well, the snake gave Eve that apple. Businesses love to give things away in the hope of snagging customers. Paper towel manufacturers give away towel hardware that only accepts paper in a proprietary size. Food companies give coolers and freezers to stores if the stores agree not to stock rival brands in them.

In fact, most industries do more than just give away free gifts to lure customers. Most share ideas, strategies, and plans between competitors because cooperation lets them all blossom. Stereo companies make components that interoperate because they adhere to the same standard. Lawyers, engineers, and doctors are just some of the people who constantly trade ideas and solutions with each other despite the fact that they work as competitors. A broad, central, unowned pool of knowledge benefits everyone in much the same way that it helps the free software community.

The real question is not "Who do these pseudo-commie pinkos think they are?" It's "What took the software industry so long to figure this out?" How did the programmers who are supposedly a bunch of whip-smart, hard-core libertarians let a bunch of lawyers lead them down a path that put them in a cubicle farm and prevented them from talking to each other?

Recipes are one of the closest things to software in the material world, and many restaurants now share them widely. While chefs once treated them like industrial secrets, they now frequently give copies to magazines and newspapers as a form of publicity. The free advertisement is worth more than the possibility that someone will start cloning the recipe. The restaurants recognized that they were selling more than unique food. Ambiance, service, and quality control are often more in demand than a particular recipe.

When the free software industry succeeds by sharing the source code now, it's capitalizing on the fact that most people don't want to use the source code to set up a take-no-prisoners rivalry. Most people just want to get their work done. The cost of sharing source code is so low that it doesn't take much gain to make it worth the trouble. One bug fix or tiny feature could pay for it.

Shareware Is Not Open Source and Open Source Isn't Free

The software industry has been flirting with how to make money off of the low cost of distributing its product. The concept of shareware began long before the ideological free software movement as companies and individual developers began sharing the software as a cheap form of advertisement. Developers without the capital to start a major marketing campaign have passed around free versions of their software. People could try it and if it met their needs, they could pay for it. Those who didn't like it were honor-bound to erase their version.

Shareware continues to be popular to this day. A few products have made a large amount of money with this approach, but most have made very little. Some people, including many of the major companies, distribute their own crippled version of their product so people can try it. Crucial functions like the ability to print or save a document to the disk are usually left out as a strong encouragement to buy the real version.

Of course, free source products aren't the same thing as shareware because most shareware products don't come with the source code. Programmers don't have the ability or the right to modify them to do what they want. This has always been one of the biggest selling points to the high-end marketplace that knows how to program.

In fact, free source software is not dirt cheap either. Anyone who's been around the open software community for a time realizes that you end up having to pay something for the lunch. Keeping some costs hidden from the consumer isn't new, and it still hasn't gone away in the free software world. The costs may not be much and they may be a much better deal than the proprietary marketplace, but the software still costs something.

The simplest cost is time. Free software is often not as polished as many commercial products. If you want to use many of the tools, you must study manuals and learn to think like a programmer. Some manuals are quite nice, but many are cursory. This may change as the free software movement aims to dominate the desktop, but the manuals and help aren't as polished as the solutions coming out of Microsoft. Of course, one free software devotee told me by way of apology, "Have you actually tried using Microsoft's manuals or help? They suck, too."

Even when it is polished, free source software requires time to use. The more options that are available, the more time it takes to configure the software. Free source gives tons of options.

The lack of polish isn't usually a problem for programmers, and it's often not an extra cost either. Programmers often need to learn a system before they find a way to revise and extend it to do what their boss wants it to do. Learning the guts of a free software package isn't much of an extra cost because they would be just trying to learn the guts of a Microsoft product instead. Plus, the source code makes the process easier.

Still, most users including the best programmers end up paying a company like Red Hat, Caldera, or a group like OpenBSD to do some of the basic research in building a Linux system. All of the distribution companies charge for a copy of their software and throw in some support. While the software is technically free, you pay for help to get it to work.

If the free source code is protected by the GNU General Public License, then you end up paying again when you're forced to include your changes with the software you ship. Bundling things up, setting up a server, writing documentation, and answering users' questions take time. Sure, it may be fair, good, and nice to give your additions back to the community, but it can be more of a problem for some companies. Let's say you have to modify a database to handle some proprietary process, like a weird way to make a chemical or manufacture a strange widget. Contributing your source code back into the public domain may reveal something to a competitor. Most companies won't have this problem, but being forced to redistribute code always has costs.

Of course, the cost of this is debatable. Tivo, for instance, is a company that makes a set-top box for recording television content on an internal hard disk. The average user just sees a fancy, easy-to-use front end, but underneath, the entire system runs on the Linux operating system. Tivo released a copy of the stripped-down version of Linux it ships on its machines on its website, fulfilling its obligation to the GNU GPL. The only problem I've discovered is that the web page (www.tivo.com/linux/) is not particularly easy to find from the home page. If I hadn't known it was there, I wouldn't have found it.

Of course, companies that adopt free source software also end up paying in one way or another because they need to hire programmers to keep the software running. This isn't necessarily an extra cost because they would have hired Microsoft experts anyway. Some argue that the free source software is easier to maintain and thus cheaper to use, but these are difficult arguments to settle.

In each of these ways, the free software community is giving away something to spark interest and then finding a way to make up the cost later. Some in the free software community sell support and others get jobs. Others give back their extensions and bug fixes. A running business is a working ecology where enough gets reinvested to pay for the next generation of development. The free source world isn't a virtual single corporation like the phone company or the cable business, but it can be thought of in that way. Therefore, the free software isn't much different from the free toasters at the banks, the free lollipops at the barber's, or the free drugs from the neighborhood pusher.

If you want to think bigger, it may be better to see the free software world as closer to the great socialized resources like the ocean, the freeway system, or the general utility infrastructure. These treat everyone equally and provide a common basis for travel and commerce.

Of course, that's the most cynical way that free software is no different from many of the other industries. There are other ways that the free source vision is just a return to the way that things used to be before the software industry mucked them up. The problem is that a mixture of licensing, copyright, and patent laws have given the software industry more ways to control their product than virtually any other industry. The free source movement is more a reaction against these controls than a brave new experiment.

Would You License a Car from These Guys?

Comparing the software industry to the car industry is always a popular game. Normally, the car industry looks a bit poky and slow off the mark because they haven't been turning out new products that are twice as fast and twice as efficient as last year's products. But many parts of the car industry are bright, shining examples of freedom compared to their software equivalents.

Consider the Saturday afternoon mechanic who likes to change the oil, put in a new carburetor, swap the spark plugs, and keep the car in running order. The car guy can do all of these things without asking the manufacturer for permission. There's nothing illegal about taking apart an engine or even putting an entirely new, souped-up engine in your car. The environmental protection laws may prohibit adding engines that spew pollutants, but the manufacturer is out of the loop. After all, it's your car. You paid for it.

Software is something completely different. You don't own most of the software you paid for on your computer. You just own a "license" to use it. The difference is that the license can be revoked at any time if you don't follow the rules, and some of the rules can be uncomfortable or onerous. There's nothing wrong with this mechanism. In the right hands, it can be very pleasant. The Berkeley Software Distribution license, for instance, has no real requirements except that you credit the university for its contributions, and the university just revoked that requirement. The GNU Public License is much stricter, but only if you want to change, modify, and distribute the code. In that case, you're only prevented from keeping these changes a secret. That's not a big problem for most of us.

Other licenses are even more stricter. One Microsoft license prevents the programmer from trying to figure out how the software works inside by saying "LICENSEE may not reverse engineer, decompile or disassemble Microsoft Agent." These clauses are popular and found in many software licenses. The company lawyers argue that they ostensibly prevent people from stealing the secrets that are bound up in the software.

These licenses have been interpreted in different ways. The video game maker Accolade, for instance, won its case against the manufacturer Sega by arguing that reverse engineering was the only way to create a clone. If companies couldn't clone, there would be no free market. On the other hand, Connectix lost some of the early court battles when Sony sued them for creating a software clone of the PlayStation. The judge decided that Connectix had violated Sony's *copyright* when they made a copy to study for reverse engineering. In February 2000, an appeals court struck down this ruling, freeing Connectix to sell the emulator again. By the time you read this, the legal landscape will probably have changed again.

In practice, license clauses like this only hurt the honest programmers who are trying to deal with a nasty bug. Most people don't want to steal secrets, they just want to be able to make their software work correctly. Decompiling or disassembling the code is a good way to figure out exactly what is going on inside the software. It can save hours and plenty of grief.

The license even borders on the absurd because the phrase "reverse engineer" is so ambiguous. It may be possible to argue that just learning to use a piece of software is reverse engineering it. Learning how a feature works means learning to predict what it will do. In many cases, the bugs and the glitches in software mean that the features are often a bit unpredictable and only a bit of black-box reverse engineering can teach us how they work. That's not much different from learning the steps that happen inside. Fiddling with shrink-wrapped software is like fiddling with a black box.

Imagine that General Motors or Ford sold their cars with such a do-not-reverse-engineer license. They would either weld the hood shut or add on a special lock and only give the keys to registered dealers who would sign lots of forms that guaranteed that they would keep the workings of the cars secret. No one could change the spark plugs, chop the hood, add a nitro tank, or do anything with the car except drive it around in a completely boring way. Some lawyers at the car companies might love to start shipping cars with such a license. Think how much more they could charge for service! The smart executives might realize that they were hurting their biggest fans, the people who liked to tune, tweak, fiddle, and futz with their machines. They would be stripping away one of the great pleasures of their devices and slowly but surely turning the cars into commodity items that put the owners in legal straitjackets.

Some software companies take the licensing requirements to even greater extremes. One of the most famous examples is the Microsoft Agent software, which allows a programmer to create little animated characters that might give instructions. Some versions of Microsoft Office, for instance, come with a talking paper clip that points out new and improved features. Microsoft released this technology to the general programmer community hoping that people would add the tools to their software and create their own talking characters.

The software is free and Microsoft posts a number of nice tools for using the code on their website. They couldn't leave well enough alone, though, because anyone who wants to use the tool with their code needs to print out and file a separate license with the Microsoft legal staff. Many of the clauses are pretty simple and do useful things like force anyone using the software to try to keep their versions up to date. But the most insidious one ensures that no one will

"...use the Character Animation Data and Image Files to disparage Microsoft, its products or services or for promotional goods or for products which, in Microsoft's sole judgment, may diminish or otherwise damage Microsoft's goodwill in the SOFTWARE PRODUCT including but not limited to uses which could be deemed under applicable law to be obscene or pornographic, uses which are excessively violent, unlawful, or which purpose is to encourage unlawful activities."

In other words, if you want to make the cute animated cartoon say something unkind about Microsoft, Microsoft can simply shut you down. And don't even think about creating a little animated marijuana cigarette for your Grateful Dead softwarepalooza. It's practically illegal just to think bad thoughts in the vicinity of a computer running Microsoft Agent.

Most software licenses are not as bad or as restrictive as the Microsoft Agent license, but many cause their own share of grief. Companies continue to try to come up with more restrictive solutions for combating piracy, and in the end they bother the legitimate users. People are often buying new computers or upgrading a hard disk, and both of these acts require making a copy of old software. Companies that make it too difficult to do these things end up rubbing salt in the wounds of legitimate users who lose a hard disk.

In this context, the free source world isn't a new flowering of mutual respect and sharing, it's just a return to the good old days when you could take apart what was yours. If you bought the software, you can fiddle with it. This isn't the Age of Aquarius, it is the second coming of *Mayberry R.F.D.*, *Home Improvement*, and the *Dukes of Hazzard*.

Other Professions Were Open from the Start

This comparison doesn't have to be limited to the car guys in the garage. Many other professions freely share ideas and operate without the very restrictive covenants of the software industry. The legal business is a great example of a world where people are free to beg, borrow, and steal ideas from others. If someone finds a neat loophole, they can't patent it or prevent others from exploiting it. Once other lawyers hear about it, they'll be filing their own lawsuits for their own clients.[1]

---

[1] The legal system is not perfect. Too many cases are now filed under seal, and the courts are too willing to act as private dispute agencies for big corporations. When the law is locked up in this way, it is not a great example for the free software world.

Consider the world of tobacco liability. Once one state advanced the legal opinion that the tobacco companies were liable for the cost of treating any disease that might emerge from smoking cigarettes, the other states and plenty of lawyers were able to jump on board. Once they settled, the lawyers turned their sights on the gun companies. By the time you read this, they'll probably have moved on to the fat delivery vehicle manufacturers in the fast-food industry and the stress induction groups, aka your employer. The exercise reduction industry, made up of a megalomaniacal consortium of moviemakers, television producers, and, yes, book writers, must be on someone's list.[2]

Free source folks are just as free to share ideas. Many of the rival Linux and BSD distributions often borrow code from each other. While they compete for the hearts and minds of buyers, they're forced by the free source rules to share the code. If someone writes one device driver for one platform, it is quickly modified for another.

The proprietary software world moves slowly in comparison. They keep their ideas secret and people spend thousands of lawyer years on projects just keeping the various licenses straight. Code is shared, but only after lawyers vet the contracts.

The legal industry is also a good example of how the free sharing of ideas, techniques, and strategies does not hurt the income of the practitioners. In fact, lawyers have managed to carve themselves a very nice slice of the nation's income. Most are not as rich as the lucky few who beat the tobacco companies, but they do all right.

Copyright, Tool of Dictators

It would be unfair to the software industry to portray the rest of society as much more sharing and giving. Most of the other industries are fran-

---

[2] The author recommends that you read this on the Stairmaster or a stationary bike, but only after checking with a registered doctor and consulting with a licensed exercise specialist who is thoroughly familiar with your medical history. These medical specialists will be able to tune your workout to provide the optimal fitness benefits so you can live long enough to get Alzheimer's disease.

tically using the legal system and any other means necessary to stay ahead of their competitors. It's just part of doing business.

One of the best examples is content production, which is led by mega-companies like Disney. In recent years, Hollywood has worked hard to get copyright laws changed so that the copyright lasts 95 years instead of 75 years. In 1998, Congress passed the Sonny Bono Copyright Term Extension Act of 1998 (CTEA) that kept works published after 1923 from passing into the public domain until 2019. The industry feels that this gives them the protection to keep creating new items. Creations like Mickey Mouse and Snow White will continue to live in the very safe place controlled by Disney and not fall into the evil hands of the public domain.

Several Harvard professors, Larry Lessig, Charles Nesson, and Jonathan Zittrain of the Berkman Center for Internet & Society at Harvard Law School, and Geoffrey Stewart of the Boston law firm Hale and Dorr filed a lawsuit contesting the act by pointing out that the Constitution provides for a "limited" term. Artists, authors, and creators were given copyright protection, but it was only for a limited amount of time. Afterward, the society could borrow and use the work freely.

There's little doubt that the major Hollywood producers recognize the value of a well-stocked collection of public domain literature. Movies based on works by William Shakespeare, Henry James, and Jane Austen continue to roll out of the studios to the welcoming patrons who buy tickets despite knowing how the story ends. Disney itself built its movie franchise on shared fables like Sleeping Beauty or Snow White. Very few of Disney's animated films (*The Lion King* was one of the first ones) were created in-house from a clean piece of paper. Most were market-tested for acceptance by their years in the public domain. Of course, Disney only pays attention to this fact when they're borrowing an idea to create their own version, not when they're defending the copyright of their own creations. They want to take, not give.

The movie industry, like the proprietary software business, seems to forget just how valuable a shared repository of ideas and solutions can be. In this context, the free source movement isn't an explosion of creative brilliance or a renaissance of cooperation, it's just a return to the good old days when Congress wouldn't slavishly answer the whims of the content industry. If a theater owner wanted to put on a Shakespeare play, the text was in the public domain. If someone wanted to rewrite Jane Austen and create the movie *Clueless*, they were free to do so. In the good old days, copyright faded after a limited amount of time and the public got something back for granting a monopoly to the artist. In the good old days, the artist got something back, too, when the monopoly of other artists faded away.

It's not like this brave new world of total copyright protection has generated superior content. The so-called original movies aren't that different. All of the action movies begin with some death or explosion in the first two minutes. They all run through a few car chases that lead to the dramatic final confrontation. The television world is filled with 30-minute sitcoms about a bunch of young kids trying to make it on their own. It's sort of surprising that Hollywood continues to suggest that the copyright laws actually promote creativity.

It's not hard to believe that we might be better off if some of the characters were protected by an open source license. Superman and Batman have both gone through several decades of character morphing as the artists and writers assigned to the strips change. Of course, that change occurred under the strict control of the corporation with the copyright.

The thousands of fan novels and short stories are better examples. Many fans of movies like *Star Trek* or *Star Wars* often write their own stories using the protected characters without permission. Most of the time the studios and megalithic corporations holding the copyright look the other way. The work doesn't make much money and is usually born out of love for the characters. The lawyers who have the job of defending the copyrights are often cool enough to let it slide.

Each of these novels provides some insight into the characters and also the novelist. While not every novelist is as talented as the original authors, it can still be fun to watch the hands of another mold the characters and shape his or her destiny. The world of the theater has always accepted the notion that directors and actors will fiddle with plays and leave their own marks on them. Perhaps it wouldn't be so bad if writers could have the same latitude after the original author enjoyed a short period of exclusivity.

There are many ways in which the free software world is strange and new to society, but sharing ideas without limitations is not one of them. Almost all businesses let people tinker and change the products they buy. The software industry likes to portray itself as a bunch of libertarians who worship the free market and all of its competition. In reality, the leading firms are riding a wave of power-grabbing that has lasted several decades. The firms and their lawyers have consistently interpreted their rules to allow them to shackle their customers with stronger and stronger bonds designed to keep them loyal and everspending.

This is all part of a long progression that affects all industries. Linus Torvalds explained his view of the evolution when he told the *San Jose Mercury-News*, "Regardless of open source, programs will become really cheap. Any industry goes through three phases. First, there's the development of features people need. Then there's the frills-and-upgrade phase, when people buy it because it looks cool. Then there's the everybody-takes-it-for-granted phase. This is when it becomes a commodity. Well, we're still in the look-cool-and-upgrade stage. In 10 or 15 years you'll be happy with software that's 5 years old. Open source is one sign that we're moving in that direction."

In this light, the free software revolution isn't really a revolution at all. It's just the marketplace responding to the overly greedy approaches of some software companies. It's just a return to the good old days when buying something meant that you owned it, not that you just signed on as a sort of enlightened slave of the system.

• • •

20. NATIONS

Microsoft is an American company. Bill Gates lives in Washington State and so do most of the programmers under his dominion. The software they write gets used around the globe in countries big and small, and the money people pay for the software comes flooding back to the Seattle area, where it buys huge houses, designer foods, and lots of serious and very competitive consumption. Through the years, this sort of economic imperialism has built the great cities of Rome, London, Tokyo, Barcelona, and many other minor cities. History is just a long series of epochs when some company comes up with a clever mechanism for moving the wealth of the world home to its cities. Britain relied on opium for a while. Rome, it might be said, sold a legal system. Spain trafficked in pure gold and silver. Microsoft is selling structured information in one of the most efficient schemes yet.

Of course, these periods of wealth-building invariably come to an abrupt end when some army, which is invariably described as "ragtag," shows up to pillage and plunder. The Mongolian hordes, the Visigoths, and the Vikings are just a few of the lightweight, lean groups that appeared over the horizon and beat the standing army of the fat and complacent society. This was the cycle of boom and doom that built and trashed empire after dynasty after great society.

Perhaps it's just a coincidence that Linus Torvalds has Viking blood in him. Although he grew up in Finland, he comes from the minority of the population for whom Swedish is the native tongue. The famous neutrality during World War II, the lumbering welfare states, the Nobel Peace Prize, and the bays filled with hiding Russian submarines give the impression that the Viking way is just a thing of the past, but maybe some of the old hack and sack is still left in the bloodlines.

The Linux movement isn't really about nations and it's not really about war in the old-fashioned sense. It's about nerds building software and letting other nerds see how cool their code is. It's about empowering the world of programmers and cutting out the corporate suits. It's about spending all night coding on wonderful, magnificent software with massive colonnades, endless plazas, big brass bells, and huge steam whistles without asking a boss "Mother, may I?" It's very individualistic and peaceful.

That stirring romantic vision may be moving the boys in the trenches, but the side effects are beginning to be felt in the world of global politics. Every time Linux, FreeBSD, or OpenBSD is installed, several dollars don't go flowing to Seattle. There's a little bit less available for the Microsoft crowd to spend on mega-mansions, SUVs, and local taxes. The local library, the local police force, and the local schools are going to have a bit less local wealth to tax. In essence, the Linux boys are sacking Seattle without getting out of their chairs or breaking a sweat. You won't see this battle retold on those cable channels that traffic in war documentaries, but it's unfolding as we speak.

The repercussions go deeper. Microsoft is not just a Seattle firm. Microsoft is an American company and whatever is good for Microsoft is usually good, at least in some form, for the United States. There may be some fraternal squabbling between Microsoft and Silicon Valley, but the United States is doing quite well. The info boom is putting millions to work and raising trillions in taxes.

The free software revolution undermines this great scheme in two very insidious ways. The first is subtle. No one officially has much control over a free software product, and that means that no country can claim it as its own. If Bill Gates says that the Japanese version of Windows will require a three-button mouse, then Japan will have to adjust. But Torvalds, Stallman, and the rest can't do a darn thing about anyone. People can just reprogram their mouse. If being boss means making people jump, then no one in the free software world is boss of anything. Free source code isn't on anyone's side. It's more neutral than Switzerland was in World War II. The United States can only take solace in the fact that many of the great free source minds choose to live in its boundaries.

The second effect is more incendiary. Free software doesn't pay taxes. In the last several centuries, governments around the world have spent their days working out schemes to tax every transaction they can find. First, there were just tariffs on goods crossing borders, then the bold went after the income, and now the sales tax and the VAT are the crowning achievement. Along the way, the computer with its selfless ability to count made this possible. But how do you tax something that's free? How do you take a slice out of something that costs nothing?

These are two insidious effects. The main job of governments is to tax people. Occasionally, one government will lust after the tax revenue of another and a war will break out that will force people to choose sides. The GPL and the BSD licenses destroy this tax mechanism, and no one knows what this will bring.

One of the best places to see this destabilization is in the efforts of the United States government to regulate the flow of encryption software around the globe. Open source versions of encryption technology are oozing through the cracks of a carefully developed mechanism for restricting the flow of the software. The U.S. government has tried to keep a lid on the technology behind codes and ciphers since World War II. Some argue that the United States won World War II and many of the following wars by a judicious use of eavesdropping. Codebreakers in England and Poland cracked the German Enigma cipher, giving the Allies a valuable clue about German plans. The Allies also poked holes in the Japanese code system and used this to win countless battles. No one has written a comprehensive history of how code-breaking shifted the course of the conflicts in Vietnam, Korea, or the Middle East, but the stories are bound to be compelling.

In recent years, the job of eavesdropping on conversations around the world has fallen on the National Security Agency, which is loath to lose the high ground that gave the United States so many victories in the past. Cheap consumer cryptographic software threatened the agency's ability to vacuum up bits of intelligence throughout the world, and something needed to be done. If good scrambling software was built into every copy of Eudora and Microsoft Word, then many documents would be virtually unreadable. The United States fought the threat by regulating the export of all encryption source code. The laws allowed the country to regulate the export of munitions, and scrambling software was put in that category.

These regulations have caused an endless amount of grief in Silicon Valley. The software companies don't want someone telling them what to write. Clearing some piece of software with a bureaucrat in Washington, D.C., is a real pain in the neck. It's hard enough to clear it with your boss. Most of the time, the bureaucrat won't approve decent encryption software, and that means the U.S. company has a tough choice: it can either not export its product, or build a substandard one.

There are branches of the U.S. government that would like to go further. The Federal Bureau of Investigation continues to worry that criminals will use the scrambling software to thwart investigations. The fact that encryption software can also be used by average folks to protect their money and privacy has presented a difficult challenge to policy analysts from the FBI. From time to time, the FBI raises the specter of just banning encryption software outright.

The software industry has lobbied long and hard to lift these regulations, but they've had limited success. They've pointed out that much foreign software is as good as if not better than American encryption software. They've screamed that they were losing sales to foreign competitors from places like Germany, Australia, and Canada, competitors who could import their software into the U.S. and compete against American companies. None of these arguments went very far because the interests of the U.S. intelligence community always won when the president had to make a decision.

The free source code world tripped into this debate when a peace activist named Phil Zimmerman sat down one day and wrote a program he called Pretty Good Privacy, or simply PGP. Zimmerman's package was solid, pretty easy to use, and free. To make matters worse for the government, Zimmerman gave away all of the source code and didn't even use a BSD or GPL license. It was just out there for all the world to see.

The free source code had several effects. First, it made it easy for everyone to learn how to build encryption systems and add the features to their own software. Somewhere there are probably several programmers being paid by drug dealers to use PGP's source code to scramble their data. At least one person trading child pornography was caught using PGP.

Of course, many legitimate folks embraced it. Network Solutions, the branch of SAIC, the techno powerhouse, uses digital signatures generated by PGP to protect the integrity of the Internet's root server. Many companies use PGP to protect their e-mail and proprietary documents. Banks continue to explore using tools like PGP to run transaction networks. Parents use PGP to protect their kids' e-mail from stalkers.

The free source code also opened the door to scrutiny. Users, programmers, and other cryptographers took apart the PGP code and looked for bugs and mistakes. After several years of poking, everyone pretty much decided that the software was secure and safe.

This type of assurance is important in cryptography. Paul Kocher, an expert in cryptography who runs Cryptography Research in San Francisco, explains that free source software is an essential part of developing cryptography. "You need source code to test software, and careful testing is the only way to eliminate security problems in cryptosystems," he says. "We need everyone to review the design and code to look for weaknesses."

Today, security products that come with open source code are the most trusted in the industry. Private companies like RSA Data Security or Entrust can brag about the quality of their in-house scientists or the number of outside contractors who've audited the code, but nothing compares to letting everyone look over the code.

When Zimmerman launched PGP, however, he knew it was an explicitly political act designed to create the kind of veil of privacy that worried the eavesdroppers. He framed his decision, however, in crisp terms that implicitly gave each person the right to control their thoughts and words. "It's personal. It's private. And it's no one's business but yours," he wrote in the introduction to the manual accompanying the software. "You may be planning a political campaign, discussing your taxes, or having an illicit affair. Or you may be doing something that you feel shouldn't be illegal, but is. Whatever it is, you don't want your private electronic mail (e-mail) or confidential documents read by anyone else. There's nothing wrong with asserting your privacy. Privacy is as apple-pie as the Constitution."

Initially, Zimmerman distributed PGP under the GPL, but backed away from that when he discovered that the GPL didn't give him much control over improvements. In fact, they proliferated and it made it hard to keep track of who created them. Today, the source code comes with a license that is very similar to the BSD license and lets people circulate the source code as much as they want.

"I place no restraints on your modifying the source code for your own use," he writes in the accompanying documentation, and then catches himself. "However, do not distribute a modified version of PGP under the name 'PGP' without first getting permission from me. Please respect this restriction. PGP's reputation for cryptographic integrity depends on maintaining strict quality control on PGP's cryptographic algorithms and protocols."

Zimmerman's laissez-faire attitude, however, doesn't mean that the software is available with no restrictions. A holding company named Public Key Partners controlled several fundamental patents, including the ones created by Ron Rivest, Adi Shamir, and Len Adleman. Zimmerman's PGP used this algorithm, and technically anyone using the software was infringing the patent.

While "infringing on a patent" has a certain legal gravitas, its real effects are hard to quantify. The law grants the patent holders the right to stop anyone from doing what is spelled out in the patent, but it only allows them to use a lawsuit to collect damages. In fact, patent holders can collect triple damages if they can prove that the infringers knew about the patent. These lawsuits can be quite a hassle for a big company like Microsoft, because Microsoft is selling a product and making a profit. Finding a number to multiply by three is easy to do. But the effects of the lawsuits on relatively poor, bearded peace activists who aren't making money is harder to judge. What's three times zero? The lawsuits make even less sense against some guy who's using PGP in his basement.

Still, the threat of a lawsuit was enough of a cudgel to worry Zimmerman. The costs, however, put a limit on what PKP could demand. In the end, the two parties agreed that PGP could be distributed for noncommercial use if it relied upon a toolkit known as RSAREF made by PKP's sister company, RSA Data Security. Apparently, this would encourage people to use RSAREF in their commercial products and act like some free advertising for the toolkit.

The patent lawsuit, however, was really a minor threat for Zimmerman. In 1994, the U.S. government started investigating whether Zimmerman had somehow exported encryption software by making it available on the Internet for download. While Zimmerman explicitly denounced violating the laws and took pains to keep the software inside the country, a copy leaked out. Some suggest it was through a posting on the Net that inadvertently got routed throughout the world. Was Zimmerman responsible? A branch of the U.S. Customs launched a criminal investigation in the Northern District of California to find out.

Of course, determining how the source code got out of the country was a nearly impossible exercise. Unless Zimmerman confessed or somehow kept some incriminating evidence around, the prosecutors faced a tough job painting him as a lawbreaker. The software was available for free to anyone inside the country, and that meant that everyone had at least an opportunity to break the law. There were no purchase records or registration records. No one knew who had PGP on their disk. Maybe someone carried it across the border after forgetting that the source code was on a hard disk. Maybe a foreigner deliberately came into the U.S. and carried it out. Who knows? Zimmerman says it blew across the border "like dandelion seeds blowing in the wind."

To make matters worse for the forces in the U.S. government that wanted to curtail PGP, the patent held by RSA wasn't filed abroad due to different regulations. Foreigners could use the software without care, and many did. This was the sort of nightmare that worried the parts of the U.S. intelligence-gathering branch that relied upon wholesale eavesdropping.

Eventually, the criminal investigation amounted to nothing. No indictments were announced. No trials began. Soon after the investigation ended, Zimmerman helped form a company to create commercial versions of PGP. While the free versions continue to be available today and are in widespread use among individuals, companies often turn to PGP for commercial products that come with a license from PKP. When the RSA patent expires in September 2000, the people will be free to use PGP again.[1]

---

[1]The GNU project has already worked around many of these impediments. Their Privacy Guard package (GNU PG) is released under the GNU license.

Zimmerman's experiences show how free source code turned into a real thorn in the side of the U.S. government. Businesses can be bought or at least leaned on. Merchandise needs to flow through stores and stores have to obey the law. Red tape can ruin everything. But free software that floats like dandelion seeds can't be controlled. People can give it to each other and it flows like speech. Suddenly it's not a product that's being regulated, but the free exchange of ideas between people, ideas that just happen to be crystallized as a computer program.

Of course, a bureaucracy has never met something it couldn't regulate, or at least something it couldn't try to regulate. Zimmerman's experience may have proved to some that governments are just speed bumps on the infobahn of the future, but others saw it as a challenge. Until the end of 1999, the U.S. government has tried to tighten up the restrictions on open source versions of encryption technology floating around the world. The problem was that many countries around the globe explicitly exempt open source software from the restrictions, and the United States has lobbied to tighten these loopholes.

The best place to begin this story may be in the trenches where system administrators for the U.S. government try to keep out hackers. Theo de Raadt, the leader of the OpenBSD team, likes to brag that the U.S. government uses OpenBSD on its secure internal network. The system designers probably made that choice because OpenBSD has been thoroughly audited for security holes and bugs by both the OpenBSD team and the world at large. They want the best code, and it's even free.

"They're running Network Flight Recorder," de Raadt says. "It's a super sniffing package and an intrusion detection system. They can tell you if bad traffic happens on your private little network that the firewall should have stopped. They have OpenBSD running NFR on every network. They run an IPSEC vpn back to a main network information center where they look and do traffic analysis."

That is, the departments watch for bad hackers by placing OpenBSD boxes at judicious points to scan the traffic and look for incriminating information. These boxes, of course, must remain secure. If they're compromised, they're worthless. Turning to something like OpenBSD, which has at least been audited, makes sense.

"They catch a lot of system administrators making mistakes. It's very much a proactive result. They can see that a sys admin has misconfig-ured a firewall," he says.

Normally, this would just be a simple happy story about the govern-ment getting a great value from an open source operating system. They paid nothing for it and got the results of a widespread, open review looking for security holes.

De Raadt lives in Canada, not the United States, and he develops OpenBSD there because the laws on the export of encryption software are much more lenient. For a time, Canada did not try to control any mass market software. Recently, it added the requirement that shrink-wrapped software receive a license, but the country seems willing to grant licenses quite liberally. Software that falls into the public domain is not restricted at all. While OpenBSD is not in the public domain, it does fit that definition as set out by the rules. The software is distributed with no restrictions or charge. By the end of 1999, senior officials realized that the stop crypt policy was generating too many ironic moments.

This is just another example of how free source software throws the traditional-instincts regulatory system for a loop. Companies sell prod-ucts, and products are regulated. Public domain information, on the other hand, is speech and speech is protected, at least by the U.S. Constitution. Relying on Canada for network security of the Internet was too much.

In January 2000, the U.S. government capitulated. After relentless pressure from the computer industry, the government recognized that high-quality encryption software like OpenBSD was common throughout the world. It also recognized that the quality was so good that many within the United States imported it. The government loos-ened restrictions and practically eliminated them for open source soft-ware. While many people are still not happy with the new regulations, open source encryption software can now flow out of the United States. The distributors need only notify the U.S. government about where the software is available. The commercial, proprietary encryption software was not as lucky. The regulations are now substantially easier on the corporations but they still require substantial review before an export license is granted.

The difference in treatment probably did not result from any secret love for Linux or OpenBSD lurking in the hearts of the regulators in the Bureau of Export Affairs at the Department of Commerce. The regulators are probably more afraid of losing a lawsuit brought by Daniel Bernstein. In the latest decision released in May 1999, two out of three judges on an appeals panel concluded that the U.S. government's encryption regulations violated Bernstein's rights of free speech. The government argued that source code is a device not speech. The case is currently being appealed. The new regulations seem targeted to specifically address the problems the court found with the current regulations.

Encryption software is just the beginning of the travails as the government tries to decide what to do about the free exchange of source code on the Net. Taxes may be next. While people joke that they would be glad to pay 10 percent sales tax on the zero dollars they've spent on GNU software, they're missing some of the deeper philosophical issues behind taxation. Many states don't officially tax the sale of an object; they demand the money for the use of it. That means if you buy a stereo in Europe, you're still supposed to pay some "use tax" when you turn it on in a state. The states try to use this as a cudgel to demand sales tax revenue from out-of-state catalog and mail-order shops, but they haven't gotten very far. But this hasn't stopped them from trying.

What tax could be due on a piece of free software? Well, the state could simply look at the software, assign a value to it, and send the user a bill. Many states do just that with automobiles. You might have a rusted clunker, but they use the Blue Book value of a car to determine the tax for the year and each year they send a new bill. This concept proved to be so annoying to citizens of Virginia that Jim Gilmore won the election for governor with a mandate to repeal it. But just because he removed it doesn't mean that others will leave the issue alone.

If governments ever decide to try to tax free software, the community might be able to fight off the request by arguing that the tax is "paid" when the government also uses the free software. If 7 out of 100 Apache servers are located in government offices, then the government must be getting 7 percent returned as tax.

One of the most difficult problems for people is differentiating between wealth and money. The free software movement creates wealth without moving money. The easy flow of digital information makes this possible. Some folks can turn this into money by selling support or assisting others, but most of the time the wealth sits happily in the public domain.

Today, the Internet boom creates a great pool of knowledge and intellectual wealth for the entire society. Some people have managed to convert this into money by creating websites or tools and marketing them successfully, but the vast pool of intellectual wealth remains open and accessible to all. Who does this belong to? Who can tax this? Who controls it? The most forward-thinking countries will resist the urge to tax it, but how many will really be able to keep on resisting?

21. WEALTH

The writer, P. J. O'Rourke, once pointed out that wealth is a particularly confusing concept to understand. It had nothing to do with being born in the right place. Africa is filled with diamonds, gold, platinum, oil, and thousands of other valuable resources, while Japan has hardly anything underground except subway tunnels and anthrax from strange cults. Yet Japan is still far wealthier even after the long swoon of their postbubble economy.

O'Rourke also pointed out that wealth has nothing to do with raw brains. The Russians play chess as a national sport while Brentwood is filled with dim bulbs like the folks we saw during the O. J. Simpson murder trial. Yet poverty is endemic in Russia, while Brentwood flourishes. Sure, people wait in line for food in Brentwood like they did in Soviet Russia, but this is only to get a table at the hottest new restaurant.

Wealth is a strange commodity, and understanding it keeps economists busy. Governments need to justify their existence in some way, and lately people in the United States use their perception of the "economy" as a measure of how well the government is doing. But many of their attempts to use numbers to measure wealth and prosperity are doomed to failure. One year, the economists seem to be frantically battling deflation, then they turn around and rattle on and on about inflation. They gave up trying to measure the money supply to follow inflation and seem, at times, to be flying the economy by the seat of their pants. Of course, they're not really in charge. One minute you can't have growth without inflation. The next minute you can. It's all a bit like ancient days of tribal living when the high priest was responsible for dreaming up reasons why the volcano did or did not erupt. Some days the money supply smiles upon us, and on other days, she is very, very angry.

Wealth in the free software world is an even slippier concept. There's not even any currency to use to keep score. Let's say we wanted to know or at least guesstimate whether the free source world was wealthy. That's not too hard. Most of the guys hacking the code just want to drink caffeinated beverages, play cool games, and write more code. The endless stream of faster and faster computer boxes makes this as close to a perfect world as there could be. To make matters better, new T-shirts with clever slogans keep appearing. It's a nerd utopia. It's Shangri-La for folks who dig computers.

Of course, deciding whether or not someone is wealthy is not really an interesting question of economics. It's more about self-esteem and happiness. Someone who has simple needs can feel pretty wealthy in a shack. Spoiled kids will never be happy no matter how big their palace. There are plenty of content people in the free software world, but there are also a few who won't be happy until they have source code to a huge, wonderful, bug-free OS with the most features on the planet. They want total world domination.

A more intriguing question is whether the free source world is wealthier than the proprietary source world. This starts to get tricky because it puts Apples up against oranges and tries to make complicated comparisons. Bill Gates is incredibly wealthy in many senses of the word. He's got billions of dollars, a huge house, dozens of cars, servants, toys, and who knows what else. Even his employees have their own private jets. All of the trappings of wealth are there. Linus Torvalds, on the other hand, says he's pretty happy with about $100,000 a year, although several IPOs will probably leave him well off. Microsoft has thousands of programmers who are paid well to write millions of lines of code a year. Most open source programmers aren't paid much to create what they do. If money were a good measure, then the proprietary source world would win hands-down.

But money is the answer only if you want piles of paper with pictures of famous Americans on them. Several countries in Latin America generate huge piles of money from drugs, oil, and other natural resources, but the countries remain quite poor. The leaders who end up with most of the money might like the huge disparity, but it has very distinct limitations. When it comes time for college or medical care, the very rich start flying up to the United States. Johns Hopkins, a hospital in Baltimore near where I live, provides wonderful medical service to the poor who live in the surrounding neighborhood. It also has a special wing with plush suites for rich people who fly in for medical treatment. Many are potentates and high government officials from poor countries around the world.

People in the United States can enjoy the synergies of living near other well-educated, creative, empowered, and engaged citizens. People in poor societies can't assume that someone else will design great roads, build airlines, create cool coffee shops, invent new drugs, or do anything except get by on the few scraps that slip through the cracks to the great unwashed poor. The ultrarich in Latin America may think they're getting a great deal by grabbing all the pie, until they get sick. Then they turn around and fly to hospitals like Johns Hopkins, a place where the poor of Baltimore also enjoy quite similar treatment. Wealth is something very different from cash.

Most folks in the free source world may not have big bank accounts. Those are just numbers in a computer anyway, and everyone who can program knows how easy it is to fill a computer with numbers. But the free source world has good software and the source code that goes along with it. How many times a day must Bill Gates look at the blue screen of death that splashes across a Windows computer monitor when the Windows software crashes? How many times does Torvalds watch Linux crash? Who's better off? Who's wealthier?

The question might be asked, "Is your software better than it was four years ago?" That is, does your software do a better job of fetching the mail, moving the data, processing the words, or spreading the sheets? Is it more intuitive, more powerful, more stable, more feature-rich, more interesting, more expressive, or just better?

The answers to these questions can't be measured like money. There's no numerical quotient that can settle any of these questions. There will always be some folks who are happy with their early-edition DOS word processor and don't see the need to reinvent the wheel. There are others who are still unhappy because their desktop machine can't read their mind.

For the devoted disciples of the open software mantra, the software in the free source world is infinitely better. Richard Stallman feels that the GNU code is better than the Microsoft code just because he has the source code and the freedom to do what he wants with it. The freedom is more important to him than whatever super-duper feature comes out of the Microsoft teams. After all, he can add any feature he wants if he has access to the basic source code. Living without the source code means waiting like a good peon for the nice masters from the big corporation to bless us with a bug fix.

There's no question that people like Stallman love life with source code. A deeper question is whether the free source realm offers a wealthier lifestyle for the average computer user. Most people aren't programmers, and most programmers aren't even the hard-core hackers who love to fiddle with the UNIX kernel. I've rarely used the source code to Linux, Emacs, or any of the neat tools on the Net, and many times I've simply recompiled the source code without looking at it. Is this community still a better deal?

There are many ways of looking at the question. The simplest is to compare features. It's hard to deny that the free software world has made great strides in producing something that is easy to use and quite adaptable. The most current distributions at the time I'm writing this come with a variety of packages that provide all of the functionality of Microsoft Windows and more. The editors are good, the browser is excellent, and the availability of software is wonderful. The basic Red Hat or Caldera distribution provides a very rich user interface that is better in many ways than Windows or the Mac. Some of the slightly specialized products like video software editors and music programs aren't as rich-looking, but this is bound to change with time. It is really a very usable world.

Some grouse that comparing features like this isn't fair to the Mac or Windows world. The GNOME toolkit, they point out, didn't come out of years of research and development. The start button and the toolbar look the same because the GNOME developers were merely copying. The GNU/Linux world didn't create their own OS, they merely cloned all of the hard commercial research that produced UNIX. It's always easier to catch up, but pulling ahead is hard. The folks who want to stay on the cutting edge need to be in the commercial world. It's easy to come up with a list of commercial products and tools that haven't been cloned by an open source dude at the time of this writing: streaming video, vector animation, the full Java API, speech recognition, three-dimensional CAD programs, speech synthesis, and so forth. The list goes on and on. The hottest innovations will always come from well-capitalized start-ups driven by the carrot of wealth.

Others point out that the free software world has generated more than its share of innovation. Most of the Internet was built upon non-proprietary standards developed by companies with Department of Defense contracts. Stallman's Emacs continues to be one of the great programs in the world. Many of the projects like Apache are the first place where new ideas are demonstrated. People who want to mock up a project find it easier to extend free source software. These ideas are often reborn as commercial products. While free source users may not have access to the latest commercial innovations, they have plenty of their own emerging from the open software world. GNOME isn't just a Windows clone—it comes with thousands of neat extensions and improvements that can't be found in Redmond.

Stallman himself says the GNU project improved many pieces of software when they rewrote them. He says, "We built on their work, to the extent that we could legally do so (since we could not use any of their code), but that is the way progress is made. Almost every GNU program that replaces a piece of Unix includes improvements."

Another way to approach the question is to look at people's behavior. Some argue that companies like Red Hat or organizations like Debian prove that people need and want some of the commercial world's hand-holding. They can't afford to simply download the code and fiddle with it. Most people aren't high school students doing time for being young. They've got jobs, families, and hobbies. They pay because paying brings continuity, form, structure, and order to the free source world. Ultimately, these Red Hat users aren't Stallman disciples, they're commercial sheep who are just as dependent on Red Hat as the Windows customers are on Microsoft.

The counterargument is that this insight overlooks a crucial philosophical difference. The Red Hat customers may be slaves like the Microsoft customers, but they still have important freedoms. Sure, many Americans are wage slaves to an employer who pays them as little as possible, but they do have the freedom to go be wage slaves of another employer if they choose. Old-fashioned slaves faced the whip and death if they tried to take that route.

Most Linux users don't need to rewrite the source, but they can still benefit from the freedom. If everyone has the freedom, then someone will come along with the ability to do it and if the problem is big enough, someone probably will. In other words, only one person has to fly the X-wing fighter down the trench and blow up the Death Star.

Some point out that the free source world is fine–if you've got the time and the attention to play with it. The source code only helps those who want to spend the time to engage it. You've got to read it, study it, and practice it to get any value from it at all. Most of us, however, just want the software to work. It's like the distinction between people who relax by watching a baseball game on television and those who join a league to play. The spectators are largely passive, waiting for the action to be served up to them. The league players, on the other hand, don't get anything unless they practice, stretch, push, and hustle. They need to be fully engaged with the game. All of us like an occasional competition, but we often need a soft couch, a six-pack, and the remote control. Free software is a nice opportunity to step up to the plate, but it's not true refreshment for the masses.

Which is a better world? A polished Disneyland where every action is scripted, or a pile of Lego blocks waiting for us to give them form? Do we want to be entertained or do we want to interact? Many free software folks would point out that free software doesn't preclude you from settling into the bosom of some corporation for a long winter's nap. Companies like Caldera and Linuxcare are quite willing to hold your hand *and* give you the source code. Many other corporations are coming around to the same notion. Netscape led the way, and many companies like Apple and Sun will follow along. Microsoft may even do the same thing by the time you read this.

Money isn't the same as wealth, and the nature of software emphasizes some of the ways in which this is true. Once someone puts the hours into creating software, it costs almost nothing to distribute it to the world. The only real cost is time because raw computer power and caffeinated beverages are very inexpensive.

Wealth and Poverty

George Gilder laid out the gap between wealth and money in his influential book *Wealth and Poverty*. The book emerged in 1981 just before Ronald Reagan took office, and it became one of the philosophical touchstones for the early years of the administration. At the time, Gilder's words were aimed at a world where socialist economies had largely failed but capitalists had never declared victory. The Soviet Union was sliding deeper into poverty. Sweden was heading for some of the highest interest rates imaginable. Yet the newspapers and colleges of the United States refused to acknowledge the failure. Gilder wanted to dispel the notion that capitalism and socialism were locked into some eternal yin/yang battle. In his mind, efficient markets and decentralized capital allocation were a smashing success compared to the plodding bureaucracy that was strangling the Soviet Union.

Although Gilder spoke generally about the nature of wealth, his insights are particularly good at explaining just why things went so right for the open software world. "Capitalism begins with giving," he says, and explains that societies flourish when people are free to put their money where they hope it will do the best. The investments are scattered like seeds and only some find a good place to grow. Those capitalists who are a mixture of smart and lucky gain the most and then plow their gains back into the society, repeating the process. No one knows what will succeed, so encouraging the bold risk-takers makes sense.

Gilder's chapter on gift-giving is especially good at explaining the success of the free software world. Capitalism, he explains, is not about greed. It's about giving to people with the implicit knowledge that they'll return the favor severalfold. He draws heavily on anthropology and the writings of academics like Claude Lévi-Strauss to explain how the best societies create capital through gifts that come with the implicit debt that people give something back. The competition between people to give better and better gifts drives society to develop new things that improve everyone's life.

Gilder and others have seen the roots of capital formation and wealth creation in this gift-giving. "The unending offerings of entrepreneurs, investing capital, creating products, building businesses, inventing jobs, accumulating inventories—all long before any return is received, all without assurance that the enterprise will not fail—constitute a pattern of giving that dwarfs in extent and in essential generosity any primitive rite of exchange. Giving is the vital impulse and moral center of capitalism," he writes.

The socialists who've railed against the injustices and brutalities of market capitalism at work would disagree with the strength of his statement, but there are plenty of good examples. The American Civil War was the battle between the northern states where workers were occasionally chained to looms during their shifts and the southern states where the workers were always slaves. In the end, the least cruel society won, in part because of the strength of its industry and its ability to innovate. Companies that discovered this fact flourished and those that didn't eventually failed. By the end of the 20th century, the demand for labor in the United States was so high that companies were actively competing in offering plush treatment for their workers.

The free software world, of course, is a perfect example of the altruistic nature of the potlatch. Software is given away with no guarantee of any return. People are free to use the software and change it in any way. The GNU Public License is not much different from the social glue that forces tribe members to have a larger party the next year and give back even more. If someone ends up creating something new or interesting after using GPL code as a foundation, then they become required to give the code back to the tribe.

Of course, it's hard to get much guidance from Gilder over whether the GPL is better than the BSD license. He constantly frames investment as a "gift" to try to deemphasize the greed of capitalism. Of course, anyone who has been through a mortgage foreclosure or a debt refinancing knows that the banks don't act as if they've given away a gift. There are legal solutions for strong-arming the folks who don't give back enough. He was trying to get readers to forget these tactics a bit and get them to realize that after all of the arms are broken, the bank is still left with whatever the loan produced. There were no ultimate guarantees that all of the money would come back.

Gilder smooths over this with a sharply drawn analogy. Everyone, he says, has experienced the uncomfortable feeling that comes from getting a gift that is the wrong size, the wrong style, or just wrong altogether. "Indeed, it is the very genius of capitalism that it recognizes the difficulty of successful giving, understands the hard work and sacrifice entailed in the mandate to help one's fellow men, and offers a practical way of living a life of effective charity," he writes. It's not enough to give a man a fish, because teaching him to fish is a much better gift. A fish farm that hires a man and gives him stock options may be offering the highest form of giving around.

Gilder does note that the cycle of gifts alone is not enough to build a strong economy. He suggests that the bigger and bigger piles of coconuts and whale blubber were all that emerged from the endless rounds of potlatching. They were great for feasting, but the piles would rot and go stale before they were consumed. The successful society reinterpreted the cycle of gifts as investment and dividends, and the introduction of money made it possible for people to easily move the returns from one investment to the start of another. This liquidity lets the cycles be more and more efficient and gives people a place to store their wealth.

Of course, Gilder admits that money is only a temporary storage device. It's just a tool for translating the wealth of one sector of the economy into the wealth of another. It's just a wheelbarrow or an ox cart. If society doesn't value the contributions of the capitalists, the transfer will fail. If the roads are too rocky or blocked by too many toll collectors, the carts won't make the trip.

At first glance, none of this matters to the free software world. The authors give away their products, and as long as someone pays a minimal amount for storage the software will not decay. The web is filled with source code repositories and strongholds that let people store away their software and let others download it at will. These cost a minimal amount to keep up and the cost is dropping every day. There's no reason to believe that the original work of Stallman will be lost to the disease, pestilence, wear, and decay that have cursed physical objects like houses, clothes, and food.

But despite the beautiful permanence of software, everyone knows that it goes bad. Programmers don't use the term "bit rot" for fun. As operating systems mature and other programs change, the old interfaces start to slowly break down. One program may depend upon the operating system to print out a file in response to a command. Then a new version of the printing code is revved up to add fancier fonts and more colors. Suddenly the interface doesn't work exactly right. Over time, these thousands of little changes can ruin the heart of a good program in much the same way worms can eat the hull of a wooden ship.

The good news is that free source software is well positioned to fix these problems. Distributing the source code with the software lets others do their best to keep the software running in a changing environment. John Gilmore, for instance, says that he now embraces the GPL because earlier experiments with totally free software created versions without accompanying source code.

The bad news is that Gilder has a point about capital formation. Richard Stallman did a great job writing Emacs and GCC, but the accolades weren't as easy to spend as cash. Stallman was like the guy with a pile of whale meat in his front yard. He could feast for a bit, but you can only eat so much whale meat. Stallman could edit all day and night with Emacs. He could revel in the neat features and cool Emacs LISP hacks that friends and disciples would contribute back to the project. But he couldn't translate that pile of whale meat into a free OS that would let him throw away UNIX and Windows.

While Stallman didn't have monetary capital, he did have plenty of intellectual capital. By 1991, his GNU project had built many well-respected tools that were among the best in their class. Torvalds had a great example of what the GPL could do before he chose to protect his Linux kernel with the license. He also had a great set of tools that the GNU project created.

The GNU project and the Free Software Foundation were able to raise money just on the strength of their software. Emacs and GCC opened doors. People gave money that flowed through to the programmers. While there was no cash flow from software sales, the project found that it could still function quite well.

Stallman's reputation also can be worth more than money when it opens the right doors. He continues to be blessed by the implicit support of MIT, and many young programmers are proud to contribute their work to his projects. It's a badge of honor to be associated with either Linux or the Free Software Foundation. Programmers often list these details on their résumés, and the facts have weight.

The reputation also helps him start new projects. I could write the skeleton of a new double-rotating, buzzword-enhanced editor, label it "PeteMACS," and post it to the Net hoping everyone would love it, fix it, and extend it. It could happen. But I'm sure that Stallman would find it much easier to grab the hearts, minds, and spare cycles of programmers because he's got a great reputation. That may not be as liquid as money, but it can be better.

The way to transfer wealth from project to project is something that the free software world doesn't understand well, but it has a good start. Microsoft struck it rich with DOS and used that money to build Windows. Now it has been frantically trying to use this cash cow to create other new businesses. They push MSN, the Microsoft Network, and hope it will stomp AOL. They've built many content-delivery vehicles like Slate and MSNBC. They've created data-manipulation businesses like Travelocity. Bill Gates can simply dream a dream and put 10,000 programmers to work creating it. He has serious intellectual liquidity.

In this sense, the battle between free and proprietary software development is one between pure giving and strong liquidity. The GPL world gives with no expectation of return and finds that it often gets a return of a thousand times back from a grateful world of programmers. The proprietary world, on the other hand, can take its profits and redirect them quickly to take on another project. It's a battle of the speed of easy, unfettered, open source cooperation versus the lightning speed of money flowing to make things work.

Of course, companies like Red Hat lie in a middle ground. The company charges money for support and plows this money back into improving the product. It pays several engineers to devote their time to improving the entire Linux product. It markets its work well and is able to charge a premium for what people are able to get for free.

No one knows if the way chosen by companies like Red Hat and Caldera and groups like the Free Software Foundation is going to be successful in the long run. Competition can be a very effective way of driving down the price of a product. Some worry that Red Hat will eventually be driven out of business by cheap $2 CDs that rip off the latest distribution. For now, though, the success of these companies shows that people are willing to pay for hand-holding that works well.

A deeper question is whether the open or proprietary model does a better job of creating a world where we want to live. Satisfying our wants is the ultimate measure of a wealthy society. Computers, cyberspace, and the Internet are rapidly taking up a larger and larger part of people's time. Television viewership is dropping, often dramatically, as people turn to life online. The time spent in cyberspace is going to be important.

Stallman wrote in *BYTE* magazine in 1986,

> *I'm trying to change the way people approach knowledge and information in general. I think that to try to own knowledge, to try to control whether people are allowed to use it, or to try to stop other people from sharing it, is sabotage. It is an activity that benefits the person that does it at the cost of impoverishing all of society. One person gains one dollar by destroying two dollars' worth of wealth.*

No one knows what life online will look like in 5 or 10 years. It will certainly include web pages and e-mail, but no one knows who will pay how much. The cost structures and the willingness to pay haven't been sorted out. Some companies are giving away some products so they can make money with others. Many are frantically giving away everything in the hope of attracting enough eyeballs to eventually make some money.

The proprietary model rewards risk-takers and gives the smartest, fastest programmers a pile of capital they can use to play the game again. It rewards the ones who satisfy our needs and gives them cash they can use to build newer and bigger models. The distribution of power is pretty meritocratic, although it can break down when monopolies are involved.

But the open source solution certainly provides good software to everyone who wants to bother to try to use it. The free price goes a long way to spreading its bounty to a wide variety of people. No one is excluded and no one is locked out of contributing to the commonweal because they don't have the right pedigree, education, racial heritage, or hair color. Openness is a powerful tool.

Richard Stallman told me, "Why do you keep talking about 'capital'? None of this has anything to do with capital. Linus didn't need capital to develop a kernel, he just wrote it. We used money to hire hackers to work on the kernel, but describing that as capital is misleading.

"The reason why free software is such a good idea is that developing software does not really need a lot of money. If we cannot 'raise capital' the way the proprietary software companies do, that is not really a problem.

"We *do* develop a lot of free software. If a theory says we can't, you have to look for the flaws in the theory."

One of the best ways to illustrate this conundrum is to look at the experiences of the workers at Hotmail after they were acquired by Microsoft. Sure, many of them were overjoyed to receive so much for their share in an organization. Many might even do the same thing again if they had the choice. Many, though, are frustrated by their new position as corporate citizens whose main job is augmenting Microsoft's bottom line.

One Hotmail founder told the PBS Online columnist Robert Cringely, "All we got was money. There was no recognition, no fun. Microsoft got more from the deal than we did. They knew nothing about the Internet. MSN was a failure. We had 10 million users, yet we got no respect at all from Redmond. Bill Gates specifically said, 'Don't screw-up Hotmail,' yet that's what they did."

• • •

22. FUTURE

David Henkel-Wallace sat quietly in a chair in a Palo Alto coffee shop explaining what he did when he worked at the free software firm Cygnus. He brought his new daughter along in a baby carriage and kept her parked alongside. Cygnus, of course, is one of the bigger successes in the free software world. He helped make some real money building and sustaining the free compiler, GCC, that Richard Stallman built and gave away. Cygnus managed to make the real money even after they gave away all of their work.

In the middle of talking about Cygnus and open source, he points to his child and says, "What I'm really worried about is she'll grow up in a world where software continues to be as buggy as it is today." Other parents might be worried about the economy, gangs, guns in schools, or the amount of sex in films, but Henkel-Wallace wants to make sure that random software crashes start to disappear.

He's done his part. The open source movement thrives on the GCC compiler, and Cygnus managed to find a way to make money on the process of keeping the compiler up to date. The free operating systems like Linux or FreeBSD are great alternatives for people today. They're small, fast, and very stable, unlike the best offerings of Microsoft or Apple. If the open software movement continues to succeed and grow, his child could grow up into a world where the blue screen of death that terrorizes Microsoft users is as foreign to them as manual typewriters.

Future

No one knows if the open software world will continue to grow. Some people are very positive and point out that all the features that made it possible for the free OSs to bloom are not going away. If anything, the forces of open exchange and freedom will only accelerate as more people are drawn into the mix. More people mean more bug fixes, which means better software.

Others are not so certain, and this group includes many of the people who are deeply caught up in the world of open source. Henkel-Wallace, for instance, isn't so sure that the source code makes much difference when 99 percent of the people don't program. Sure, Cygnus had great success sharing source code with the programmers who used GCC, but all of those guys knew how to read the code. What difference will the source code make to the average user who just wants to read his e-mail? Someone who can't read the source code isn't going to contribute much back to the project and certainly isn't going to put much value in getting it. A proprietary company like Microsoft may be able to maintain a broad base of loyalty just by offering better hand-holding for the folks who can't program.

Free software stands at an interesting crossroads as this book is being written. It won over a few hackers in garages in the early 1990s. By the mid-1990s, webmasters embraced it as a perfectly good option. Now everyone wonders whether it will conquer the desktop in the next century.

It's always tempting for an author to take the classic TV news gambit and end the story with the earnest punt phrase, "Whether this will happen remains to be seen." That may be the most fair way to approach reporting the news, but it's not as much fun. I'm going to boldly predict that open source software will win the long-term war against proprietary companies, but it will be a bloody war and it will be more costly than people expect. Over the next several years, lawyers will spend hours arguing cases; people will spend time in jail; and fortunes will be lost to the struggle.

While it seems difficult to believe, some people have already spent time in jail for their part in the free software revolution. Kevin Mitnick was arrested in 1995 amid accusations that he stole millions if not billions of dollars' worth of source code. There was no trial, nor even a bail hearing. Finally, after almost five years in prison, Mitnick pled guilty to some charges and received a sentence that was only a few months longer than the time he served while waiting for a trial. Mitnick was accused of stealing millions of dollars from companies by breaking into computers and stealing copies of their source code.

In the statement he made following his release, he said, "... my crimes were simple crimes of trespass. I've acknowledged since my arrest in February 1995 that the actions I took were illegal, and that I committed invasions of privacy—I even offered to plead guilty to my crimes soon after my arrest."

He continued, "The fact of the matter is that I never deprived the companies involved in this case of anything. I never committed fraud against these companies. And there is not a single piece of evidence suggesting that I did so."

This trespass, of course, would be breaking the rules. The irony is that in 1999, Sun announced that it was sharing its source code with the world. They begged everyone to look at it and probe it for weaknesses. The tide of opinion changed and Sun changed with it.

Of course, breaking into a company's computer system will always be bad, but it's hard to view Mitnick's alleged crimes as a terrible thing. Now that source code is largely free and everyone digs public sharing, he begins to look more like a moonshine manufacturer during Prohibition. The free source revolution has given him a rakish charm. Who knows if he deserves it, but the zeitgeist has changed.

There are more arrests on the way. In January 2000, a young Norwegian man was detained by the Norwegian police who wanted to understand his part in the development of software to unscramble the video data placed on DVD disks. Motion picture producers who released their movies in this format were worried that a tool known as DeCSS, which was floating around the Internet, would make it easier for pirates to make unlicensed copies of their movies.

The man, Jan Johansen, did not write the tool, but merely helped polish and circulate it on the Net. News reports suggest an anonymous German programmer did the actual heavy lifting.

Still, Johansen made a great target for the police, who never officially arrested him, although they did take him in for questioning.

At this writing, it's not clear if Johansen officially broke any laws. Some argue that he violated the basic strictures against breaking and entering. Others argue that he circulated trade secrets that were not legimately obtained.

Still others see the motion picture industry's response as an effort to control the distribution of movies and the machines that display them. A pirate doesn't need to use the DeCSS tool to unlock the data on a DVD disk. They just make a verbatim copy of the disk without bothering with the encryption. That leads others to suspect that the true motive is to sharply limit the companies that produce machines that can display DVD movies.

One group that is locked out of the fray is the Linux community. While software for playing DVD movies exists for Macintoshes and PCs, there's none for Linux. DeCSS should not be seen as a hacker's tool, but merely a device that allows Linux users to watch the legitimate copies of the DVDs that they bought. Locking out Linux is like locking in Apple and Microsoft.

The battle between the motion picture community and the Linux world is just heating up as I write this. There will be more lawsuits and prehaps more jail time ahead for the developers who produced DeCSS and the people who shared it through their websites.

Most of the battles are not so dramatic. They're largely technical, and the free source world should win these easily. Open source solutions haven't had the same sophisticated graphical interface as Apple or Windows products. Most of the programmers who enjoy Linux or the various versions of BSD don't need the graphical interface and may not care about it. The good news is that projects like KDE and GNOME are great tools already. The open source world must continue to tackle this area and fight to produce something that the average guy can use.

The good news is that open source software usually wins most technical battles. The free versions of UNIX are already much more stable than the products coming from Microsoft and Apple, and it seems unlikely that this will change. The latest version of Apple's OS has free versions of BSD in its core. That battle is won. Microsoft's version of NT can beat these free OSs in some extreme cases, but these are getting to be rarer by the day. Sun's Solaris is still superior in some ways, but the company is sharing the source code with its users in a way that emulates the open source world. More attention means more programmers and more bug fixes. Technical struggles are easy for open source to win.

Microsoft's greatest asset is the installed base of Windows, and it will try to use this to the best of its ability to defeat Linux. At this writing, Microsoft is rolling out a new version of the Domain Name Server (DNS), which acts like a telephone book for the Internet. In the past, many of the DNS machines were UNIX boxes because UNIX helped define the Internet. Windows 2000 includes new extensions to DNS that practically force offices to switch over to Windows machines to run DNS. Windows 2000 just won't work as well with an old Linux or UNIX box running DNS.

This is a typical strategy for Microsoft and one that is difficult, but not impossible, for open source projects to thwart. If the cost of these new servers is great enough, some group of managers is going to create its own open source clone of the modified DNS server. This has happened time and time again, but not always with great success. Linux boxes come with Samba, a program that lets Linux machines act as file servers. It works well and is widely used. Another project, WINE, started with the grand design of cloning all of the much more complicated Windows API used by programmers. It is a wonderful project, but it is far from finished. The size and complexity make a big difference.

Despite these tactics, Microsoft (and other proprietary companies) will probably lose their quest to dominate the standards on the Internet. They can only devote a few programmers to each monopolistic grab. The free software world has many programmers willing to undertake projects. The numbers are now great enough that the cloners should be able to handle anything Microsoft sends its way.

The real battles will be political and legal. While the computer world seems to move at a high speed with lots of constant turnover, there's plenty of inertia built into the marketplace. Many people were rather surprised to find that there was plenty of COBOL, FORTRAN, and other old software happily running along without any idea of how to store a date with more than two digits. While Y2K incidents fell far short of the media's hype, the number of systems that required reprogramming was still much larger than conventional wisdom predicted. IBM continues to sell mainframes to customers who started buying mainframes in the 1960s. Once people choose one brand or product or computer architecture, they often stay with it forever.

This is bad news for the people who expect the free OSs to take over the desktop in the next 5 or 10 years. Corporate managers who keep the machines on people's desktops hate change. Change means reeducation. Change means installing new software throughout the plant. Change means teaching folks a new set of commands for running their word processors. Change means work. People who manage the computer networks in offices get graded on the number of glitches that stop workflow. Why abandon Microsoft now?

If Microsoft has such an emotional stranglehold on the desktop and the computer industry takes forever to change, will free software ever grow beyond the 10 million or so desktops owned by programmers and their friends?

Its strongest lever will be price. Freedom is great, but corporations respond better to a cost that is close to, if not exactly, zero. Big companies like Microsoft are enormous cash engines. They need a huge influx of cash to pay the workers, and they can't let their stock price slip. Microsoft's revenues increased with a precision that is rare in corporate America. Some stock analysts joke that the stock price suggests that Microsoft's revenues will grow faster than 10 percent forever. In the past, the company accomplished this by absorbing more and more of the market while finding a way to charge more and more for the software they supply. Businesses that lived quite well with Windows 95 are now running Windows NT. Businesses that ran NT are now using special service packs that handle network management and data functions. The budget for computers just keeps going up, despite the fact that hardware costs go down.

Something has to give. It's hard to know how much of a lever the price will be. If the revenue at Microsoft stops growing, then the company's stock price could take a sharp dive. The company manages continually to produce greater and greater revenues each quarter with smooth precision. The expectation of the growth is built into the price. Any hiccup could bring the price tumbling down.

The biggest question is how much people are willing to pay to continue to use Microsoft products. Retooling an office is an expensive proposition. The cost of buying new computers and software is often smaller than the cost of reeducation. While the free software world is much cheaper, shifting is not an easy proposition. Only time will tell how much people are willing to pay for their reluctance to change.

The first cracks are already obvious. Microsoft lost the server market to Apache and Linux on the basis of price and performance. Web server managers are educated computer users who can make their own decisions without having to worry about the need to train others. Hidden computers like this are easy targets, and the free software world will gobble many of them up. More users mean more bug fixes and propagations of better code.

The second crack in Microsoft's armor will be appliance computers. Most people want to browse the web and exchange some e-mail. The basic distribution from Red Hat or FreeBSD is good enough. Many people are experimenting with creating computers that are defined by the job they do, not the operating system or the computer chip. Free source packages should have no trouble winning many battles in this arena. The price is right and the manufacturers have to hire the programmers anyway.

The third breach will be young kids. They have no previous allegiances and are eager to learn new computer technology. Microsoft may ask "Where do you want to go today?" but they don't want to talk with someone whose answer is "The guts of your OS." The best and brightest 13-year-olds are already the biggest fans of free software. They love the power and the complete access.

The fourth crack will be the large installations in businesses that are interested in competitive bidding. Microsoft charges a bundle for each seat in a company, and anyone bidding for these contracts will be able to charge much less if they ship a free OS. It's not uncommon for a company to pay more than a million dollars to Microsoft for license fees. There's plenty of room for price competition when the bill gets that high. Companies that don't want to change will be hard to move from Windows, but ones that are price-sensitive will be moved.

Of course, free software really isn't free. A variety of companies offering Linux support need to charge something to pay their bills. Distributions like Red Hat or FreeBSD may not cost much, but they often need some customization and hand-holding. Is a business just trading one bill for another? Won't Linux support end up costing the same thing as Microsoft's product?

Many don't think so. Microsoft currently wastes billions of dollars a year expanding its business in unproductive ways that don't yield new profits. It spent millions writing a free web browser to compete with Netscape's and then they just gave it away. They probably gave up millions of dollars and untold bargaining chips when they twisted the arms of competitors into shunning Netscape. The company's successful products pay for these excursions. At the very least, a free OS operation would avoid these costs.

Free OS systems are inherently cheaper to run. If you have the source, you might be able to debug the problem yourself. You probably can't, but it doesn't hurt to try. Companies running Microsoft products can't even try. The free flow of information will help keep costs down.

Of course, there are also hard numbers. An article in *Wired* by Andrew Leonard comes with numbers originally developed by the Gartner Group. A 25-person office would cost $21,453 to outfit with Microsoft products and $5,544.70 to outfit with Linux. This estimate is a bit conservative. Most of the Linux cost is debatable because it includes almost $3,000 for 10 service calls to a Linux consultant and about $2,500 for Applixware, an office suite that does much of the same job as Microsoft Office. A truly cheap and technically hip office could make do with the editor built into Netscape and one of the free spreadsheets available for Linux. It's not hard to imagine someone doing the same job for about $3, which is the cost of a cheap knockoff of Red Hat's latest distribution.

Of course, it's important to realize that free software still costs money to support. But so does Microsoft's. The proprietary software companies also charge to answer questions and provide reliable information. It's not clear that Linux support is any more expensive to offer.

Also, many offices large and small keep computer technicians on hand. There's no reason to believe that Linux technicians will be any more or less expensive than Microsoft technicians. Both answer questions. Both keep the systems running. At least the Linux tech can look at the source code.

The average home user and small business user will be the last to go.

These users will be the most loyal to Microsoft because they will find it harder than anyone else to move. They can't afford to hire their own Linux gurus to redo the office, and they don't have the time to teach themselves.

These are the main weaknesses for Microsoft, and the company is already taking them seriously. I think many underestimate how bloody the battle is about to become. If free source software is able to stop and even reverse revenue growth for Microsoft, there are going to be some very rich people with deep pockets who feel threatened. Microsoft is probably going to turn to the same legal system that gave it such grief and find some wedge to drive into the Linux community. Their biggest weapon will be patents and copyright to stop the cloners.

Any legal battle will be an interesting fight. On the one hand, the free software community is diverse and spread out among many different entities. There's no central office and no one source that could be brought down. This means Microsoft would fight a war on many fronts, and this is something that's emotionally and intellectually taxing for anyone, no matter how rich or powerful.

On the other hand, the free software community has no central reservoir of money or strength. Each small group could be crippled, one by one, by a nasty lawsuit. Groups like OpenBSD are always looking for donations. The Free Software Foundation has some great depth and affection, but its budget is a tiny fraction of Sun's or Microsoft's. Legal bills are real, and lawyers have a way of making them blossom. There may be hundreds of different targets for Microsoft, but many of them won't take much firepower to knock out.

The free software community is not without some deep pockets itself. Many of the traditional hardware companies like IBM, Compaq, Gateway, Sun, Hewlett-Packard, and Apple can make money by selling either hardware or software. They've been hurt in recent years by Microsoft's relentless domination of the desktop. Microsoft negotiated hard contracts with each of the companies that controlled what the user saw. The PC manufacturers received little ability to customize their product. Microsoft turned them into commodity manufacturers and stripped away their control. Each of these companies should see great potential in moving to a free OS and adopting it. There is no extra cost, no strange meetings, no veiled threats, no arm-twisting.

Suddenly, brands like Hewlett-Packard or IBM can mean something when they're slapped on a PC. Any goofball in a garage can put a circuit board in a box and slap on Microsoft Windows. A big company like HP or IBM could do extra work to make sure the Linux distribution on the box worked well with the components and provided a glitch-free existence for the user.

The hardware companies will be powerful allies for the free software realm because the companies will be the ones who benefit economically the most from the free software licenses. When all of the software is free, no one controls it and this strips away many of Microsoft's traditional ways of applying leverage. Microsoft, for instance, knocked the legs out from underneath Netscape by giving away Internet Explorer for free. Now the free software world is using the same strategy against Microsoft. It's hard for them to undercut free for most users.

The university system is a less stable ally. While the notion of free exchange of information is still floating around many of the nation's campuses, the places are frighteningly corporate and profit-minded. Microsoft has plenty of cash at its disposal and it hasn't been shy about spreading it around places like MIT, Harvard, and Stanford. The computer science departments on those campuses are the recipients of brand-new buildings compliments of Bill Gates. These gifts are hard to ignore.

Microsoft will probably avoid a direct confrontation with the academic tradition of the institutions and choose to cut their prices as low as necessary to dominate the desktops. Universities will probably be given "free," tax-deductible donations of software whenever they stray far from the Microsoft-endorsed solution. Lab managers and people who make decisions about the computing infrastructure of the university will probably get neat "consulting" contracts from Microsoft or its buddies. This will probably not mean total domination, but it will buy a surprisingly large amount of obedience.

Despite these gifts, free software will continue to grow on the campuses. Students often have little cash and Microsoft doesn't get any great tax deduction by giving gifts to individual students (that's income). The smartest kids in the dorms will continue to run Linux. Many labs do cutting-edge work that requires customized software. These groups will naturally be attracted to free source code because it makes their life easier. It will be difficult for Microsoft to counteract the very real attraction of free software.

Of course, Microsoft is not without its own arms. Microsoft still has patent law on its side, and this may prove to be a very serious weapon. The law allows the patent holder the exclusive right to determine who uses an idea or invention over the course of the patent, which is now 20 years from the first filing date. That means the patent holder can sue anyone who makes a product that uses the invention. It also means that the patent holder can sue someone who simply cobbles up the invention in his basement and uses the idea without paying anything to anyone. This means that even someone who distributes the software for free or uses the software can be liable for damages.

In the past, many distrusted the idea of software patents because the patent system wasn't supposed to allow you to lay claim to the laws of nature. This interpretation fell by the wayside as patent lawyers argued successfully that software combined with a computer was a separate machine and machines were eligible for protection.

Today, it is quite easy to get patent protection for new ideas on how to structure a computer network, an operating system, or a software tool. The only requirement is that they're new and nonobvious. Microsoft has plenty of these.

If things go perfectly for Microsoft, the company will be able to pull out one or two patents from its huge portfolio and use these to sue Red Hat, Walnut Creek, and a few of the other major distributors. Ideally, this patent would cover some crucial part of the Linux or BSD operating system. After the first few legal bills started arriving on the desk of the Red Hat or Walnut Creek CEO, the companies would have to settle by quitting the business. Eventually, all of the distributors of Linux would crumble and return to the small camps in the hills to lick their wounds. At least, that's probably the dream of some of Microsoft's greatest legal soldiers.

This maneuver is far from a lock for Microsoft because the free software world has a number of good defenses. The first is that the Linux and BSD world do a good job of publicizing their advances. Any patent holder must file the patent before someone else publishes their ideas. The Linux discussion groups and source distributions are a pretty good public forum. The ideas and patches often circulate publicly long before they make their way into a stable version of the kernel. That means that the patent holders will need to be much farther ahead than the free software world.

Linux and the free software world are often the cradle of new ideas. University students use open source software all the time. It's much easier to do way cool things if you've got access to the source. Sure, Microsoft has some smart researchers with great funding, but can they compete with all the students?

Microsoft's ability to dominate the patent world may be hurt by the nature of the game. Filing the application first or publishing an idea first is all that matters in the patent world. Producing a real product is hard work that is helped by the cash supply of Microsoft. Coming up with ideas and circulating them is much easier than building real tools that people can use.

The second defense is adaptability. The free software distributions can simply strip out the offending code. The Linux and BSD disks are very modular because they come from a variety of different sources. The different layers and tools come from different authors, so they are not highly integrated. This makes it possible to remove one part without ruining the entire system.

Stallman's GNU project has been dealing with patents for a long time and has some experience programming around them. The GNU Zip program, for instance, was written to avoid the patents on the Lempel-Ziv compression algorithm claimed by UNISYS and IBM. The software is well-written and it works as well as, if not better than, the algorithm it replaces. Now it's pretty standard on the web and very popular because it is open source and patent-free. It's the politically correct compression algorithm to use because it's open to everyone.

It will be pretty difficult for a company like Microsoft to find a patent that will allow it to deal a fatal blow to either the Linux or BSD distributions. The groups will just clip out the offending code and then work around it.

Microsoft's greatest hope is to lock up the next generation of computing with patents. New technologies like streaming multimedia or Internet audio are still up for grabs. While people have been studying these topics in universities for some time, the Linux community is further behind. Microsoft will try to dominate these areas with crucial patents that affect how operating systems deal with this kind of data. Their success at this is hard to predict. In any event, while they may be able to cripple the adoption of some new technologies like streaming multimedia, they won't be able to smash the entire world.

The third and greatest defense for the free source ideology is a loophole in the patent law that may also help many people in the free software world. It is not illegal to use a patented idea if you're in the process of doing some research on how to improve the state of the art in that area. The loophole is very narrow, but many users of free software might fall within it. All of the distributions come with source code, and many of the current users are programmers experimenting with the code. Most of these programmers give their work back to the project and this makes most of their work pretty noncommercial. The loophole probably wouldn't protect the corporations that are using free software simply because it is cheap, but it would still be large enough to allow innovation to continue. A noncommercial community built up around research could still thrive even if Microsoft manages to come up with some patents that are very powerful.

The world of patents can still constrain the world of free software. Many companies work hard on developing new technology and then rely upon patents to guarantee them a return on investment. These companies have trouble working well with the free software movement because there's no revenue stream to use. A company like Adobe can integrate some neat new streaming technology or compression algorithm and add the cost of a patent license to the price of the product. A free software tool can't.

This does not preclude the free software world from using some ideas or software. There's no reason why Linux can't run proprietary application software that costs money. Perhaps people will sell licenses for some distributions and patches. Still, the users must shift mental gears when they encounter these packages.

There are no easy solutions to patent problems. The best news is that proprietary, patented technology rarely comes to dominate the marketplace. There are often ways to work around solutions, and other engineers are great at finding them. Sure, there will be the occasional brilliant lightbulb, transistor, radio, or other solution that is protected by a broad patent, but these will be relatively rare.

There are a few things that the open source community can do to protect themselves against patents. Right now, many of the efforts at developing open source solutions come after technology emerges. For instance, developing drivers for DVD disks is one of the current challenges at the time that I'm writing this chapter even though the technology has been shipping with many midpriced computers for about a year.

There is no reason why some ivory-tower, blue-sky research can't take place in a patent-free world of open source. Many companies already allow their researchers to attend conferences and present papers on their open work and classify this as "precompetitive" research. Standards like JPEG or MPEG emerge from committees that pledge not to patent their work. There is no reason why these loose research groups can't be organized around a quasi-BSD or GNU license that forces development to be kept in the open.

These research groups will probably be poorly funded but much more agile than the corporate teams or even the academic teams. They might be organized around a public newsgroup or mailing list that is organized for the purpose of publicly disclosing ideas. Once they're officially disclosed, no patents can be issued on them. Many companies like IBM and Xerox publish paper journals for defensive purposes.

Still, the debate about patents will be one that will confound the entire software industry for some time. Many for-profit, proprietary firms are thrown for a loop by some of the patents granted to their competitors. The open source world will have plenty of allies who want to remake the system.

The patents are probably the most potent legal tool that proprietary software companies can use to threaten the open source world. There is no doubt that the companies will use it to fend off low-rent competition.

One of the biggest challenges for the free software community will be developing the leadership to undertake these battles. It is one thing to mess around in a garage with your buddies and hang out in some virtual he-man/Microsoft-haters clubhouse cooking up neat code. It's a very different challenge to actually achieve the world domination that the Linux world muses about. When I started writing the book, I thought that an anthem for the free software movement might be Spinal Tap's "Flower People." Now I think it's going to be Buffalo Springfield's "For What It's Worth," which warns, "There's something happening here / What it is ain't exactly clear."

Tim O'Reilly emphasizes this point. When asked about some of the legal battles, he said, "There's definitely going to be a war over this stuff. When I look back at previous revolutions, I realize how violent they became. They threatened to burn Galileo at the stake. They said 'Take it back,' and he backed down. But it didn't make any difference in the end. But just because there's a backlash doesn't mean that open source won't win in the long run."

Companies like Microsoft don't let markets and turf just slip away. They have a large budget for marketing their software. They know how to generate positive press and plenty of fear in the hearts of managers who must make decisions. They understand the value of intellectual property, and they aren't afraid of dispatching teams of lawyers to ensure that their markets remain defended.

The open source community, however, is not without a wide variety of strengths, although it may not be aware of them. In fact, this diffuse power and lack of self-awareness and organization is one of its greatest strengths. There is no powerful leadership telling the open source community "Thou shalt adopt these libraries and write to this API." The people in the trenches are testing code, proposing solutions, and getting their hands dirty while making decisions. The realm is not a juggernaut, a bandwagon, a dreadnought, or an unstoppable freight train roaring down the track. It's creeping kudzu, an algae bloom, a teenage fad, and a rising tide mixed together.

The strength of the free price shouldn't be underestimated. While the cost isn't really nothing after you add up the price of paying Red Hat, Slackware, SuSE, Debian, or someone else to provide support, it's still much cheaper than the proprietary solutions on the market. Price isn't the only thing on people's minds, but it will always be an important one.

In the end, though, I think the free software world will flourish because of the ideals it embraces. The principles of open debate, broad circulation, easy access, and complete disclosure are like catnip to kids who crackle with intelligence. Why would anyone want to work in a corporate cubicle with a Dilbert boss when you can spend all night hacking on the coolest tools? Why would you want to join some endless corporate hierarchy when you can dive in and be judged on the value of your code? For these reasons, the free software world can always count on recruiting the best and the brightest.

This process will continue because the Dilbert-grade bosses aren't so dumb. I know more than a few engineers and early employees at start-up firms who received very small stock allowances at IPO time. One had written three of the six systems that were crucial to the company's success on the web. Yet he got less than 1 percent of the shares allocated to the new CEO who had just joined the company. The greed of the non-programming money changers who plumb the venture capital waters will continue to poison the experience of the programmers and drive many to the world of free software. If they're not going to get anything, they might as well keep access to the code they write.

The open source ideals are also strangely empowering because they force everyone to give up their will to power and control. Even if Richard Stallman, Linus Torvalds, Eric Raymond, and everyone else in the free software world decides that you're a scumbag who should be exiled to Siberia, they can't take away the code from you. That freedom is a very powerful drug.

The free software movement is rediscovering the same notions that drove the American colonists to rebel against the forces of English oppression. The same words that flowed through the pens of Thomas Paine, Thomas Jefferson, and Benjamin Franklin are just as important today. The free software movement certifies that we are all created equal, with the same rights to life, liberty, and the pursuit of bug-free code. This great nation took many years to evolve and took many bad detours along the way, but in the end, the United States tends to do the right thing.

The free software movement has many flaws, blemishes, and weaknesses, but I believe that it will also flourish over the years. It will take wrong turns and encounter great obstacles, but in the end the devotion to liberty, fraternity, and equality will lead it to make the right decisions and will outstrip all of its proprietary competitors.

In the end, the lure of the complete freedom to change, revise, extend, and improve the source code of a project is a powerful drug that creative people can't resist. Shrink-wrapped software's ease-of-use and prepackaged convenience are quite valuable for many people, but its world is static and slow.

In the end, the power to write code and change it without hiring a team of lawyers to parse agreements between companies ensures that the free software world will gradually win. Corporate organization provides money and stability, but in technology the race is usually won by the swiftest.

In the end, free software creates wealth, not cash, and wealth is much better than cash. You can't eat currency and you can't build a car with gold. Free software does things and accomplishes tasks without crashing into the blue screen of death. It empowers people. People who create it and share it are building real infrastructure that everyone can use. The corporations can try to control it with intellectual property laws. They can buy people, hornswoggle judges, and co-opt politicians, but they can't offer more than money.

In the end, information wants to be free. Corporations want to believe that software is a manufactured good like a car or a toaster. They want to pretend it is something that can be consumed only once. In reality, it is much closer to a joke, an idea, or gossip. Who's managed to control those?

For all of these reasons, this grand free-for-all, this great swapfest of software, this wonderful nonstop slumber party of cooperative knowledge creation, this incredible science project on steroids will grow in strange leaps and unexpected bounds until it swallows the world. There will be battles, there will be armies, there will be spies, there will be snakes, there will be court cases, there will be laws, there will be martyrs, there will be heroes, and there will be traitors. But in the end, information just wants to be free. That's what we love about it.

• • •

GLOSSARY

Apache License   A close cousin of the BSD License. The software comes with few restrictions, and none prevent you from taking a copy of Apache, modifying it, and selling binary versions. The only restriction is that you can't call it Apache. For instance, C2Net markets a derivative of Apache known as Stronghold.

AppleScript   A text language that can be used to control the visual interface of the Macintosh. It essentially says things like "Open that folder and double click on Adobe Photoshop to start it up. Then open the file named 'Pete's Dog's Picture.'"

architecture   Computer scientists use the word "architecture" to describe the high-level, strategic planning of a system. A computer architect may decide, for instance, that a new system should come with three multiplier circuits but not four after analyzing the sequence of arithmetic operations that a computer will likely be called upon to execute. If there are often three multiplications that could be done concurrently, then installing three multiplier circuits would increase efficiency. Adding a fourth, however, would be a waste of effort if there were few occasions to use it. In most cases, the term "computer architect" applies only to hardware engineers. All sufficiently complicated software projects, however, have an architect who makes the initial design decisions.

Artistic License   A license created to protect the original PERL language. Some users dislike the license because it is too complex and filled with loopholes. Bruce Perens writes, "The Artistic License requires you to make modifications free, but then gives you a loophole (in Section 7) that allows you to take modifications private or even place parts of the Artistic-licensed program in the public domain!"

BeOS   An operating system created by the Be, a company run by ex-Apple executive Jean Louis Gassée.

BSD   An abbreviation for Berkeley Software Distribution, a package first released by Bill Joy in the 1970s. The term has come to mean both a class of UNIX that was part of the distribution and also the license that protects this software. There are several free versions of BSD UNIX that are well-accepted and well-supported by the free source software community. OpenBSD, NetBSD, and FreeBSD are three of them. Many commercial versions of UNIX, like Sun's Solaris and NeXT's OS, can trace their roots to this distribution. The BSD was originally protected by a license that allowed anyone to freely copy and modify the source code as long as they gave some credit to the University of California at Berkeley. Unlike the GNU GPL, the license does not require the user to release the source code to any modifications.

BSD License   The original license for BSD software. It placed few restrictions on what you did with the code. The important terms forced you to keep the copyright intact and credit the University of California at Berkeley when you advertise a product. The requirement to include credit is now removed because people realized that they often needed to publish hundreds of acknowledgments for a single CD-ROM. Berkeley removed the term in the hopes that it would set a good example for the rest of the community.

copyleft   Another term that is sometimes used as a synonym for the GNU General Public License.

Debian Free Software Guidelines   See **Open Source**.
(www.debian.org)

driver   Most computers are designed to work with optional devices like modems, disk drives, printers, cameras, and keyboards. A driver is a piece of software that translates the signals sent by the device into a set of signals that can be understood by the operating system. Most operating systems are designed to be modular, so these drivers can be added as an afterthought whenever a user connects a new device. They are usually designed to have a standard structure so other software will work with them. The driver for each mouse, for instance, translates the signals from the mouse into a standard description that includes the position of the mouse and its direction. Drivers are an important point of debate in the free software community because volunteers must often create the drivers. Most manufacturers write the drivers for Windows computers because these customers make up the bulk of their sales. The manufacturers often avoid creating drivers for Linux or BSD systems because they perceive the market to be small. Some manufacturers also cite the GNU GPL as an impediment because they feel that releasing the source code to their drivers publishes important competitive information.

FreeBSD   The most popular version of BSD. The development team, led by Jordan Hubbard, works hard to provide an easy-to-use tool for computers running the Intel x86 architecture. In recent years, they've tried to branch out into other lines. (www.freebsd.org)

Free Software Foundation   An organization set up by Richard Stallman to raise money for the creation of new free software. Stallman donates his time to the organization and takes no salary. The money is spent on hiring programmers to create new free software.

GIMP   The GNU Image Manipulation Program, which can manipulate image files in much the same way as Adobe Photoshop. (www.gimp.org)

GNOME   The GNU Network Object Model Environment, which might be summarized as "All of the functionality of Microsoft Windows for Linux." It's actually more. There are many enhancements that make the tool easier to use and more flexible than the prototype from Redmond. See also **KDE,** another package that accomplishes much of the same. (www.gnome.org)

GNU   A recursive acronym that stands for "GNU is Not UNIX." The project was started by Richard Stallman in the 1980s to fight against the tide of proprietary software. The project began with several very nice programs like GNU Emacs and GCC, the C compiler that was protected by Stallman's GNU General Purpose License. It has since grown to issue software packages that handle many different tasks from games (GNU Chess) to privacy (GNU Privacy Guard). See also **GPL** and **Free Software Foundation** (www.gnu.org). Its main goal is to produce a free operating system that provides a user with the ability to do everything they want with software that comes with the source code.

GNU/Linux   The name some people use for Linux as a way of giving credit to the GNU project for its leadership and contribution of code.

GPL   An abbreviation that stands for "General Purpose License." This license was first written by Richard Stallman to control the usage of software created by the GNU project. A user is free to read and modify the source code of a GPL-protected package, but the user must agree to distribute any changes or improvements if they distribute the software at all. Stallman views the license as a way to force people to share their own improvements and contribute back to the project if they benefit from the project's hard work. See also **BSD.**

higher-level languages   Modern computer programmers almost always write their software in languages like C, Java, Pascal, or Lisp, which are known as higher-level languages. The word "higher" is a modifier that measures the amount of abstraction available to a programmer. A high-level language might let a programmer say, "Add variable revenues to variable losses to computer profits." A high-level language would be able to figure out just where to find the information about the profits and the losses. A low-level programming language would require the software author to point directly to a location in the memory where the data could be found.

KDE   The K desktop environment is another toolkit that offers much of the same functionality as Windows. It is controversial because it originally used some proprietary software and some users needed a license. See also **GNOME,** a similar package that is distributed under the GNU GPL. (www.kde.org)

kernel   The core of an OS responsible for juggling the different tasks and balancing all of the demands. Imagine a short-order cook who scrambles eggs, toasts bread, chops food, and somehow manages to get an order out in a few minutes. A kernel in an OS juggles the requests to send information to a printer, display a picture on the screen, get data from a website, and a thousand other tasks.

Linux   The name given to the core of the operating system started by Linus Torvalds in 1991. The word is now generally used to refer to an entire bundle of free software packages that work together. Red Hat Linux, for instance, is a large bundle of software including packages written by many other unrelated projects.

Mozilla Public License   A cousin of the Netscape Public License that was created to protect the public contributions to the source tree of the Mozilla project. Netscape cannot relicense the modifications to code protected by the MPL, but they can do it to the NPL. See also Netscape Public License.

NetBSD   One of the original free distributions of BSD. The team focuses on making sure that the software works well on a wide variety of hardware platforms, including relatively rare ones like the Amiga. (www.netbsd.org)

Netscape Public License   A license created by Netscape when the company decided to release their browser as open source. The license is similar to the BSD License, but it provides special features to Netscape. They're allowed to take snapshots of the open source code and turn them back into a private, proprietary project again. Bruce Perens, one of the unpaid consultants who helped Netscape draft the license, says that the provision was included because Netscape had special contracts with companies to provide a proprietary tool. See also **Mozilla Public License**.

OpenBSD   One of the three major versions of BSD available. The development team, led by Theo de Raadt, aims to provide the best possible security by examining the source code in detail and looking for potential holes. (www.openbsd.org)

open source   A broad term used by the Open Source Initiative (www.opensource.org) to embrace software developed and released under the GNU General Public License, the BSD license, the Artistic License, the X Consortium, and the Netscape License. It includes software licenses that put few restrictions on the redistribution of source code. The Open Source Initiative's definition was adapted from the Debian Free Software Guidelines. The OSI's definition includes 10 criteria, which range from insisting that the software and the source code must be freely redistributable to insisting that the license not discriminate.

Open Source Initiative   A group created by Eric Raymond, Sam Ockman, Bruce Perens, Larry Augustin, and more than a few others. The group checks licenses to see if they match their definition of open source. If the license fits, then it can wear the term "certified by the OSI."

Symmetric Multi-Processing   Much of the recent work in operating system design is focused on finding efficient ways to run multiple programs simultaneously on multiple CPU chips. This job is relatively straightforward if the different pieces of software run independently of each other. The complexity grows substantially if the CPUs must exchange information to coordinate their progress. The kernel must orchestrate the shuffle of information so that each CPU has enough information to continue its work with a minimum amount of waiting time. Finding a good way to accomplish this SMP is important because many of the new machines appearing after 2000 may come with multiple processors.

UNIX An operating system created at AT&T Bell Labs by Ken Thompson and Dennis Ritchie. The system was originally designed to support multiple users on a variety of different hardware platforms. Most programs written for the system accept ASCII text and spit out ASCII text, which makes it easy to chain them together. The original name was "unics," which was a pun on the then-popular system known as Multics.

BIBLIOGRAPHY

Abelson, Reed. "Among U.S. Donations, Tons of Worthless Drugs." *New York Times,* June 29, 1999.

Ananian, C. Scott. "A Linux Lament: As Red Hat Prepares to Go Public, One Linux Hacker's Dreams of IPO Glory Are Crushed by the Man." *Salon* magazine, July 30, 1999. (http://www.salon.com/tech/feature/1999/07/30/redhat_shares/index.html)

————. "Questions Not to Ask on Linux-Kernel." May 1998. (http://lwn.net/980521/a/nonfaq.html)

Aragon, Lawrence, and Matthew A. De Bellis. "Our Lunch With Linus: (Almost) Everything You Need to Know About the World's Hottest Programmer." *VAR Business,* April 12, 1999.

Betz, David, and Jon Edwards. "GNU's NOT UNIX." *BYTE,* July 1986.

Brinkley, Joel. "Microsoft Witness Attacked for Contradictory Opinions." *New York Times,* January 15, 1999. (http://www.nytimes.com/library/1999/01/biztech/articles/15soft.html)

Bronson, Po. "Manager's Journal Silicon Valley Searches for an Image." *Wall Street Journal,* June 8, 1998.

————. *Nudist on the Late Shift: And Other True Tales of Silicon Valley.* New York: Random House, 1999.

Brown, Zack. "The 'Linux' vs. 'GNU/Linux' Debate." *Kernel Traffic,* April 13, 1999. (http://www.kt.opensrc.org/kt19990408_13.html#editorial)

Caravita, Giuseppe. "Telecommunications, Technology, and Science."
    Il Sole 24 Ore, March 5, 1999.
    (http://www.ilsole24ore.it/24oreinformatica/speciale_3d.199903
    05/INFORMATICA/Informatica/A.html)

Chalmers, Rachel. "Challenges Ahead for the Linux Standards Base."
    LinuxWorld, April 1999. (http://www.linuxworld.com/ linux-
    world/lw-1999-04/lw-04-lsb.html)

Coates, James. "A Rebellious Reaction to the Linux Revolution."
    Chicago Tribune, April 25, 1999.
    (http://www.chicagotribune.com/business/printedition/arti-
    cle/0,1051,SA-Vo9904250051,00.html)

Cox, Alan. "Editorial." *Freshmeat,* July 18, 1999. (http://www.fresh-
    meat.net/news/1998/07/18/900797536.html)

Cringely, Robert X. "Be Careful What You Wish For: Why Being
    Acquired by Microsoft Makes Hardly Anyone Happy in the
    Long Run." *PBS Online,* August 27, 1999.
    (http://www.pbs.org/cringely/pulpit/pulpit19990826.html)

D'Amico, Mary Lisbeth. "German Division of Microsoft Protests
    'Where Do You Want to Go Tomorrow' Slogan: Linux Site
    Holds Contest for New Slogan While Case Is Pending."
    LinuxWorld, April 13, 1999. (http://www.linuxworld.com/linux-
    world/lw-1999-04/lw-04-german.html)

Diamond, David. "Linus the Liberator." *San Jose Mercury News.*
    (http://www.mercurycenter.com/svtech/news/special/linus/story
    .html)

DiBona, Chris, Sam Ockman, and Mark Stone. *Open Sources: Voices from
    the Open Source Revolution.* San Francisco: O'Reilly, 1999.

Freeman, Derek. *Margaret Mead and Samoa: The Making and Unmaking
    of an Anthropological Myth.* Cambridge, MA: Harvard University
    Press, 1988.

Gilder, George. *Wealth and Poverty.* Institute for Contemporary
    Studies. San Fransisco: CA, 1981.

Gleick, James. "Control Freaks." *New York Times,* July 19, 1998.

———. "Broken Windows Theory." *New York Times,* March 21, 1999.

"Interview with Linus Torvalds." FatBrain.com, May 1999. (http://www.kt.opensrc.org/interviews/ti19990528_fb.html)

Jelinek, Jakub. "Re: Mach64 Problems in UltraPenguin 1.1.9." *Linux Weekly News,* April 27, 1999. (http://www.lwn.net/1999/0429/a/up-dead.html)

Johnson, Richard B., and Chris Wedgwood. "Segfault in syslogd [problem shown]." April 1999. (http://www.kt.opensrc.org/kt19990415_14.html#8)

Joy, Bill. "Talk to Stanford EE 380 Students." November 1999.

Kahn, David. *The Codebreakers.* New York: Macmillan, 1967.

Kahney, Leander. "Open-Source Gurus Trade Jabs." *Wired News,* April 10, 1999. (http://www.wired.com/news/news/technology/story/19049.html)

———. "Apple Lifts License Restrictions." *Wired News,* April 21, 1999. (http://www.wired.com/news/news/technology/story/19233.html)

Kidd, Eric. "Why You Might Want to Use the Library GPL for Your Next Library." *Linux Gazette,* March 1999. (http://www.linuxgazette.com/issue38/kidd.html)

Kohn, Alfie. "Studies Find Reward Often No Motivator; Creativity and Intrinsic Interest Diminish If Task Is Done for Gain." *Boston Globe,* January 19, 1987.

Leonard, Andrew. "Open Season: Why an Industry of Cutthroat Competition Is Suddenly Deciding Good Karma Is Great Business." *Wired News,* May 1999.

Linksvayer, Mike. "Choice of the GNU Generation." *Meta Magazine.* (http://gondwanaland.com/meta/history/interview.html)

"Linux Beat Windows NT Handily in an Oracle Performance Benchmark." *Linux Weekly News,* April 29, 1999. (http://rpmfind.net/veillard/oracle/)

Liston, Robert. *The Pueblo Surrender: A Covert Action by the National Security Agency.* New York: Evans, 1988.

Little, Darnell. "Comdex Q&A: Linus Torvalds on the Battle Against Microsoft." *Chicago Tribune* April 19, 1999. (http://chicagotribune.com/business/businessnews/ws/item/0,1267,26746-27007-27361,00.html)

Lohr, Steve. "Tiny Software Maker Takes Aim at Microsoft in Court." *New York Times,* May 31, 1999.

Mauss, Marcel. "Gift: The Form and Reason for Exchange in Archaic Societies," trans. W. D. Halls. New York: W.W. Norton & Company (of reissue in US), 1950.

McKusick, Marshall Kirk. "Twenty Years of Berkeley Unix." In *Open Sources: Voices from the Open Source Revolution.* San Francisco: O'Reilly, 1999.

McKusick, Marshall Kirk, Keith Bostic, and Michael J. Karels, eds. *The Design and Implementation of the 4.4BSD Operating System (Unix and Open Systems Series).* Reading, MA: Addison-Wesley, 1996.

McMillan, Robert, and Nora Mikes. "After the 'Sweet Sixteen': Linus Torvalds's Take on the State of Linux." *LinuxWorld,* March 1999. (http://www.linuxworld.com/linuxworld/lw-1999-03/lw-03-torvalds.html)

Metcalfe, Bob. "Linux's '60s Technology: Open-Sores Ideology Won't Beat W2K, but What Will?" June 19, 1999. (http://www.infoworld.com/articles/op/xml/990621opmetcalfe.xml)

Nolan, Chris. "Microsoft Antitrust: the Gassée Factor: U.S. Reportedly Looks into Obstacles for Be Operating System." *San Jose Mercury News,* February 11, 1999. (http://www.sjmercury.com/svtech/columns/talkischeap/docs/cn021199.html)

Oakes, Chris. "Netscape Browser Guru: We Failed." *Wired News*, April 2, 1999. (http://www.wired.com/news/news/technology/story/18926.html)

Ousterhout, John. "Free Software Needs Profit." *Dr. Dobb's Journal* website, 1999. (http://www.ddj.com/oped/1999/oust.htm)

Perens, Bruce, Wichert Akkerman, and Ian Jackson. "The Apple Public Source License—Our Concerns." March 1999. (http://perens.com/APSL.html/)

————. "The Open Source Definition." In *Open Sources: Voices from the Open Source Revolution*, ed. Chris DiBona, Sam Ockman, and Mark Stone, 171–85. San Francisco: O'Reilly, 1999.

Picarille, Lisa, and Malcolm Maclachlan. "Apple Defends Open Source Initiative." March 24, 1999. (http://www.techweb.com/wire/story/TWB19990324S0027)

Raymond, Eric. *The Cathedral and the Bazaar: Musings on Linux and Open Source by an Accidental Revolutionary*. San Francisco: O'Reilly, 1999.

Reilly, Patrick. "Nader's Microsoft Agenda: Progressive Nonprofit Plan for 'Free' Software." *Capital Research Center*, April 1, 1999. (http://www.capitalresearch.org/trends/ot-0499a.html)

Rubini, Alessandro. "Tour of the Linux Kernel Source." Linux Documentation Project.

Rusling, David A. "The Linux Kernel." (http://metalab.unc.edu/mdw/LDP/tlk/tlk-title.html)

Schmalensee, Richard. "Direct Testimony in the Microsoft Anti-Trust Case of 1999." (http://www.courttv.com/trials/ microsoft/legal-docs/ms_wit.html)

Schulman, Andrew. *Unauthorized Windows 95*. Foster City, CA: IDG Books, 1995.

Searles, Doc. "It's an Industry." *Linux Journal*, May 21, 1999. (http://www.linuxresources.com/articles/conversations/001.html)

Slind-Flor, Victoria. "Linux May Alter IP Legal Landscape: Some Predict More Contract Work if Alternative to Windows Catches On." *National Law Journal,* March 12, 1999. (http://www.lawnewsnetwork.com/stories/mar/e030899q.html)

Stallman, Richard. "The GNU Manifesto." 1984. (http://www.gnu.org/gnu/manifesto.html)

———. "Why Software Should Not Have Owners." 1994. (http://www.gnu.org/philosophy/why-free.html)

Thompson, Ken, and Dennis Ritchie. "The UNIX Time-Sharing System." *Communications of the ACM,* 1974.

Thygeson, Gordon. *Apple T-Shirts: A Yearbook of History at Apple Computer.* Cupertino, CA: Pomo Publishing, 1998

Torvalds, Linus. "Linus Torvalds: Leader of the Revolution." Transcript of Chat with Linus Torvalds, creator of the Linux OS. ABCNews.com.

———. "Linux's History." July 31, 1992. (http://www.li.org/li/linuxhistory.shtml)

Valloppillil, Vinod. "Open Source Software: A (New?) Development Methodology." Microsoft, Redmond, WA, August 1998.

Wayner, Peter. "If SB266 Wants Plaintext, Give Them Plaintext . . . ," *Risks Digest,* May 23, 1991. (http://catless.ncl.ac.uk/Risks/11.71.html#subj2)

———. "Should Hackers Spend Years in Prison?" *Salon,* June 9, 1999. (http://www.salon.com/tech/feature/1999/06/09/hacker_penalties/index.html)

———. "Netscape to Release New Browser Engine to Developers." *New York Times,* December 7, 1999.

———. "Glory Among the Geeks." *Salon,* January 1999. (http://www.salon.com/21st/feature/1999/01/28feature.html)

Whitenger, Dave. "Words of a Maddog." *Linux Today,* April 19, 1999. (http://linuxtoday.com/stories/5118.html)

"Web and File Server Comparison: Microsoft Windows NT Server 4.0 and Red Hat Linux 5.2 Upgraded to the Linux 2.2.2 Kernel." *Mindcraft,* April 13, 1999. (http://www.mindcraft.com/whitepapers/nts4rhlinux.html)

Williams, Sam. "Linus Has Left the Building." *Upside,* May 5, 1999. (http://www.upside.com/Open_Season/)

Williams, Riley. "Linux Kernel Vertsion History." (http://ps.cus.umist.ac.uk/~rhw/kernel.versions.html)

Zawinski, Jamie. "Resignation and Postmortem." (http://www.jwz.org/gruntle/nomo.html)

INDEX